# The Project Manager's Guide to Making Successful Decisions

# The Project Manager's Guide to Making Successful Decisions

*COL Robert A. Powell, PhD*

*Dennis M. Buede, PhD*

**MANAGEMENT**CONCEPTS

**♩♩♩**
**MANAGEMENT**CONCEPTS

8230 Leesburg Pike, Suite 800
Vienna, VA 22182
(703) 790-9595
Fax: (703) 790-1371
www.managementconcepts.com

Library of Congress Cataloging-in-Publication Data

Powell, Robert A., 1961–
    The project manager's guide to making successful decisions / Robert A. Powell,
Dennis M. Buede.
        p. cm.
    ISBN 978-1-56726-234-6
1. Project management.  2. Decision making.  I. Buede, Dennis M.  II. Title.
HD69.P75P64 2009
658.4'03—dc22

                                                                        2008038271


Printed in the United States of America

10      9      8      7      6      5      4      3      2      1

# About the Authors

COL Robert A. Powell, PhD, was Academy Professor and Deputy Department Head of the Department of Systems Engineering at the U.S. Military Academy at West Point. He received a PhD in systems engineering from Stevens Institute of Technology, an MS in operations research from George Mason University, and a BS in industrial engineering from Texas A&M. He was a member of the Military Operations Research Society, the American Society of Engineering Education, and the International Council on Systems Engineering. Sadly, COL Powell passed away shortly before this book was published.

**Dennis M. Buede, PhD,** is president of Innovative Decisions, Inc., a consulting firm in northern Virginia. Dr. Buede was formerly a professor at Stevens Institute of Technology and George Mason University. He received a PhD and an MS in engineering-economic systems from Stanford University. He has written numerous journal articles on decision-making, as well as two books: *The Engineering Design of Systems* and *Decision Synthesis: The Principles and Practice of Decision Analysis.* Dr. Buede is a Fellow of the International Council on Systems Engineering and belongs to the Military Operations Research Society, the Institute of Electrical and Electronic Engineers, and the American Society of Engineering Education.

This book is dedicated to the memory of COL Robert A. Powell. Bob was a bright and inquisitive student, a tireless researcher, a trusted colleague, and a great friend. He was devoted to his family and was an enthusiastic volunteer in his community. We all miss him dearly.

# Contents

# Preface

This is not another traditional book on project management. There are an adequate number of books on managing projects, and adding another one will not necessarily increase project manager skills or contribute to project success. What project managers need most is a resource that will help them become better decision makers.

In traditional project management training, project managers are taught how to plan projects according to business objectives, how to gather requirements, how to develop a management plan, how to assign resources, how to track progress, how to handle conflict, and how to maintain control. We have found, however, that project managers receive very little education or training focused on the decision-making required to successfully manage complex, large-scale projects.

The objective of this book is to show how successful decision-making significantly contributes to project success. We highlight the hundreds of decisions project managers have to make to support the project management life cycle, and we present various techniques that facilitate the decision-making process. We also provide an overview of decision analysis as it relates to project management.

## Decision-Making in Project Management

Project managers make many decisions during the project life cycle, including:

- Defining the project organization

- Selecting the team

- Planning, budgeting, and scheduling the project

- Conducting needs analysis

- Conducting product analysis and concept design

- Allocating resources to the project

- Executing the project

- Monitoring and controlling the project

- Performing test management

- Evaluating and terminating the project.

Faulty decision-making in any area can have huge financial consequences. Other negative effects can include demoralization of staff, loss of staff, wasted resources, and missed opportunities. Despite this significant impact on projects and people, project management books and training don't give much attention to decision-making. As a result, project managers might overlook the most critical element in managing projects—the decisions that are required to accomplish project objectives.

Project management training materials commonly cover risk management, which focuses on minimizing risks by identifying uncertainties that could prevent a project from achieving cost, schedule, and performance objectives. In addition to cost, schedule, and performance risks, however, risk management training should also cover the specific risks associated with decision-making. To increase the probability of project success, project managers must have an understanding of both the risk to project objectives and the risk to project decisions.

Managing decisions is the key to managing successful projects. Root-cause analysis or failure analysis often identifies a poor decision, an untimely decision, or the absence of a decision as the cause of a failed project. A project can survive without adequate resources, but it can never survive faulty decision-making.

## How This Book Is Organized

Chapter 1 begins with an exploration of why making good decisions is essential to good project management. It explains why a decision context is required for making effective decisions and presents the three cornerstones of decision-making. Next, the chapter focuses on reasons for project success before presenting the anatomy of a project failure. Making decisions is no easy task. The chapter ends with a recommendation for a planned process for handling the difficult task of making decisions.

Chapter 2 introduces the anatomy of a project management decision and the impact of such decisions on project success. The chapter identifies what happens when good and bad decisions are made: good decisions lead to good outcomes and bad decisions lead to bad outcomes. It also covers reasons for project success and failure and concludes with case studies that highlight project successes and project failures.

Chapter 3 presents the project management life cycle as a framework that guides decision-making and provides a representative set of sample decisions unique to each stage of the life cycle. This summary of project management gives the basis for the discussion of decision-making throughout the rest of the book.

Chapter 4 describes decision-making—its history, what makes good decisions, the different approaches to decision-making—and how to avoid project failure. The chapter distinguishes good decisions and good outcomes—good outcomes are never guaranteed. Good decisions result from a good decision-making process in which the decision maker carefully considers the values and objectives associated with the decision context and seeks out alternative courses of action.

Chapter 5 is the heart of this book: It identifies those decisions required for successful project management. Decision categories are initially divided into product system and development system. The product system is the focus of the project. The development system is the organization of people and support tools that constitutes the project. Each category is further decomposed into the many decisions made during the project life cycle.

Chapter 6 focuses on framing decisions—clarifying the most important decision elements to consider when selecting the best solution—and describes the distinct elements of a decision. The chapter presents a new qualitative decision support tool that can serve as a template for framing a decision. A case study of the 1950s Sidewinder missile illustrates the concept of a decision frame.

Chapter 7 presents several techniques for generating decision alternatives. The chapter also demonstrates how to apply the decision frame to alternatives. Two case studies—the Cuban Missile Crisis and the Windows NT development—illustrate these concepts.

Chapter 8 continues with a presentation of several qualitative approaches to analyzing decision alternatives. Well-known cognitive biases and heuristics are summarized to caution against overconfidence in decision-making. The chapter ends with a summary of the requirements for good decisions.

Chapter 9 discusses risk and uncertainty in projects. Risk analysis must be incorporated into the decision-making process. A case study and decision frame for the Hubble Space Telescope project illustrate some of the important points about risk and uncertainty.

Chapter 10 highlights why it's important to focus on decision-making and decision analysis in current project management training and recommends a curriculum to integrate into such training.

The appendixes provide additional case studies, tools, and checklists for making project decisions, as well as an introduction to decision trees.

We hope that this book will help readers make better project decisions that lead to greater project success.

*Robert A. Powell*
West Point, New York

*Dennis M. Buede*
Reston, Virginia

# Acknowledgments

We want to thank Robert Dees and Ken Gilliam for contributing the valuable appendix on decision analysis.

We also want to acknowledge the many colleagues who have provided guidance, inspiration, and support over the years. They know who they are.

# CHAPTER 1

# Good Decision-Making: The Key to Project Success

Successful projects are everywhere—and so are failed projects. We are surrounded by thousands of successful projects. The cars we drive, the houses we live in, the buildings we work in, and the technology we use are all examples. We are also surrounded by numerous failed projects. The examples of failure presented in this book include the Segway personal transportation system, the Mars Climate Orbiter of the National Aeronautics and Space Administration (NASA), and the Minneapolis I-35W bridge, which collapsed in 2007. In each of these projects, the problem was not the quality of the available resources. Each project had highly talented and dedicated managers, the best professional teams, the best project management tools, and total support from top management. It is the *decisions* that were made—or not made—that account for their failure.

When decisions are of poor quality, untimely, or altogether absent, the result is frequently a failed project. That is, projects stand a far greater chance of succeeding when quality decisions are made. It can be stated with certainty, then, that good decision-making leads to successful projects. A project might survive without adequate resources, but it can never survive faulty decision-making.

Project managers must understand the importance of decision-making and then consider each of their decisions carefully. When they do so, they will encounter fewer surprises, handle challenges better, and keep the project management team focused on the project objectives, the organizational strategy, and the overall organizational mission.

This chapter presents the following sections:

- Good Decision-Making Begins with a Decision Context

- The Three Cornerstones of Decision-Making

- Why Projects Fail

- A Planned Process for Decision-Making

- A General Framework for Making Decisions.

## Good Decision-Making Begins with a Decision Context

Projects traditionally have three overarching *objectives*—meeting the budget, finishing on schedule, and meeting client specifications (product performance). These objectives establish the control parameters and discipline by which a project is managed. When these three project objectives are achieved, the project is usually considered a success.

Meeting project objectives requires action. *Decisions* can be thought of as the action or momentum that enables project managers to move their projects toward success.

## What Is a Decision Context?

A *decision context* is the setting in which decisions occur (Clemen and Reilly 2001). Each specific decision calls for a specific objective. Here, "setting" refers to the situation faced by the decision maker, including the decision maker's current status in terms of resources, obligations, opportunities, and desires. The setting can also include the resources, obligations, opportunities, and desires of the decision maker's organization, family, friends, and associates. From this setting, the decision maker develops a set of alternative courses of action, considers some objectives on which to evaluate these courses of action, and ponders issues such as uncertainty, time preference, and risk preference.

For example, a decision context might be the setting surrounding a decision of where to build a new residential subdivision. In this case, the objectives that relate to how much money can be made by the organization that is considering building the residential subdivision might include minimal commute time, educational needs, and accessibility to shopping areas for the homeowners.

The following example is a simple case involving the selection of a supercomputer.

## Which Supercomputer?

Boeing Corporation is a large-scale manufacturer of sophisticated defense systems, commercial aircraft, and other assorted technology products, as well as a premiere research organization. As such, Boeing needs significant computing power for computer-aided design, inventory control and tracking, and manufacturing support. When key managers of the engineering department were considering various supercomputer alternatives, these managers found that organizing their concerns or objectives focused the task of collecting information needed to evaluate competing alternatives. Figure 1-1 shows the result of this process of organizing their concerns and objectives (Barnhart 1993).

In this case, Boeing was confronted with a decision to expand its high-power computing capacity. The decision was essentially about the acquisition of a supercomputer. In the decision context, several objectives associated with the decision. Based on the given scenario, the objectives include (1) satisfying user needs, (2) maximizing performance, (3) minimizing costs, (4) satisfying organizational needs, and (5) satisfying management issues. These objectives can be further broken down into different aspects, as shown in Figure 1-1.

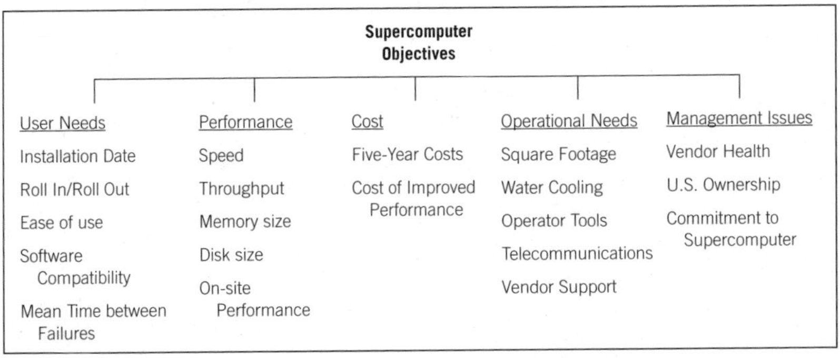

| | | Supercomputer Objectives | | |
|---|---|---|---|---|
| User Needs | Performance | Cost | Operational Needs | Management Issues |
| Installation Date | Speed | Five-Year Costs | Square Footage | Vendor Health |
| Roll In/Roll Out | Throughput | Cost of Improved Performance | Water Cooling | U.S. Ownership |
| Ease of use | Memory size | | Operator Tools | Commitment to Supercomputer |
| Software Compatibility | Disk size | | Telecommunications | |
| Mean Time between Failures | On-site Performance | | Vendor Support | |

Clemen and Reilly, *Making Hard Decisions with Decision Tools Suite Update Edition,* 1E. Copyright © 2001 by South-Western, a part of Cengage Learning, Inc. Figure reprinted with permission.

**FIGURE 1-1:** Objectives for Boeing's Supercomputer

An important issue in understanding the decision context is determining which comes first, the objective(s) or the decision. When objectives come first, the project manager is well prepared to make the decisions necessary for project success and to entertain new decision opportunities as they arise. When decisions come first, because every decision situation involves a specific context, the context helps the project manager determine what objectives need to be considered. The notion is that objectives and decisions go hand in hand.

In project management it is best to begin with objectives because projects are managed according to a set of predefined objectives. Therefore, it is important that all of the *appropriate* objectives are considered upfront. Appropriate objectives are those that are relevant to the success of the project. *Inappropriate* objectives are those that are tangential or irrelevant to the project's success; inappropriate objectives will result in inappropriate choices for what could be key decisions. On the other hand, when appropriate objectives are developed, decisions can be aligned with the objectives. Clemen and Reilly (2001) have found that when the decision context is specified and appropriate objectives align with the context, decision makers know what the situation is and exactly why they care about making a decision in that situation. The project manager, as the decision maker, should view the decision context as one of the key cornerstones for project success.

## The Three Cornerstones of Decision-Making

There are three cornerstones of decision-making: the *decision*, the *decision process*, and the *decision maker* or *actor*. For Bocquet, Cardinal, and Mekhilef (1999), a decision is "any action taken by an actor(s) that will consume resources and affect other actors in the pursuit of achieving objectives within constraints." The decision process is the planned process that is followed when decisions are made. A decision maker (or an actor) is a person who participates in the making of decisions, such as the CEO, program manager, project manager, contractors, consultants, clients, workers, and customers. While every actor is responsible for making decisions, the emphasis in this book is on the *project manager* (the person who manages the entire project) and the decisions that person makes. Decisions made by project managers have a clear impact on the use of resources and on other project actors. More specifically, the decisions made by the project manager have a clear impact on project success.

Jim Johnson of Standish Group International identifies ten top reasons for project success, as follows (Hartmann 2006):

1. User involvement

2. Executive management support

3. Clear business objectives

4. Optimizing scope

5. Agile process

6. Project manager expertise

7. Financial management

8. Skilled resources

9. Formal methodology

10. Standard tools and infrastructure.

The third reason relates directly to objectives for evaluating decision alternatives and therefore is critical to good decision-making. User involvement, executive management support, optimizing scope, agile process, and financial management may all impact the definition of the objectives and will be critical in evaluating the alternatives in a proper and timely manner. Project manager expertise, skilled resources, a formal methodology, and standard tools and infrastructure relate to the decision process and the decision maker.

## Why Projects Fail

As we have discussed, project failure can often be traced to poor decisions, which result more often than not from poor decision-making processes by the project manager and staff. In this section we review the more general reasons given for project failures and relate these general reasons back to decision-making.

Many projects end successfully, many fail, and a majority end somewhere in the middle. Cobb's Paradox (Standish Group International 2001) asks, "We know why projects fail; we know how to prevent their failure—so why do they still fail?" Why is traditional project management training not resulting in greater success? And why do even well-managed projects fail? Consider the following (Shenhar and Dvir 2007):

> Denver International Airport was initiated in 1989 to take over Denver's Stapleton Airport, which had outgrown its maximum capacity. But the project suffered an extensive delay of sixteen months and an enormous cost overrun of $1.5 billion. As it turned out, one component—the automatic bag-handling system—had a higher risk than the project's other elements, but it was treated as a standard, well-proven subsystem, just like any other part of the project.

> The Segway personal transportation system, deployed in 2001, was expected to change the way people traveled, particularly in big cities. With high sales expectations, its builders prepared a substantial infrastructure for mass production. Although the product was well designed and fun to ride, it did not fulfill its business forecasts; sales were short of predictions; stakeholder expec-

tations were not met; there were legal issues on its use, and, in retrospect, the extensive investment in production capabilities seemed unjustified.

NASA's Mars Climate Orbiter (MCO) was supposed to circle the planet Mars and collect weather data as well as act as a relay communication station to a second vehicle, Mars Polar Lander. MCO was launched by NASA as planned on December 11, 1998, but after nine and a half months in space, its signal was lost just as it began its final insertion maneuver. The failure was later described as a technical error due to a failure to use metric units in the coding of one of the ground software files.

We can assume these projects were run by experienced managers and highly regarded organizations. Yet they all still failed to meet expectations. When project managers understood what went wrong and why, it was too late to correct the problems. All of the projects failed because of poor decision-making.

Many projects fail because at least one of the following three overarching objectives, which were cited at the beginning of this chapter, has been missed: meeting the budget, finishing on schedule, or meeting client specifications (product performance).

Some project teams lose sight of the business rationale behind their projects—that they must satisfy a customer and achieve business results, and not just meet technical project requirements (Shenhar and Dvir 2007). Other projects fail because enterprises are driven by financial requirements—that is, return on investment, earnings, stakeholder value, and so on—and are, therefore, forced to make business decisions with limited knowledge (Clarke 2000). Project managers need knowledge to make decisions, but there will never be enough knowledge to totally prevent failure, and risk and uncertainty are always there to threaten a project.

The success of a project thus turns on the decisions that are made, not the knowledge and not the absence of risk. Regardless of the amount of knowledge available, it is the decisions that are made that keep the project moving in the right direction. The knowledge that does make a difference to a project is knowledge about what decisions are most critical to successful project management. In fact, this type of knowledge is essential.

In the software development industry, failure appears to be the norm for large-scale software system development projects. Data for the year 2000 reveal that the average failure rate of software system projects was 85 percent (Bronzite 2000). An assessment of 8,380 computer applications by the Standish Group International (2001) revealed similar results. This survey categorized projects by three types:

**Resolution Type 1—project success:** The project was completed on time and on budget, with all features and functions as initially specified.

**Resolution Type 2—project challenged:** The project was completed and operational but was over budget, was over the time estimate, and has fewer features and functions than originally specified.

**Resolution Type 3—project impaired:** The project was canceled at some point during the development cycle.

Of the projects surveyed by the Standish Group International in 2001, 16 percent achieved success, challenged projects accounted for 53 percent, and 31 percent were impaired or failed. Nearly 85 percent of the projects surveyed, as shown in Figure 1-2, fell short of achieving success. Data from another assessment in 2004 indicate that 71 percent of the projects did not achieve success (Hartmann 2006).

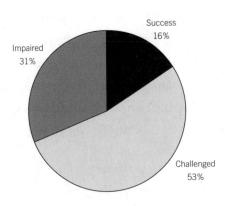

Michael Bronzite, *System Development: A Strategic Framework* (London: Springer, 2000).
Reprinted with permission from Springer Science and Business Media.

**FIGURE 1-2:** Project Resolution Types

An earlier assessment of software system development projects in various countries carried out in the 1990s yielded interestingly similar results. Table 1-1 presents a composite of those results (Bronzite 2000). The average system development failure rate, based on this survey, is also about 85 percent.

**TABLE 1-1:** Summary of Survey Results

| Location | Year | Source | No. Samples | Success Rate (percent) |
|---|---|---|---|---|
| London, UK | 1990 | Kearney | 400 | 11 |
| London, UK | 1994 | Pagoda | 100 | 11 |
| Dennis, MA (USA)* | 1995 | Standish-small | 365 | 28 |
| | 1995 | Standish-medium | | 16 |
| | 1995 | Standish-large | | 9 |
| Sheffield, UK** | 1996 | OASIG | 45 | 15 |
| Toronto, Canada | 1997 | KPMG | 176 | 16 |

\* Total number of samples for all three types
\*\* Reported success rate between 10 and 20 percent

Michael Bronzite, Table 2.1, "Formulating the Problem," *System Development: A Strategic Framework* (London: Springer, 2000): 22. Copyright © 2000 Springer Science and Business Media. Reprinted with permission.

In the 1990s, the focus in project management was placed on managing projects faster, better, and cheaper. The idea was that providing products to market faster would give companies a competitive edge. Many projects during that time period, however, were failing at an alarming rate. Why? One reason is this: Making the decision to starve projects of time and resources is seldom helpful in meeting project objectives. This lack of time and resources is a common threat faced by many project managers. Some projects will naturally take more time and possibly more resources. In some cases, the success of a project directly correlates to the availability of the required resources. Thus, the decision to starve a project should not be made without extensive knowledge of the side effects of such an action.

## A Planned Process for Decision-Making

Objectives provide the logical basis for the decisions that occur in managing a project (Powell 2002); decisions provide the basis for guiding and controlling the *management process* in reaching defined objectives. A project manager's management process includes (1) planning, (2) organizing, (3) directing, and (4) monitoring project work. The most consequential of these is *planning*, a process that permeates all the other processes—that is, organizing the project is planned, directing the project is planned, and monitoring the project is planned as well.

Successful planning depends on effective decision-making, and to make effective decisions, *a decision process*—a planned process for decision-making—must also exist. Such a planned decision-making process helps the project manager to make successful decisions while planning, organizing, directing, and monitoring projects. The many decisions made during project execution rely on high-quality planning, and it is clear that project objectives cannot be successfully achieved without a decision process.

But why is a planned process necessary? A process is needed because making decisions can be very complex. Decisions involve many stakeholders; require consideration of competing objectives, risk, and uncertainty; and may involve large financial investments with the returns having a long time horizon before success can be determined. Furthermore, not all decisions require only common sense. Of the 10,000 hypothetical decisions posited by Keeney (2004) and shown in Figure 1-3, approximately 7,000 have such small consequences that they require very little thought. Another 2,000 can be classified as "No Brainers." The remaining 1,000 decisions require the application of some systematic process. Due to the complex nature of such decisions, the expertise of a trained decision analyst would be very helpful to the project manager in most circumstances.

The sequence of decisions and associated choices available to the project manager at the beginning of a project has a nearly uncountable number of paths (Powell and Buede 2006). Buede (2000) makes the following argument:

> To be successful, the engineering design of systems must embrace the notion that many decisions are made during the development process. This is not a controversial position to take. However, adopting the notion that these decisions should be made via a rational, explicit process is not consistent with much of the current practice in the engineering of systems.

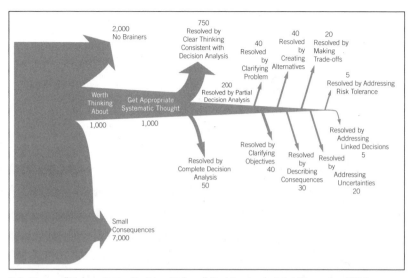

R. L. Keeney, "Making Better Decision Makers," *Decision Analysis* 1:4 (December 2004): 193–204. Reprinted with permission from the Institute for Operations Research and the Management Sciences (INFORMS), 7240 Parkway Drive, Suite 310, Hanover, MD 21076 USA.

**FIGURE 1-3:** Resolving Decisions

Assuming that many decisions are going to be made in the course of a project, *a random or unplanned and unstructured decision-making process* correlates to a random pathway into the future rather than a well-planned one. A decision pathway or sequence that is random is more likely to lead to failure than to success. Achieving success requires that a *rational and explicit or structured decision process be developed and used.* When a rational and explicit process is absent, decisions are not well structured, not discussed widely, and not well documented.

The project manager is likely to emphasize cost in some decisions and schedule or performance in others. When this type of decision-making occurs, dysfunctions occur and success is elusive. A colleague of ours once said that a good sign of a well-managed project is clear evidence that all of the staff know the key project objectives and use them to guide their daily activities.

Decision-making should occur as part of a dynamic process, but not a random one. When a planned process is used, mistakes are minimized because there are opportunities built into the process to correct errors. Projects thus stand a greater chance of succeeding when a process provides for self-correction. Because many decisions in the real world are made in an unstructured way, this notion of a process-oriented approach might seem quite novel. It is, in fact, very true that it is different from traditional ways of arriving at a choice, but the very difference a structured approach entails seems certain to improve managerial decision-making within an organization by virtue of its ability to catch and correct errors (Harrison 1987).

## A General Framework for Making Decisions

Figure 1-4 presents a general framework for making decisions. The framework organizes the tasks of decision-making and makes performing those tasks simpler. Using this framework ensures that all the important tasks are addressed in a consistent manner.

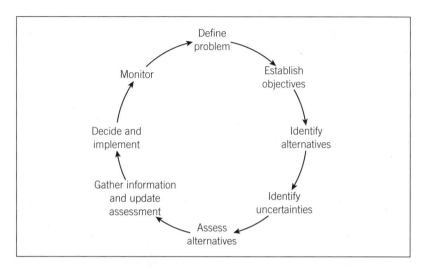

**FIGURE 1-4:** Decision-Making Process

The project manager should remember that the framework is simply a tool; the tool cannot replace common sense, judgment, evidence, quantitative analysis, or leadership. The framework can also be used as an audit trail to explain why specific decisions were made. The framework is not a panacea for bad decisions; it is intended to organize and improve the decision-making process.

- **Step 1: Define the problem**—Define the context of the problem. This context includes such things as the time horizon, constraints on cost and other factors, and key project imperatives.

- **Step 2: Establish objectives**—Define the project objectives. The project manager must identify the decision situation and understand the objectives in that situation. Project objectives define project decisions; it is thus important that the right objectives are defined. Addressing the wrong objective or objectives will lead to the wrong decisions and the wrong decision outcomes.

■ **Step 3: Identify alternatives**—Canvas key people and conduct brainstorming sessions to identify as many feasible alternatives as possible. Then whittle these alternatives down to a reasonable number of solution candidates, modifying the alternatives as necessary to make them different from each other and more attractive in terms of the objectives.

■ **Step 4: Identify uncertainties**—Find the major factors that connect the alternatives to the known objectives and try to collect as much data and expert judgment on these factors as is cost-effective.

■ **Step 5: Assess alternatives**—Collect the necessary facts, data, and judgments to assess how well each alternative course of action meets all of the objectives. Complete this assessment and identify the strengths and weaknesses of each alternative.

■ **Step 6: Gather information and update the assessment**—Assess which information might be most useful in determining that the recommended alternative in Step 5 is NOT the best alternative. Gather this information if possible, and collect this information to move on to the final stage of assessment.

■ **Step 7: Decide and implement**—Determine which alternative best meets the defined objectives and assign the necessary responsibilities and authorities to begin the implementation of the chosen alternative.

■ **Step 8: Monitor**—Establish and implement a data collection plan to assess progress towards the objectives and to plan changes to the implementation if necessary.

No one ever reached an objective without using some type of process to make decisions. "If you do not know where you are going, any road will get you there" is a classic observation.

Regardless of the nature of their individual achievements, successful people tend to have one thing in common: They make effective decisions that are the result of an effective process. The runner who trains for a long-distance marathon, the student trying to get into medical school, the platoon leader preparing for combat, and the project manager who successfully manages a project all use a process for making effective decisions. A process helps the decision maker or project manager produce the decisions necessary to reach the desired objectives. As mentioned earlier, a process helps the project manager identify and organize the tasks and decisions that are required to manage winning projects.

A planned decision process not only helps to guide and control decisions but also influences events that occur in managing projects. A planned process is also a tool that can help project managers to make good decisions. Achieving success in project management comes at a high price. A mistake made in one key decision can hinder an entire project's success. A project manager must thus be proactive and must guide the project team and all stakeholders through the decision-making process.

- Project managers are aware of their responsibilities for managing projects but receive very little training on decision-making.

- Project managers make hundreds, if not thousands, of decisions that support the project management process.

- A project can survive without adequate resources, but it will never survive faulty decision-making.

- Defining a decision context is necessary to make good decisions.

- The three vital cornerstones of decision-making are (1) the decision, (2) the decision process, and (3) the decision maker or actor.

- Project success is traditionally measured by whether a project meets budget and schedule estimates and whether the project achieves client specifications. This book focuses on the decisions that are necessary to prevent project failure.

- Decisions provide the basis for guiding and controlling the management process in reaching defined objectives.

- A planned decision process not only helps guide and control decisions but also influences events that occur in managing projects.

# CHAPTER 2

# Managerial Decision-Making

$\mathbf{A}$re project management decisions different from the types of everyday decisions that we make? Indeed they are. They are not traditional common-sense decisions like those we make in the normal course of living. They are complex decisions about problems that require a great deal of analysis. Project management decisions have a large impact on project success. Projects such as designing new products, building a house, installing new systems, constructing new facilities, designing information systems, and designing a political campaign are good examples of projects that require a great deal of management decision-making. Project management decisions include not just decisions about spending and specifications, but also decisions about achieving long-term goals such as customer satisfaction and larger business goals.

In project management, decisions cannot be random and must be planned in support of project, product, and organizational objectives. Managerial decisions, based on their specific context and nature, have a significant effect on the organization (Braverman 1980) and require a commitment of fiscal, physical, or human resources (Harrison 1987).

This chapter presents the nature of managerial decisions, the importance of planning managerial decisions, and several examples of successful and failed projects. We also look at some of the specific decisions that project managers have to make. Several case studies are presented that highlight decisions that contributed to project success or project failure.

This chapter presents the following sections:

- Managerial Decisions Defined

- Strategic, Operational, and Tactical Decisions

- Generic Project Management Decisions

- The Importance of Project Management Decisions

- Project Management Decisions Contribute to Project Success

- A Management Perspective on Failed Projects: Two Case Studies

- The Solution—Good-Quality Decisions.

## Managerial Decisions Defined

As stated in Chapter 1, project managers are generally concerned with three objectives:

- Meeting the budget

- Finishing on schedule

- Meeting client specifications (product performance).

Project managers are also responsible for successfully achieving these additional objectives:

- Successfully managing stakeholders (e.g., CEO, program manager, contractors, consultants, clients)

- Successfully managing the project team (e.g., finding the right people, finding the right number of people, assigning the right people to the right tasks at the right time with the right information)

- Successfully managing risks.

Projects run the risk of failing when these six project, product, organizational, and business objectives are not attained. Project managers must not assume, however, that they are responsible for making *all* the decisions that are required to successfully manage projects. Some decisions will be made by others. For example, program managers are responsible for making decisions about project resources, and clients and end-users are responsible for making decisions that affect the operation of the product or system being managed.

It is, therefore, a major responsibility of the project manager to make sure that members of the project management team use a structured decision process that uses a consistent set of objectives and a planned methodology.

In short, project managers are specifically responsible for making project management decisions (decisions related to the six objectives presented earlier in this section). Some decisions result in short-term success, while others effect long-term success. Project management includes both short-term and long-term objectives.

Table 2-1 shows the categorization of project management decisions. Project management decisions are broad in nature and affect the project, the product, and the organization. Project and product decisions are narrow in scope, while organizational decisions are broad in scope. Project decisions focus on meeting project requirements—cost, schedule, and product performance. Organizational decisions focus on meeting organizational objectives.

**TABLE 2-1:** Categorization of Project Management Decisions

|  | Actor (s) | Decision Scope | Decision Impact |
|---|---|---|---|
| **Project management decisions** | Project manager | Broad | Performance of the project, the product, and the organization |
| **Project decisions** | Project manager; program managers | Narrow | Achieving cost, schedule, and product performance |
| **Product decisions** | Product manager; clients | Narrow | Achieving product specifications and customer expectations |
| **Organizational decisions** | Project manager | Broad | Performance of product team |

Project management decisions focus on achieving business results and include budget, schedule, and product performance decisions. They are decisions that (1) relate to defining processes, activities, and events that have to be carried out to attain the objectives specified for the project, product, and organization; (2) reflect the overall management and discipline of the project; and (3) define the necessary resources for product development and resources for operation (Powell 2002). These decisions are used as the control parameter during management of the integrity of the development process and quality of the product. As a result, each decision made must be a conscious decision intended to guide and control all events occurring in the project management process that satisfy project, product, and organizational objectives.

Managerial decisions tend to focus on at least the following five dimensions that contribute to a project's success (Shenhar and Dvir 2007):

- Project efficiency: Meeting time and budget goals

- Impact on customer: Meeting requirements and achieving customer satisfaction, benefits, and loyalty

- Impact on team: Satisfaction, retention, and personal growth

- Business and direct success: Return on investment, market share, and growth

- Preparation for the future: New technologies, new markets, and new capabilities

Each dimension includes several possible submeasures, shown in Figure 2-1 (Shenhar and Dvir 2007). Making effective decisions within each dimension is a complex task. For example, there are schedule decisions and budget decisions, and there are requirements decisions and customer-related decisions. There are decisions related to the team and additional decisions that impact the organization.

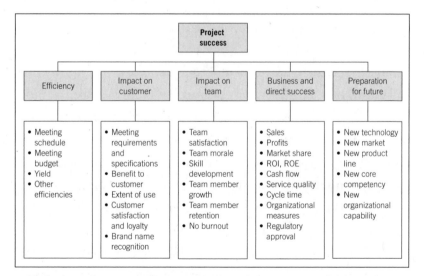

Aaron Shenhar and Dov Dvir, Table 2.1, *Reinventing Project Management: The Diamond Approach to Successful Growth and Innovation* (Boston: Harvard Business School Press, 2007): 27. Copyright © 2007 by Harvard Business School Press. Reprinted with permission.

**FIGURE 2-1:** Dimensions and Submeasures that Contribute to Project Success

Because project managers concern themselves with the future, decisions must be made that impact an organization's future. Due to the dynamic nature of the decision-making required, it is easy to understand why effective decision-making is no easy task. Project managers must simultaneously focus on all five dimensions because decisions made in one dimension will have an impact on decisions that need to be made in another dimension. For example, schedule decisions have an impact on decisions related to customer decisions, and customer decisions affect project team decisions.

## Strategic, Operational, and Tactical Decisions

Every organization has a structure—flat or hierarchical. Companies involved in project management traditionally have a hierarchical structure. Because decisions are made at every level of the organization, we can classify project management decisions into three categories—*strategic decisions, operational decisions,* or *tactical decisions.*

Strategic decisions are broad in scope, affect the entire organization, and usually have long-term consequences. By "broad in scope," we mean that strategic decisions can be high-level thematic decisions or choices that will drive other decisions. Organizational objectives, for example, reside at the strategic level. An example of a strategic decision is the identification and description of the unique features of the business that will make it competitive. Choosing those features, that is, deciding upon which features will make the business competitive, is a decision that is on a high level and thus demands no specific action explicitly. But it does drive other decisions that must be made to implement the organization's strategic business plan.

Operational decisions are less broad in scope, affect middle management, and are also usually long-term decisions. Choosing product objectives resides at the operational level. An example of an operational decision is choosing the materials that are required to design and develop product components.

Tactical decisions are narrow in scope, are short-term, and are driven by strategic and operational decisions. Choosing project objectives resides at the tactical level. An example of a tactical decision is choosing among various alternatives how a project can best be managed. Strategic, operational, and tactical decisions are interrelated, and decision makers exchange information with other decision makers as shown in Figure 2-2. Strategic decisions are made first and help to define operational decisions. Both strategic and operational decisions then affect or drive the tactical decisions that are made. Tactical decisions are made more frequently and routinely than either strategic or operational decisions.

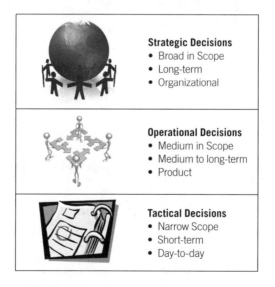

**FIGURE 2-2:** Relationship between Decisions

# Generic Project Management Decisions

We now turn our attention to some of the specific decisions that project managers have to make. The example we use is decisions we would need to make if we started our own company—a company called Powell and Buede's Bakery, which will produce nutritional almond cookies. In Table 2-2, column 1 presents the decisions that must be made (specific to cookie production), column 2 presents the actual decisions that were made, and column 3 presents the stage in the project management life cycle in which the decision was made. (See the section "The Project Management Life Cycle Guides Decision-Making" later in this chapter.) Some decisions are strategic in nature, while others are operational and tactical. The decisions shown are appropriate for just about any type of project.

**TABLE 2-2:** Generic Project Management Decisions

| Types of Decisions to be Made (Specific to Cookie Production) | Exemplary Decisions Made | Project Management Life-Cycle Stage |
|---|---|---|
| What are the market needs? | Consumers like cookies that are super-size and that are loaded with extra-large crunchy almonds. | Conception |
| What are the unique features of the business that will make it competitive? | The company offers freshly baked homemade cookies. | Conception |
| What are the business risks? | The risks are lack of an interest in the cookie and a short supply of almonds on hand when they are needed. | Feasibility Analysis |
| What is the expected demand for the project? | The expected demand for the cookie will be highest during the weekday and at lunch. | Feasibility Analysis |
| What are the organizational requirements? | The company will need to have a manager, shift managers, counter workers, and a number of bakers. | Planning |
| Where will the facility be located? | The fast-food facility will be located in the food court of a shopping mall. | Planning |

| Types of Decisions to be Made (Specific to Cookie Production) | Exemplary Decisions Made | Project Management Life-Cycle Stage |
|---|---|---|
| What costing method will be used? | A top-down costing approach will be used. | Planning |
| What are the operational risks? | The risks are a lack of employees and a natural disaster. | Implementation |
| What are the training requirements? | Workers will need training on newly purchased and installed technology. | Implementation |
| How will managers ensure the quality of the product, measure quality, and identify quality problems? | Managers will check the quality of almonds—size and freshness. All ingredients will be checked for freshness. The dough will be checked for texture. The cookie will be checked for overall quality. | Monitor and Controlling |
| How will the inventory of raw materials be monitored? | An economic order quantity model will be used to track resources. | Monitor and Controlling |
| What termination documents are required? | A project final report is required at the end of the project. | Termination |
| What are the termination criteria? | The project will end when the costs outstrip the profit over a 9-month period. | Termination |

# The Importance of Project Management Decisions

Making managerial decisions is one of the most important functions a project manager must perform. The primary reason for the importance of this function is that the competitive advantage of an organization often depends on project success. Project managers must keep decision quality high while locating limited project resources and performing other highly visible tasks.

The natural tendency is for project managers to place strict emphasis on the management of a project instead of focusing on the type, nature, and impact of the decisions made in the project management process. In some cases, a decision-making process is altogether absent. Because project management decisions usually affect many people and are made in a dynamic and uncertain environment that involves cost, time, and performance trade-offs, making the best decision is critical to successful project management (Mazda 1998). (It should be noted that this book does not address decision-making styles, such as authoritative or participatory styles. The authors think that each project manager should use the style that's most comfortable.)

*Decision analysis* is a process that assists in determining whether a decision is good or bad. Not analyzing the effect of a decision is definitely not good business. Even when decision analysis is conducted, because risk and uncertainty are present, an exact outcome can never be known ahead of time. What we do know is that when proper and improper decisions are made, several things occur, respectively.

When proper decisions are made, three things are certain (Kerzner 2006):

■ Functional units understand their total responsibilities toward achieving project needs.

■ Problems resulting from scheduling and allocation of critical resources are known beforehand.

■ Problems that might jeopardize successful project completion are identified early in the process, so that effective corrective action can be taken and replanning can occur to prevent or resolve problems.

When improper decisions are made, three things are certain (Kerzner 2006):

- Company and/or project policies, procedures, and directives are continually revised and/or established.

- Organizational responsibility is continually shifting and unnecessary restructuring may occur.

- Staff requires skill development and new knowledge.

It is logical that poor-quality decisions have a greater probability of schedule delays, exceeded budgets, poor product quality, a lack of proper management skills, inadequate risk analysis, and improper validation methods. The list goes on.

## Project Management Decisions Contribute to Project Success

Project management decisions focus directly on the project, the product, and the organization. The Dell computer, Microsoft Office software, the Internet, the Unmanned Aerial Vehicle (the U.S. Predator aircraft), and the Abrams tank are all very good examples of recent projects that have succeeded. The success of the projects was not necessarily judged on how well the projects met cost and schedule objectives but on how well the projects achieved the long-term business goals for which they were initiated—how much value they delivered to their organizations or customers. In each example, the focus was on the project, the product, and the organization, but the primary focus was anchored to the business results.

In traditional project management, project success depends on satisfying the three constraints—time, budget, and specifications (product performance). The focus in traditional project management is on the project efficiency. In some cases, the success of a project is still evaluated solely on project efficiency—how well it meets cost, schedule, and specifications (product performance).

A judgment of project success should not be based only on how well it satisfies the three constraints; a judgment of project success should be based on how well the project delivers long-term value to the organization and to customers. We understand that in some cases a project can be successful even though it fails to meet the time, budget, and performance objectives. In business organizations, projects are not generated to meet cost, schedule, and product performance but to achieve the long-term business goals for which they are initiated, so there needs to be some flexibility when assessing the success of projects—even when using the three fundamental objectives of all projects with which this book began.

Project managers must focus on more than just meeting time goals, budget goals, and product specifications (project efficiency). They must also focus on other dimensions of project management that are necessary to produce success: (1) customer impact, (2) impact on the team, (3) business results, and (4) preparation for the future. Customer impact deals with improving the customer's life or business. Team impact decisions focus on team learning and team growth. Business results target commercial success. Preparation for the future addresses the long-range benefits of the project.

Some dimensions, such as project efficiency, can be assessed in the very short term, while preparation for the future can be assessed only much later. Project management decisions thus have two objectives: short-term and long-term. Short-term success is achieved by or defined as meeting cost, schedule, and product performance objectives. Long-term success is defined as achieving long-term business goals—delivering value to the organization and the customer. As already stated, although a project might not satisfy the three constraints, it can still be considered a success. Consider the following cases (Shenhar and Dvir 2007).

- **Case 1**  When the first generation of the Ford Taurus was introduced in 1986, it quickly became the best-selling car in America and one of the most successful cars in Ford's history. Its revolutionary design and exceptional quality created a new standard in the U.S. automobile industry, and customers simply loved the car. Yet when the development project was completed, its project manager was demoted because the project was completed three months later than scheduled.

- **Case 2**  The first Windows software launched by Microsoft suffered enormous delays, with continuous redirection of resources and people. But Windows turned out to be one of Microsoft's most profitable products and an enormous source of revenue.

- **Case 3**  Before introducing its big hit, the Macintosh, in 1984, Apple Computer completely failed with its predecessor, the Lisa computer. Apple's managers acknowledged later that without the lessons learned and technologies developed on the Lisa project, the Mac's success would not have been possible—calling into question whether Lisa was indeed a complete failure.

In each of these cases, the project was eventually considered a success based on the value delivered to the organization and to the customer—long-term success. Evaluated against traditional—short-term—means, each project would have been considered a failure. Shenhar and Dvir have made the following observation (2007):

> Meeting time and budget goals is only a small part of the picture. Adhering to a project plan tells us nothing about achieving the long-term business goals for which the project was initiated. Most projects are part of the strategic management of their organizations, and they should be assessed based on their contribution to overall business results, and not only on their ability to meet time, budget or performance goals. An organization must therefore set

project goals in advance to reflect its expectation, both in the short term and in the long term.

What is important to keep in mind is that although a project may fail to meet time and budget goals, it can be judged successful based on product and organizational success. We now consider another case (Shenhar and Dvir 2007).

## CASE STUDY

### The Sydney Opera House

One of the world's greatest tourist attractions is the Sydney Opera House, an architectural wonder visited every year by millions of travelers. The original project plan, as envisioned by the New South Wales government in the 1950s, included an estimated budget of about seven million Australian dollars and a schedule of five years. But getting there was tough. The construction project experienced enormous difficulties—extensive delays, bitter conflicts, and painful budget overruns. Sixteen years passed before the opera house opened its doors, and its final price tag was more than 100 million dollars. Judging it purely on time and budget and performance, you might conclude that the Sydney Opera House project was a textbook example of project failure. But no one really cares anymore how the project was managed, and almost everyone sees the Opera House as a success story. It provides continuous income and fame to the city of Sydney, and it remains one the most fascinating buildings in the world.

Aaron Shenhar and Dov Dvir, *Reinventing Project Management: The Diamond Approach to Successful Growth and Innovation* (Boston: Harvard Business School Press, 2007): 21. Copyright © 2007 by Harard Business School Press. Reprinted with permission.

The next case study presents a detailed overview of a project that eventually succeeded—but not until it first failed. Both the project and the product successes are noted. Some of the decisions mentioned earlier (see the bold questions in the case study) are considered in the decision-making process. The case study presents the implementation of the Prospective Student Information System at the University of Oklahoma and includes all phases of the project life cycle, which is described in Chapter 3. The problem is defined, stakeholder analysis is conducted, alternatives are generated, a system solution is selected, and the system solution is implemented. This case depicts the integration of a number of concepts addressed in this book and brings to the reader's attention a number of challenging issues that might be encountered in the implementation of a product or system solution.

Several failures within the project were noted before the overall project was considered a success. First, the system did not meet user needs. Second, the budget did not adequately support the project requirements. Third, there was a requirement that people who used the system contribute some of their own resources. Fourth, the system's interaction with various stakeholders (e.g., students, faculty) was not well defined. Fifth, there was no way to modify the system after flaws were found. These failures can be easily traced back to a lack of good project management. A review of the case reveals the key decisions that contributed to project success—but only after time and valuable resources had been wasted by poor decisions earlier.

# CASE STUDY

## Design and Implementation of the Prospective Student Information System

*Dr. Bobbie L. Foote, Professor Emeritus, University of Oklahoma*

## The Project Beginning

**(What is the problem?)** In 1967 the University of Oklahoma decided to venture into the new computer technology to consider automating their student admissions system. The University at this time was making a commitment to utilize commercial computing power instead of continuing full-scale development of their own computer, the OSAGE, which was designed and built from conception by University faculty. They had realized that they did not have the resources to develop the myriad software applications necessary to run the University information needs based on the one-of-a-kind operating system for the OSAGE. The University had bought an IBM 650 computer by 1957 and after 1962 had purchased an IBM 1620 and had started developing the software and operating specialists to run a punch card operation.

**(What skills are required?)** A young professor in Industrial Engineering was selected to design and implement the new system. **(Who are the project team members?)** A team of administrators was formed to advise him. A bright young graduate student who was an employee of a local air-conditioning manufacturing firm and had an undergraduate degree in Industrial Engineering from the University of Oklahoma was hired to gather information and write demo software to show feasibility.

**(Who are the users?)** In the early planning stages, a standard Industrial Engineering analysis was performed. A survey was sent out to determine potential users. **(What is the source and method for determining requirements?)** These users were interviewed as to what information they wanted. This led to a listing of actions and decisions that they needed to make. A standard IE flowchart was developed to look at timing.

This was an admissions system. So the first day of enrollment in the summer or fall served as one of the drop-dead time goals. To be admitted, the student had to supply high school transcripts, a copy of a medical exam, records of immunizations, religious preferences, housing preferences, and their interest in various academic programs. There were deadlines for these submissions. If a student failed to submit the required information, the University manually went through the file and noted omissions and sent out a letter with boxes marked to indicate the information shortage. Some students went through several cycles. Students who showed late interest were a problem as the University needed to expedite their record analysis and to communicate decisions quickly. Appeals had to be handled.

**(What is the problem?)** Another problem was the exponential growth of the applications as more and more people realized the value of a college education. This led to a big problem with applications for a scholarship as the donors and other supervisors had deadlines to make decisions. Scholarship applications required extra information such as letters of recommendation and student essays. This put a real burden on the manual system.

**(What are use case studies?)** As a part of the routine information gathering, histories of other processing applications were sought. It was at this point [that] an unpleasant realization occurred. Over 90 percent of the past projects had either failed or never even started. An investigation of these failures ensued.

**The Pause**

At this point a series of meetings with upper-level managers, including the Vice President (later Provost) for Academics was initiated. A series of surveys was sent out to get information about these failures. The returns indicated a variety of reasons: The system did not meet their needs; low budget, hence a requirement that people who used the system kick in from their resources; awkward means of interacting with the system; inability to modify the systems after flaws were found.

**(What are the product requirements?)** During this time the student research assistant created a system to handle the requirements as understood. **(What is the solution concept?)** This system consisted of: a set of decisions required by each user, the time deadlines, and the information required by the decisions; a set of actions required that were to be automated such as letters of acceptance; letters asking for more information; letters reminding students of deadlines; and most importantly, a system flow diagram that pinpointed interactions among future users of the system. Student letters asking for information were separated into two groups: one that required a form answer and [one dealing with] more complex issues that required a personal answer. **(What are the feasibility criteria?)** This list was reviewed by University software developers and feasibility was assessed. IBM had an interest and donated time to help assess feasibility.

**(What are owner and user requirements?)** The above study highlighted the amount of cooperation required from University functions and their clerical personnel to use the system successfully. Everyone realized that a training package had to be developed before the system could be activated.

**The Implementation Plan**

The chairman of the IE department and the study manager had a series of meetings to address the problem of implementation. **(What are implementation requirements?)** The need for training was determined to be an easy problem to design and manage. **(What are training cost requirements?)** The major problem was the financial issue and the perceived quality issues that plagued previous projects. A series of personal interviews with users and system designers revealed a further problem: the selective memory of users. After a new system was begun, users would frequently say that they had unmet needs that had been communicated to designers but ignored in the final product. Users also had little concept of the changes in operating protocol that would be needed.

**(How will user requirements be managed?)** The following solution emerged. If you wanted help, you had to pay, but the Provost would match the dollars from the managers' budget from his own. **(What is the test plan?)** The final part of the implementation protocol was to circulate the plan to the managers (users) and then meet personally with them. The provost required one of two responses: the plan suits my need or it fails and here is what is missing. Time deadlines for responses were given. A new plan was devised and the same process was carried out. When no gaps were found by users, […] a final document [was] circulated which required the signature of the user. They either signed saying that the system met their needs or the system failed. If the system failed, they had to give reasons. Those users with problems met with the study manager and the Provost to discuss their problems. In front of the Provost, managers were candid and cooperative. After this meeting, every user who had not signed, signed. **(Who is responsible for development and testing?)** The head of the computer center took responsibility for developing and testing the software in time for implementation just after Christmas.

### The Outcome

The resulting system was programmed and proved to be a rousing success. The offload on users and their clerical staff was huge. **(What are the future require-ments?)** The growth of the University was enabled and further data processing projects grew rapidly. PSIP proved to be the basis of the complex information system that encompasses the University today.

Appendix A includes additional examples of project successes.

# A Management Perspective on Failed Projects: Two Case Studies

We eat, sleep, and breathe decisions. Decision-making is what we do daily, whether in the conscious or unconscious realm. Our ability to make decisions is exercised in many ways—through trial and error, intuition, empiricism, and process methods. Often, decisions are categorized as small decisions and big decisions; small decisions receive less attention than big decisions. This concept might work when dealing with everyday decisions, but in managing projects a decision is a decision. Overlooking what might be a small decision can have as devastating an effect as overlooking a big decision and can cause a project to fail or fall short of achieving its objectives.

For example, delaying a project review might be considered a small decision, but the delay can have huge consequences for the project schedule, the project budget, and the technical specifications of the product being managed. In essence, all decisions are equally important. Nonetheless, there are clearly some decisions that require much more attention than others. One of the goals of this book is to motivate the reader to consider more decisions to be worthy of careful, conscious attention.

The reason for a project failure is always tied to a decision that is impaired, made too early, made too late, or not made at all. In many cases, the decision to retire a project is always better than allowing a project to fail. Retiring a project saves valuable resources that can be used elsewhere in the organization. Although the decision to retire or discontinue a project is never an easy one, the decision becomes much more complicated when the project begins to exceed both schedule and budget. We present two case studies to illustrate these points.

The first case study reviews a project that failed after five years and after investments totaling $26 million (Plas 2006). A number of key project decisions were not made. Those absent decisions contributed to the project failure.

The University of Wisconsin (UW) has been implementing a system-wide payroll and benefit software at its many campuses across the state.

After five years and $26 million, UW decided to switch from a new development project by Lawson Software to Oracle/PeopleSoft, aligning with the state Department of Administration's decision to implement an information system initiative with Oracle/PeopleSoft. The UW project's implementation problems have been well-documented, including millions of dollars of cost overruns, a disbanded project management team, and the retirement of key decision makers (Plas 2006).

The main reason for failure was a lack of good project management. In an article about the project, UW project management consultant Diane Haubner faulted the entire planning process (Kleefeld 2005). That process included a number of project management decisions that were made poorly or should have been made but were not (Kleefeld 2005):

- The use of a committee-made task list as opposed to development of an overall project plan and the naming of a project manager

- People in charge of the project who knew a lot about software but not a whole lot about actual project management

- Poorly planned testing of database systems

- Lack of communication between testers and management.

The second case study is a review of a project that failed to consider the importance of fitting the right organization to the right project (Shenhar and Dvir 2007). As stated earlier, the reason for a project failure is always tied to a decision that is impaired, made too early, made too late, or not made at all. Throughout the case study, we highlight decisions that should have been made but were not.

# CASE STUDY

## The FCS Project

FCS was a third-generation fire control system developed by a well-known defense contractor in Israel. The main challenge for the FCS project was to improve the hit accuracy of weapons mounted on moving vehicles. Because the contractor was experienced in building components and subsystems for similar previous generations, its executives *assumed* that they had the capability to compete for an entire system. **(What are the required skills?)**

The major technical innovation in the FCS was a new stabilization technique, which promised to improve performance substantially. However, it would also require the use of technology that was totally new to the company, as well as an entirely different operational doctrine.

Nevertheless, company managers *assumed* that they could manage the development of this new system in the same way as their previous, less comprehensive projects. **(What are the management requirements?)** They also *assumed* they could use existing modules, with minor modifications, as building blocks for the new system. **(What are new technology requirements?)** In addition, they *assumed* that after they had developed, tested, and validated all the subsystems, it would be a straightforward matter to assemble them into a functioning integrated system. **(What is the assembly process and methodology?)** Based on these assumptions, they put together a team in the way they always had, and they set about the new project with the same general mind-set and methodology to which they were accustomed. **(What is the best form of organizational design and what are the organizational components?)**

Aaron Shenhar and Dov Dvir, *Reinventing Project Management: The Diamond Approach to Successful Growth and Innovation* (Boston: Harvard Business School Press, 2007): 37–39. Copyright © 2007 by Harard Business School Press. Reprinted with permission.

However, most of the engineers working on the program had no experience with the crucial new stabilization technology. Furthermore, none of the team members had built entire systems, with responsibility for overall performance to meet the system's end-user expectations. **(What are the required experience levels?)** On top of that, the whole project was new to the customer, and this meant that the ultimate performance objectives (and minimum requirements) were somewhat uncertain. **(What is the method for requirements validation?)** The plan was to start delivering initial units after 16 months and to begin full-scale production in three and a half years.

It soon became clear that the original project schedule was unrealistic. **(What is the method for determining task durations?)** The project plan was therefore rewritten—twice. Still, the project steadily fell behind. After the first year, the company initiated emergency procedures and started to funnel additional resources to the program. Yet it took two full years for company managers to realize that the whole program needed to address two major problems, which lay outside the scope of the original plan altogether. By this time the crisis was full blown.

The first problem was that developing the stabilization technology would require much more time, because the new units needed additional design cycles to accommodate greater technological uncertainty.

The second problem was more profound: A complex system does not simply function as a collection of subsystems. The program needed an extensive period of system integration, together with the development of a new combat doctrine. Those activities were not part of the original project plan. **(Define the organization for validating the project plan.)**

A drastic change in project management style was needed. After the intervention of top management, new systems engineering and integration groups were added to the team. In addition, the company mobilized specific hand-picked experts, including external consultants, to help the team in its efforts. And top management involvement became much more extensive, with daily briefings and almost instant reporting of new problems and solutions. **(When are the required project reviews?)** This change resulted in a breakthrough, and it led, after 38 months, to the delivery of the first fully functioning system. Production started after five years, with a final delay of 21 months and cost overruns of almost twice the original budget.

As noted, the project team finally got its act together, but not until valuable time and resources were wasted. This case clearly reveals what happens when the right decisions are not made. It is critically important that project managers be aware of what managerial decisions need to be made in order to produce project success.

## The Solution—Good-Quality Decisions

As noted in the case studies just presented, most project problems are managerial, not technical. When technical errors do cause projects to fail, it is usually management that failed to make the right decisions. Managerial decisions are critical to successful project management and therefore must be managed in a way that produces desired results. Unfortunately, great management does not necessarily lead to successful projects. Many projects under well-experienced management and management teams often end in failure or fall short of achieving managerial and product objectives.

The current trend is project failures continuing at an alarming rate. Why do projects continue to fail? Mismanagement and the decisions that management makes are the answer to this question. The success of a project essentially hinges on the quality of the decisions made. When decisions are of poor quality or are dysfunctional, the result is often a failed or impaired project; however, when decisions are of good quality, projects stand a far greater chance of being successful and contributing to organizational goals. The goal of this book is to assist the project manager in the task of identifying those decisions that will enable project, product, and organizational success.

This chapter introduced the nature of project management decisions. First, we presented an overview of project management decisions. We then presented a set of project management decisions using project life-cycle terminology. Because decisions can mean life or death for an organization, we stated why making project management decisions are an important responsibility. Decisions are made at every level within project management organizations. Although this text focuses on decisions at the project or tactical level, we defined two additional levels—strategic and operational. In addition, we showed the results of proper and improper project management decisions. The next topic addressed long-term and short-term decisions. We ended the chapter by highlighting decisions that contributed to project success and those decisions that contribute to project failure.

The following specific points were made in this chapter:

■ Project management decisions include decisions that (1) relate to defining processes, activities, and events that have to be carried out to attain the objectives specified for the project, product, and organization; (2) reflect the overall management and discipline of the project, and (3) define the necessary resources for product development and resources for operation.

■ During management, project management decisions are used as the control parameter of the integrity of the development process and the quality of the product.

■ Making managerial decisions is one of the most important functions a project manager must perform, because the competitive advantage of an organization often depends on project success.

■ Project management decisions fall into three categories—strategic decisions, operational decisions, or tactical decisions.

■ The reason for a project failure is always tied to a decision that is impaired, made too early, made too late, or not made at all.

■ Managerial decisions tend to focus on at least five dimensions: (1) project efficiency, (2) impact on the customer, (3) impact on the team, (4) business results, and (5) preparation for the future.

■ Many projects under experienced management and management teams often end in failure or fall short of achieving managerial and product objectives because the ideas and decisions that worked well the last time did not work so well this time.

In Chapter 3, we present the project management life cycle as a mechanism that guides and controls decision-making. We also provide examples of decisions unique to each life-cycle stage.

# CHAPTER 3

# Decisions and the Project Management Life Cycle

Success is the objective during project management, and good decision-making is the "yellow brick road" that leads to success. The project management life cycle guides decision-making. Project managers need a structure that helps to logically sequence their decision-making activities. Because early decisions impact later decisions, a project management life cycle identifies early activities that might have a bearing on later activities. Mistakes due to poor decision-making during the front end of the project management life cycle can have significant negative effects on the total cost of the product and its success with users and those who fund product development (often called bill payers) (Powell and Buede 2006).

Many problems surface late in the project due to earlier mistakes in decision-making, and this often results in a much higher cost to correct as well as increased project risk. Quality decisions made in the front end of the project management life cycle contribute to project, product, and organizational success and result in fewer conflicts when later decisions are made.

This chapter presents the project management life cycle, examples of decisions unique to each stage of the life cycle, decision gates within the life cycle, and examples of other life-cycle models.

This chapter presents the following sections:

- The Project Management Life Cycle

- Milestones within the Project Management Life Cycle

- Stakeholder Decisions in the Project Management Life Cycle

- Other Life-Cycle Models.

## The Project Management Life Cycle

The project management life cycle provides a framework for the project manager to use to manage the project in an organized manner. The life cycle describes how a project progresses through a succession of stages; it is a logical sequence of activities needed to accomplish a project's goals or objectives. Project activities must be grouped into stages because by doing so the project manager and the project team can efficiently and effectively plan and organize resources for each activity. This also allows the project manager and the project team to objectively measure the achievement of goals and justify their decisions to move the project to the next stage, make modifications to the project plans, or terminate the project. The project management life-cycle structure is of use to the project manager for the following reasons:

■ The project manager can use the project management life cycle to organize project management activities and to identify resources needed to support each stage.

■ The project manager can identify the collection of activities for each stage before proceeding to the next stage.

■ The project manager can effectively consider the impact that early decisions have on later stages of the project management life cycle, particularly with regard to various risks. (Precedence in decision-making is covered in greater detail in Chapter 5.)

Success in the project management life cycle requires establishing the management process for the entire life cycle of the project that is needed to reach the project's objectives (Forsberg, Mooz, and Cotterman 2000). In this vein we propose a management process for the life cycle of the project that consists of six stages, as depicted in Figure 3-1: (1) Conception, (2) Feasibility Analysis, (3) Planning, (4) Implementation, (5) Controlling, and (6) Termination.

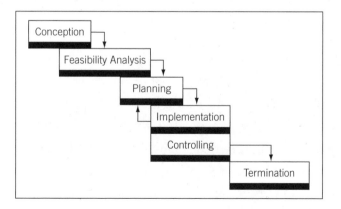

**FIGURE 3-1:** Project Management Life Cycle

Within the life cycle, the project transitions from its conception to its eventual termination in a logical sequence that facilitates project decision-making. Many decisions occur in each stage and must be adequately addressed as a project progresses.

It's important to consider the decision-making sequence. Not considering the impact of early decisions on later decisions within the project management life cycle can have devastating results. Each life-cycle stage has a set of activities and a prescribed decision gate. The activities describe what work is to be done, and the corresponding stage defines when the work needs to be done. The life-cycle stage of the project dictates what, when, how, and why work should be accomplished during the project (Driscoll 2008).

Decision gates are used to determine the appropriate time to move forward to the next life-cycle stage. They serve as project milestones. The project can only pass through these gates by satisfying specific requirements, which are usually set by the project manager based on information obtained by project staff from potential users, production representatives, design staff, and management.

Table 3-1 presents the six project management life-cycle stages and connects them with respective activities and decision gates. Looking at this table, readers can infer the types of decisions project managers should address at different life-cycle stages. For example, during the conception stage the project staff must establish the high-level requirements for performance (race car acceleration capability), cost (race car operating cost) and schedule (race car repair time for specific repairs) for both the product (race car) and the project (design of the race car). These decisions influence whether the project work will result in the overall project success.

**TABLE 3-1:** Project Management Life-Cycle Stages

| Stage | Activities | Decision Gates |
|---|---|---|
| Conception | Define the project<br>Identify stakeholder needs<br>Define project, product, and organizational goals<br>Identify preliminary cost, schedule, and performance risks<br>Establish high-level cost, schedule, and performance requirements for the project and also for the product | Requirements approval for both the project and product |
| Feasibility Analysis | Assess project, product, and organizational feasibility<br>Assess resource capabilities<br>Assess cost, schedule, and performance risks<br>Define cost benefits<br>Perform risk analysis | Required cost benefit and risk mitigation measures justified |
| Planning | Define project tasks<br>Schedule tasks<br>Resource tasks<br>Develop project organization<br>Continue risk analysis | Project management plan approval |
| Implementation | Perform project according to plan<br>Mitigate cost, schedule, and performance risk<br>Perform project testing<br>Develop a training plan<br>Develop a deployment plan<br>Continue risk analysis | High-level requirements for the project and product verified and validated |
| Controlling | Monitor and control project resources<br>Monitor and control project progress<br>Monitor and control project performance<br>Continue risk analysis | Performance measures met |
| Termination | Measure project success<br>Terminate project<br>Develop lessons learned<br>Identify remaining resources | Project completion approved |

The decision-making that occurs in each stage can be defined as either an *activation* or a *conversion*. An activation decision determines that some new activity should begin, based on the progress on other activities. A conversion decision establishes that some set of resources (typically money and information but not always) should proceed or continue with the goal of producing another set of resources or the final product. Each stage in the project receives available information and resources—or *inputs*. During each stage decisions are made that determine how the inputs are converted by selected actions into outputs (including information and resources). If a stage does not produce the right outputs, a poorly managed project will result. Mistakes in activation decision-making result when new activities are started with inappropriate resources. Mistakes in conversion decisions occur when inappropriate activities are selected for the resources available and the resources desired.

High-quality projects require that a vast array of decisions be made such that reasonably attractive alternatives are selected for most of these decisions. Attractive alternatives are those that result in reasonably good outcomes in most cases. Project managers must understand the broader context of a project in order to determine not only the processes, tools, and techniques necessary but also the decisions appropriate for each stage. Sample decisions for each stage are presented in the sections that follow.

## Conception Stage

The first stage of the project management life cycle is Conception or Initiation. In this stage, the problem and project objectives are defined. The project objectives are sometimes referred to as user needs or requirements. Stakeholders who have a relationship to the project are also identified.

The Conception stage consists of steps that must be performed before starting the detailed planning and implementation stages of the project. The focus is on establishing and defining the project's goals, objectives, deliverables, and requirements (Haugan 2006)—that is, the product and organizational goals. More important, this stage should produce a preliminary analysis of risks and the resulting impacts those risks could have on the time, budget, and performance requirements (Kerzner 2006). Key potential trade-offs among time, budget, and performance requirements should also be identified at this stage to guide future decisions.

## Feasibility Analysis Stage

The Feasibility Analysis stage provides information on whether the project should be undertaken. Many decisions are made during this stage that should support whether to proceed with or terminate the project.

The Feasibility Analysis stage essentially entails "counting up the cost"—determining whether the project can be done. Key decisions in this stage include those about (1) required resources, (2) resource availability, (3) inherent risks to successful project completion, (4) expected costs and benefits of the project, (5) likelihood of completing the project on time and within the budget, and (6) project requirements and/or objectives.

An initial risk analysis is also performed during this stage. To achieve project success, a thorough analysis of every element that could potentially derail or cause the project to fail must occur. These and other elements (according to the nature of the project) must be considered.

Additional relevant decisions during this stage include determining how the feasibility analyses should be conducted to ensure that they are effective and efficient and defining a "feasible" project—i.e., a project with the right balance of cost, schedule, and performance. This balance needs to be defined at an abstract level very early in the project. For example, when designing a race car the early design team must establish the kinds of acceleration (and deceleration) desired before the concept for the car has really been defined at the level of detail needed to determine whether these requirements can be met.

## Planning Stage

The Planning stage can be a continuation of or a parallel effort to the Feasibility Analysis stage; however, if it is determined that the project is feasible and should be pursued, the bulk of decision-making will occur in the Planning stage. Some aspects of project planning will naturally be considered when performing project feasibility analyses because such information is critical to identifying, at a minimum, what trade-offs need to occur in future decisions for performance, cost, and schedule, for both the product and project.

Project planning includes the project management techniques of identifying, scheduling, and resourcing tasks. In project planning, several documents are created, including resource plans, financial plans, monitoring plans, risk plans, acceptance plans, and communications plans. In addition, a decision-making process (or plan) should be identified. This decision-making process should establish which types of decisions are going to be made by whom, as well as what types of information should be available for the various types of decisions. For each of these plans, more detail is provided for the near term, but each plan should address the entire project management life cycle on some level.

Risk analysis should continue in this stage: Risks to the project, the product, and the organization should be defined. Also, a definition of the criteria for successful project completion should be developed.

Key decisions in this stage include those about (1) required tasks to accomplish project objectives, (2) required tasks to satisfy product performance, (3) best team organization to support project objectives, (4) resource requirements, (5) best approach for meeting schedule objectives, (6) skills required, and (7) elements of the project management plan. The level of planning is commensurate with the nature, scope, and requirements of the project. Project managers have a suite of tools (e.g., Primavera®, MS Project®) at their fingertips to make the tasks of project planning simpler and efficient. These tools do not replace decision-making, but they do aid in the decision-making process.

## Implementation Stage

The Conception stage gets the project started in the right direction; the Feasibility stage demonstrates the project can be done; the Planning stage defines the tasks and determines when and how the tasks will be performed. The Implementation stage is the stage in which the detailed tasks are implemented and performed—the stage in which project, product, and organizational objectives are realized. In this stage, the project manager is responsible for overseeing implementing the decisions made during the Planning stage. The project manager must also ensure that decisions are adequately resourced, as needed. Project planning continues to occur during this stage to handle the unexpected and unforeseen events that arise during the Implementation stage.

Key decisions in this stage include those about (1) time that resources are required, (2) design changes required to meet key performance objectives, (3) operational requirements, (4) key constraints and limitations, (5) all risks, (6) changes in the environment that affect the project, and (7) changes in business needs that affect the project.

## Controlling Stage

The Controlling stage is intended to monitor activities performed during the Implementation stage and identify necessary changes to the plan as the project progresses. All projects require a set of control mechanisms. These control mechanisms assist the project in meeting schedule, meeting budget, developing the product, and monitoring the progress made in achieving project objectives. Besides performance, cost, and schedule, special attention must be paid to the management of risk, changes to the design of the product and project, communications inside the project team and outside to key stakeholders, and the test or acceptance process.

For this stage to occur, project performance during the Implementation stage must be monitored. Specific elements of the project must be defined by the project manager as critical to keeping project performance as close as possible to expected performance. After those elements are defined, data must be collected on actual performance, and that data must be compared to planned performance.

Next, significant trends and variances should be identified along with their impact on project objectives. Corrective actions, if any, should occur as the process continues. Several management processes, such as change and risk management, should be undertaken to monitor and control the project deliverables. Key decisions in this stage include those about (1) control mechanisms, (2) control parameters, (3) test requirements, (4) data collection requirements, and (5) change procedures.

## Termination Stage

A project can be terminated at any time. To properly terminate a project when objectives have been successfully achieved, consider three essentials things: (1) the time needed to terminate the project, (2) estimated and budgeted costs that support termination, and (3) any other termination objectives such as documentation. During this stage, pay attention to remaining resources that can be reallocated to other projects or other services within the company. The major activities of this stage are project closure and a review of project completion.

Key decisions in this stage include those about (1) termination criteria, (2) project termination authorization, (3) termination requirements, (4) termination objectives, (5) reports required, and (6) lessons learned. The last decision, lessons learned, is critical to the success of future projects so that other projects learn from the successes and failures found in this project.

# Control Gates within the Project Management Life Cycle

The purpose of *control gates* is to measure the progress of a project and to determine whether the project should be terminated. Another term for control gates is *transition reviews* (Forsberg, Mooz, and Cotterman 2000). Control gates are structured *decision points* (events or milestones) in the project management life cycle and are routinely found at the beginning and end of each stage, as shown in Table 3-1. Control gates provide an assessment of the elements of each stage and provide project baseline control. They are needed to assist the project manager in effectively managing the project and to control the business, budget, and technical aspects of the project (Forsberg, Mooz, and Cotterman 2000).

At the end of each life cycle stage, the control gates produce unique outputs, such as reports, prototypes, and test results. The outputs are used by the project manager and other decision makers to determine whether the project has met the goals for that stage or milestone and is ready to move forward to the next stage. As a result these outputs are often called exit criteria for the stage just ending (or entry criteria for the next stage) (Forsberg, Mooz, and Cotterman 2000). The project manager oversees the activities in each stage and is responsible for the project's progress through each stage. The project manager must be careful assessing whether the goals of a stage have been achieved because flexibility to make adjustments as development continues may mean the difference between success and failure. Each stage consists of groups of activities that can be performed either in series or in parallel, which can determine which of the various outputs can be achieved and the relative cost-effectiveness for achieving each output.

Control gates also require decisions. For any selected control gate, the decision alternatives include (Archibald 2004):

- Proceed with the remaining work in the current stage.
- Start work on the next stage.

- Replan and restart a stage already completed.

- Revise the project objectives, plans, and schedules.

- Terminate the project.

- Place the project on hold.

A number of factors determine whether a project continues to the next stage, the most important of which is often *risk*. The decisions made in each stage of the project management life cycle possess a certain degree of risk. Risk types include administrative risk, financial risk, technical risk, schedule risk, programmatic risk, and management risk. To minimize the risks faced during the project, a complete risk analysis that addresses all stages of the project should be conducted in the Conception stage. However, once this initial risk analysis has been completed, further risk analyses should be periodically performed. Existing risks should be re-defined and updated, and new risks should be identified and defined as information becomes available. The project proceeds to the next life cycle stage only when there is an acceptable level of risk across the project. Both risk and uncertainty are covered in greater detail in Chapter 9.

Every project is unique and each one must be managed according to the nature of the project. Although we have presented the use of decision gates at the end of each stage, you might find they are needed at other points during the life-cycle stage. What is important is the presence of a clear management approach for ensuring progress and baseline approval (Forsberg, Mooz, and Cotterman 2000).

## Stakeholder Decisions in the Project Management Life Cycle

Stakeholders play a key role in the life of a project. They are essentially the reason why a project exists. It is the interest of the future users of the product that motivate the initiation of the project. The willingness of the bill payers to fund the development constitutes a critical veto on initiation and continuation of the project. Finally, all other stakeholders must demonstrate some interest and excitement or the bill payers will back out. Thus, the primary focus of any project management effort in every life cycle stage is on the stakeholders—their needs, wants, and desires.

What is a stakeholder? A *stakeholder* can be defined as an individual or an organization that is actively involved in a project or whose interests can be affected by the outcome of a project. In each life-cycle stage, stakeholders can assist the project manager in making critical decisions that will cause a project to succeed or fail. Stakeholders also provide feedback throughout the project management life cycle that is used to improve project performance, satisfy product requirements, and contribute to organizational goals.

Key stakeholders include the CEO, program manager, project manager, customers/users, performing organization, project team members, management team, financial sponsor, contractors, consultants, and project management office. Although all stakeholders are important, they are not equally important. Their vested interest in and relationship to the project, product, or organization determine their relative importance. Stakeholders exist both within and outside the project environment. Identifying the obvious stakeholders—those internal to the project environment—is usually a minor task. However, identifying stakeholders that are not so obvious—those external to the project—is somewhat more challenging. We can more easily identify the stakeholders who are not obvious by viewing the project and treating it as a system.

The International Council on Systems Engineering defines a system as

> [A]n integrated set of elements that accomplishes a defined objective. These elements can include products (hardware, software, firmware), processes (policies, laws, procedures), people (managers, analysts, skilled workers), information (data, reports, media), techniques (algorithms, inspections, maintenance), facilities (hospitals, manufacturing plants, mail distribution centers), services (evacuation, telecommunications, quality assurance), and other support elements.

In their introduction to the book *Decision Making in Systems Engineering and Management* (2008), Gregory Parnell and Patrick Driscoll note systems have the following important attributes that apply to project management (3):

- They have interconnected and interacting elements that perform systems functions to meet the product and service needs of stakeholders and consumers.

- They have objectives that are achieved by system functions.

- They interact with their environment, thereby effecting stakeholders.

- They use technology that is developed by engineering experts.

- They have a system life cycle containing elements of risk that are managed by project managers.

■ They require systems decisions, analysis by qualified persons, and decisions made by project managers.

When we view the project as a system, we realize that a project affects and is affected by environmental factors—both internal and external—and that it has an effect on all stakeholders. As mentioned earlier, the stakeholders who are not obvious tend to fall within the external environment. When we understand a project's external environment, we have a better idea of additional stakeholders who should be considered in the project management life cycle. External environmental factors are shown in Figure 3-2. These environmental factors are useful in identifying stakeholders who are not so obvious.

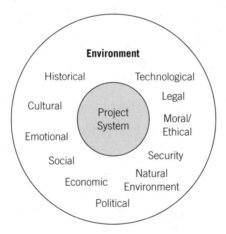

**FIGURE 3-2:** Environmental Factors

A complete taxonomy of stakeholders includes five types (Parnell and Driscoll 2008):

■ **Decision Authority:** The stakeholder(s) with decision-gate authority to move the project forward and to terminate the project

- **Client:** The person or organization that solicited support to manage the project; the source of project compensation; the stakeholder that principally defines product requirements

- **Owner:** The person or organization responsible (and hopefully accountable) for the proper development of the product or system. This person or organization may become responsible (and accountable) for keeping the product or system operating once it becomes deployed and available.

- **User:** The person or organization that will use or operate the product or system once it becomes deployed and available. This person or organization may also become responsible (and accountable) for keeping the product or system operating once it becomes deployed and available.

- **Consumer:** In some cases, such as commercial products, the consumer and the user are the same. In other cases, the consumer is the person(s) or organization(s) that have created intentional dependencies on the products or services delivered by the project. For example, if the product is a commercial airplane, the user is the airline and the consumers are the people who pay the airline to fly on the airplane.

In project management, there are usually two decision authorities—one for the project and one for whom the project is being performed. The relationship between Sikorsky—an aircraft development firm in the United States—and the Saudi government presents a good example of the differences between the two decision authorities. The Saudi government desired an aircraft that could transport its royal officials. They contracted with Sikorsky to build the aircraft. In this case, representatives of the

Saudi government acted as the decision authority for the verification, validation, and acceptance of the aircraft based on how well it satisfied their needs. The general manager within Sikorsky acted as the decision authority for resources allocated to the project, as well as for ensuring the project satisfied the objectives of each life cycle stage. Continuing with this example, the client was the Saudi government; the owner was the maintenance organization; the users were the pilots and other flight crew; and the government officials were the consumers.

Stakeholders can perform multiple roles. In many projects, the user and consumer are the same. In some cases, the decision authority and client can be the same. The roles and levels of responsibility for stakeholders tend to change over the course of the project's life cycle. For example, in the Conception stage, consumers and clients assist the project manager in defining their needs, wants, and expectations. Consumer and client involvement in the project is naturally highest during this stage. In the Feasibility Analysis and Planning stages, stakeholders help to identify environmental factors that have a bearing on the project. Stakeholders assign resources to the project in the Implementation stage. In the Controlling stage, stakeholders verify and validate that the project is meeting its objectives. In the Termination phase, stakeholders evaluate whether the project satisfies schedule, cost, and product performance objectives.

## Other Life-Cycle Models

Using the specific project management life cycle presented in this chapter is not the only possible approach to project management; it is presented simply as one model and methodology for possible use. The life-cycle model we present has the advantage of being a simple representation of how a project proceeds; the model is structured, promotes concurrency—several activities proceeding in parallel, is cyclic, provides feedback, supports ongoing changes, and if properly used, delivers value to stakeholders.

Two other life-cycle management approaches can be useful in managing projects. The Design for Life Cycle approach produces designs in which many facets of the product's life cycle are considered concurrently. The Life Cycle Management approach is an integrated approach that assists in managing the total life cycle of products and services.

Two systems engineering approaches are the waterfall life-cycle model, depicted in Figure 3-3, and the spiral life-cycle model, depicted in Figure 3-4. The waterfall life-cycle model allows for recycling through earlier stages to solve problems that arise in subsequent stages. The spiral life-cycle model presents the notion of repeated cycling through a development process; each spiral produces increasingly complex prototypes, leading to full-scale development.

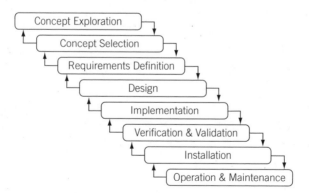

**FIGURE 3-3:** Waterfall Life-Cycle Model

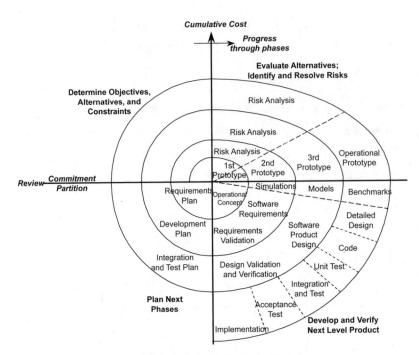

**FIGURE 3-4:** Spiral Life-Cycle Model

One great source of information on project management and systems engineering life-cycle models is the website "Max's Project Management Wisdom" (Archibald 2004). Table 3-2 provides a good summary of project life-cycle models from www.maxwideman.com.

**TABLE 3-2:** Project Life-Cycle Models

| Project Categories | Life Cycle Models and References |
|---|---|
| Generic Project Models: All (or many) project categories below. | Generic, Waterfall, Parallel-Work, Evolutionary Models. Standard, Waterfall, Cyclical, Spiral Models. |
| **1. Aerospace/Defense Projects**<br>1.1 Defense systems<br>1.2 Space<br>1.3 Military operations | Defense Acquisition Model.<br>Process Based Mission Assurance (PMBA) Program Life Cycle, 8 phases:<br>1. Program Mgt<br>2. Concept Development<br>3. Acquisition<br>4. Hardware Design<br>5. Software Design<br>6. Manufacturing<br>7. Pre-Operations Integration and Test<br>8. Operations |
| **2. Business & Organization Change Projects**<br>2.1 Acquisition/Merger<br>2.2 Management process improvement<br>2.3 New business venture<br>2.4 Organization re-structuring<br>2.5 Legal proceeding | See above generic models. |
| **3. Communication Systems Projects**<br>3.1 Network communications systems<br>3.2 Switching communications systems | See above generic models. |
| **4. Event Projects**<br>4.1 International events<br>4.2 National events | See above generic models. |
| **5. Facilities Projects**<br>5.1 Facility decommissioning<br>5.2 Facility demolition<br>5.3 Facility maintenance and modification<br>5.4 Facility design/procurement/construction | See above generic models. |

Russell D. Archibald, Table 2.4, *Managing High-Technology Programs and Projects,* 3rd edition (Hoboken, NJ: John Wiley & Sons, Inc.): 47. Copyright © 2003 by Russell D. Archibald. Reprinted with permission.

| Project Categories | Life Cycle Models and References |
|---|---|
| **6. Information Systems (Software) Projects** | Predictive (Waterfall, Prototyping, RAD, Incremental Build, Spiral) and Adaptive (ASD, XP, SCRUM) Models. Code and Fix, Waterfall, Incremental, Iterative Model. Spiral Software Development Model. "V " Software Development Model. Formula-IT Development Model. Refined Process Spiral Model. |
| **7. International Development Projects** 7.1 Agriculture/rural development 7.2 Education 7.3 Health 7.4 Nutrition 7.5 Population 7.6 Small-scale enterprise 7.7 Infrastructure: energy (oil, gas, coal, power generation and distribution), industrial, telecommunications, transportation, urbanization, water supply and sewage, irrigation) | People and process intensive projects in developing countries funded by The World Bank, regional development banks, US AID, UNIDO, other UN, and government agencies; and Capital/civil works intensive projects—often somewhat different from 5. Facility Projects as they may include, as part of the project, creating an organizational entity to operate and maintain the facility, and lending agencies impose their project life cycle and reporting requirements. |
| **8. Media & Entertainment Projects** 8.1 Motion picture 8.2 TV segment 8.2 Live play or music event | |
| **9. Product and Service Development Projects** 9.1 Information technology hardware 9.2 Industrial product/process 9.3 Consumer product/process 9.4 Pharmaceutical product/ process 9.5 Service (financial, other) | Stage-Gate® Process Model. Stage/Gate Product Development Model. Phase-Gate Process Model. Pharmaceutical Model. |
| **10. Research and Development Projects** 10.1 Environmental 10.2 Industrial 10.3 Economic development 10.4 Medical 10.5 Scientific | Technical Acquisition: Basic Model, Phased Model, Multi-Solution Model. |

Life-cycle models guide a project as it moves from concept to termination. They help project managers and other professionals on the project management team make the proper decisions necessary to deliver value to project stakeholders.

The project management life cycle introduced in this chapter has six stages: Conception, Feasibility Analysis, Planning, Implementation, Control, and Termination. The structure of the life cycle promotes discipline and order when managing projects, and it facilitates the identification of all risks within each stage by encouraging continuous risk assessments.

The following specific points were made in this chapter:

- Quality decisions made at the front end of the life cycle contribute to project success and result in fewer conflicts later, which prevents unbudgeted costs and risks.

- The project management life cycle provides a framework to manage the project and product development in an organized manner.

- The life cycle has logical sequencing that facilitates decision-making. Many decisions occur during each stage and must be adequately addressed as projects are managed.

- Control gates are structured decision points (events or milestones) in the project management life cycle and are routinely found at the beginning and end of each stage.

- At the end of each life-cycle stage, unique outputs determine whether the project has met the goals for that stage and is ready to proceed to the next stage (exit and entry criteria).

- Stakeholders assist the project manager in making critical decisions that contribute to success.

- Knowing a project's environment facilitates an understanding of factors that can impact success.

In Chapter 4, we provide an overview of decision-making and describe its history and the different approaches to decision-making, define a good decision, and state how to avoid project failure. Good decisions result from a good decision-making process that carefully considers the values and objectives associated with the context and that seeks out the available alternative courses of action. We explain why the decision-making process must be dynamic to successfully deal with the many decisions that occur during the course of a project, and we consider the need to learn from our successes and failures.

# CHAPTER 4

# Overview of Decision-Making

A s stated earlier, decisions are common in life and in project management. The purpose of decisions, of course, is to accomplish a goal or objective. We normally pick one option or alternative (a course of action or a product) from among several options we are considering. We then proceed to select what we believe to be the best option among the ones we are considering.

People make two types of decisions—(1) instinctive decisions, which are split-second decisions based on immediate perception (and intuition), and (2) thoughtful decisions, which are decisions that are based on our thinking about the consequences of specific decisions. Both types of decisions have their place in our lives. People often use anatomical terms to refer to an instinctual decision, for example, describing a decision made quickly as being made "by the seat of the pants," "based on a gut feeling," or "off the top of my head." With these types of decisions, there is typically much less of a search for good options than there is with thoughtful decisions. Simon (1955) described one version of this process as *satisficing*; one thinks of an option and assesses whether it is "good enough," and if it is, one stops thinking about alternatives; if it not good enough, one thinks of another option and repeats the process until an option is good enough.

Project managers will make both types of decisions during the course of their project leadership. While both instinctive decisions and thoughtful decisions are needed, this book focuses on the latter, thoughtful decisions based on cognitive processes—that is, cognitive decision-making.

Cognitive decision-making usually considers many options and addresses their relative pros and cons to some degree. The authors hold that too many people (including project managers) make instinctive decisions when thoughtful decisions would serve them better.

This chapter is intended to help them and others become more conscious of how best to tackle any kind of decision.

This chapter presents the following sections:

- The Basics
- Literary Views of Decision-Making
- Decision Quality
- History of Decision-Making
- Approaches to Decision-Making
- Decision-Making Methods and Aids
- Implementing the Decision.

## The Basics

So what is a decision? *The American Heritage Dictionary of the English Language,* 4th edition (2000) provides several definitions, the first three of which are:

1. The passing of judgment on an issue under consideration.

2. The act of reaching a conclusion or making up one's mind.

3. A conclusion or judgment reached or pronounced.

Howard (1968), who coined the term *decision analysis,* defines a decision as "an irrevocable allocation of resources."

Resources that can be allocated irrevocably are money, time, and physical entities such as cars and manufacturing equipment. Recall our modification of Bocquet, Cardinal, and Mekhilef's (1999) definition of decision: any action taken by an actor(s) that will consume resources and affect other actors in the pursuit of achieving objectives within constraints.

A further revision of our modification of the definition of *decision* will build upon both of these definitions but will emphasize that decisions are typically made to allocate current resources in the hope of achieving a return in future resources. Thus, we now define a *decision* as the following: An irrevocable allocation of resources at one point (or at specific points) in time by one or more actors, in order to affect the world and other actors so as obtain a more desired state in the future for the original actors.

The future in this definition might be seconds, minutes, or hours—or it could be months and years. For issues regarding nuclear power, for example, the benefits might be obtained in years and decades, but the potential negative effects might not be realized for generations.

In Chapter 2, we described types of decisions that pertain to project management and its life cycle: decisions oriented to the conception of the project, how to do the feasibility analyses, what plans and plan steps to create, how and when to perform detailed work, what milestones and gates to create for controlling, and how to terminate the project. In these types of decisions, and in all decision situations, the following three elements are always present:

1.  **Alternatives or things the decision maker can choose:** If there is only one alternative available, the decision maker does not have a decision but a problem (either a good one or bad one). Problems often can be turned into decisions by the decision maker's creativity, which could include accepting something that is less preferred on one objective to gain on another objective.

2.  **Values that tell the decision maker which option might be most or least preferred:** Values are the hardest part of decision-making for most decision makers because values are purely subjective— they pertain to what people care about. We are all used to making cost versus performance trade-offs when we buy something at the store; that is, should we get the store-brand item or the name-brand item that costs more but presumably has higher reliability or better taste? Project managers should already be familiar with the cost-time-performance trade-offs that are commonly part of introductory project management courses.

    A well-known maxim of success in project management is that a stranger should be able to walk through the project management office asking what is really important to this project and find that every answer will be the same and will contain no more than three or four topics. Nonetheless, even in successful projects it is common for the key people on the program *not* to know what the key cost, schedule, or performance parameters are. If the project manager and his senior people have not agreed on what the key factors are and communicated this information to everyone in the project office and to the contractors, then many decisions may be made at cross purposes to each other.

As all project managers know, a decision that is oriented toward project success can have negative and positive effects on both the people that are part of the organization and the project office within the larger organization's context. So, in these cases, the issues of people and organization must also be included in the value structure, along with those issues of project success.

3. **Knowledge (facts, guesses, ideas, etc.) about the world now and in the future:** Finally, there is knowledge. What do we know for sure and what do we not know? For those things that are not known, how uncertain about the answers are we? Are there known unknowns and unknown unknowns? Good project managers are able to identify many of the latter and turn them into the former. How do we deal with unknowns of any type in decision-making? This is where risks come from; risk is another topic with which project managers should be familiar.

Chapter 6 describes how to create a decision frame that addresses the alternatives, values, and knowledge for a decision, as well as the context associated with the decision. Chapter 7 covers the topics of values and knowledge in more detail.

## Literary Views of Decision-Making

Dogbert is a familiar cartoon character in the *Dilbert* cartoon strip by Scott Adams. Dogbert has identified any number of approaches to decision-making over the years:

- Act confused.

- Form a task force of people who are too busy to meet.

- Send employees to find more data.

- Lose documents submitted for your approval.

- Say you are waiting for some other manager to "get up to speed."

- Make illegible margin scrawls on the documents requiring your decision.

Decisions have also been addressed in classical literature for centuries. The Roman statesman and philosopher named Seneca said, within decades of Christ's birth, "If one does not know to which port one is sailing, no wind is favorable." Shakespeare in 1602 addressed the ultimate decision faced by people in Hamlet—"To be or not to be. ..." Lewis Carroll, paraphrasing Seneca for a new and younger audience, wrote in *Alice's Adventures in Wonderland* in 1865:

One day Alice came to a fork in the road and saw a Cheshire cat in a tree.
"Which road do I take?" she asked.
"Where do you want to go?" was his response.
"I don't know," Alice answered.
"Then," said the cat, "it doesn't matter."

Frost (1916) continued the association between decisions and selecting a road/path/port when he wrote the following well-known poem:

### The Road Not Taken

Two roads diverged in a yellow wood,
And sorry I could not travel both
And be one traveler, long I stood
And looked down one as far as I could
To where it bent in the undergrowth;

Then took the other, as just as fair,
And having perhaps the better claim,
Because it was grassy and wanted wear;
Though as for that the passing there
Had worn them really about the same,

And both that morning equally lay
In leaves no step had trodden black.
Oh, I kept the first for another day!
Yet knowing how way leads on to way,
I doubted if I should ever come back.

I shall be telling this with a sigh
Somewhere ages and ages hence:
Two roads diverged in a wood, and I—
I took the one less traveled by,
And that has made all the difference.

Here Frost points out a defining issue in the study of decision-making: When we make a decision, it is possible with hindsight to evaluate what happened as a result of that decision. But it is not possible to evaluate what might have happened if our decision had been different because we can never be sure about what might have happened at that time. Sometimes there can be little difference between the choices. At other times there can be a very big difference. Unfortunately, it is not always possible to predict whether a difference will be small or large. There has been little empirical research on comparing one decision or decision process to another because it is not possible to compare the outcomes of the selected choice to the those of choices that were not selected.

Perhaps the most relevant quote for this book on decision-making for project managers is by Rosa Parks, the African American who was ordered to give up her seat on a bus for a white person by the bus driver, but refused. She says in her book *Quiet Strength* (1994):

> When one's mind is made up, this diminishes fear;
> knowing what must be done does away with fear.

## Decision Quality

Is there a way to measure decision quality? It is always tempting to say that getting a good outcome after a decision is made means that a good decision was made. The converse of this is that a bad decision means that a bad outcome is obtained. But consider the following strategies used by two different project managers, each facing a decision about whom to select for a key position in the project management office:

> Jack: I chose Bill because he seemed affable and went to a good school. Bill was the first person to respond to my ad.

> Jill: I chose Ed because he met my major criteria concerning people skills, knowledge of the key topics needed for the job, experience in the field, and contacts with other people that could prove useful. I interviewed a dozen people, asked my deputy to screen two dozen applications, asked several of my key people to talk to the four most promising people, and asked my boss to interview the two best candidates.

Now, which of these decision processes do you think was best? We think Jill has the best defined decision process and has thought about the pros and cons of the candidates in more detail and with more clarity. Is Ed (the person selected by Jill) guaranteed to be a success in his position? No. Could Bill perform far better than expected and end up taking Jack's job when Jack gets promoted? Yes. But which of these decision processes is *most likely* to produce the best outcome? While there is no appropriate way (at this time) to do controlled research on this topic, the authors (and many other decision analysis professionals) believe that, by and large, good decision-making processes will generate a higher percentage of good outcomes than will poor decision-making processes. *Good decisions must be based on the process that was used, not the outcome that was obtained.*

Good outcomes can and do result from low-quality decision processes, and bad outcomes occur more often than we would like when high-quality decision processes are followed. Figure 4-1 illustrates the philosophy that good decision-making is the careful generation and consideration of the alternatives, values, and knowledge associated with the choice. Inherent in this careful consideration are the examination of trade-offs across multiple objectives, across time periods, and across risk positions. Consideration must be given to postponing the decision in order to gather more information; but consideration here only means that the decision is postponed if it is reasonably likely that valuable information could be collected.

In the real world, the person or group involved in actually making decisions considers the current decision, selects an alternative, implements it, and discovers the outcomes. However, there is a lot more to making

Time leads to evolving uncertain events;
Happiness/sadness as a function of outcomes

Which road is
most likely to
lead to the best
outcomes?

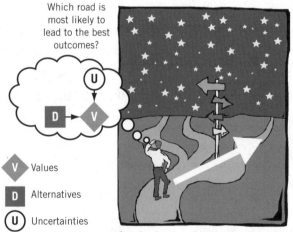

V Values

D Alternatives

U Uncertainties

Time leads to evolving uncertain events;
Happiness/sadness as a function of outcomes

**FIGURE 4-1:** Philosophy of Good Decision-Making (continues)

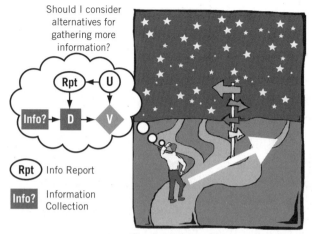

Should I consider
alternatives for
gathering more
information?

Rpt ) Info Report

Info? Information
Collection

Time leads to evolving uncertain events;
Happiness/sadness as a function of outcomes

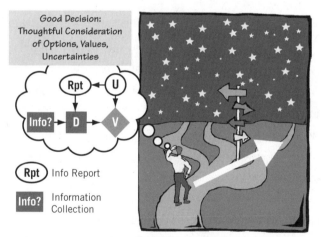

Good Decision:
Thoughtful Consideration
of Options, Values,
Uncertainties

Rpt ) Info Report

Info? Information
Collection

"Your act was
unwise," I exclaimed,
"as you can see by the
outcome."

He solemnly eyed me.
"When choosing the
course of my action,"
said he, "I had not the
outcome to guide
me."
–Ambrose Bierce

Time leads to evolving uncertain events;
Happiness/sadness as a function of outcomes

**FIGURE 4-1:** (continued) Philosophy of Good Decision-Making

a "good" decision. First, we should examine what decisions could be made now (e.g., hire more personnel, create a research program focused on a key technology) and select the appropriate decision to address (e.g., choose to create the research program because it has more immediate consequences for postponing and there are some important differences among the research programs under consideration). This is called making the *meta-decision*—deciding what decision to make. Next, it is time to identify our values or objectives for this decision and a reasonable set of alternatives, each of which could fulfill those objectives. Then, some type of evaluation of the alternatives relative to the objectives is conducted, considering any uncertainties. This evaluation should guide the decision maker in finding the best (or at least a very good) alternative.

Before implementing the alternative, the decision maker should ask if there is any important information that could be collected that might change the selection of the desired alternative or how that alternative is to be implemented. The cost and delay associated with this information collection should also be considered. When all relevant information has been collected and further considered, it is time to implement the selected alternative. In fact, a lot of activity and further decision-making are wrapped up in the task of implementation.

At one extreme, there is the case where the decision maker makes a bet at the gaming table and waits to see the result. Decision makers in real life who use this approach are bound to be disappointed quite often. At the other extreme is JR (the rich rascal from the old *Dallas* television show); JR would bribe and kill anyone who stood between him and a good outcome. This is not the kind of behavior that leads to good outcomes in the long-run; jail or death is the most likely long-run outcome here. Standing somewhere in the middle, a good decision maker determines who has the power to veto and makes sure they are in agreement or that compromise is possible. The decision maker also identifies who could slow the decision process down or cause changes to be made and then "sells" them on the proposed solution or makes appropriate compromises. The random activities that could occur are also identified, and risk mitigation plans are put in place in case they are needed. Much of this can be done mentally for simple, low-risk decisions. But for high-stakes decisions, a more formal process is appropriate.

Figure 4-2 depicts the elements of good decision-making for a current, single decision. The boxes in Figure 4-2 represent the two extremes (good versus bad) of four important concepts (Decisions, Random Events, Implementation, and Outcomes). The point of this figure is that good or bad outcomes can be caused by some combination of random events, the decision made by the project manager, and the implementation effort associated with the decision. It is possible to find cases of great decisions, well-conceived and well-conducted implementation efforts, and positive unforeseen events that still resulted in less-than-desired outcomes. Similarly, there are a few poorly made decisions with poor or no implementation efforts and disastrous unforeseen events that resulted in positive outcomes for the decision maker. The point remains that we are not guaranteed success by being smart and industrious, but we do have a far greater chance of success if we are smart and industrious.

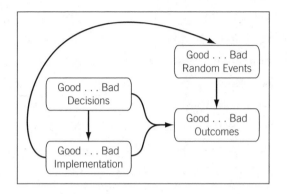

**FIGURE 4-2:** Good versus Bad Decisions and Outcomes

A good decision must include the following:

- A good decision-making structure for gathering and integrating information, finding the preferred decision, and creating and conducting the implementation efforts

- A good review of the possible decisions (the topics to be addressed) and the selection of the appropriate decision given the situation; this could be a good meta-decision (a decision about the right decision to be considered)

- A good process for finding the preferred alternative among the many that are being considered.

The next section, "History of Decision-Making," includes a description of the kind of decision-making structure that has been developed in some military organizations to ensure that a set of activities are in place for making decisions in an evolving situation. Such a process can be found in some project management organizations. The delineation of project management decisions and when they are relevant was presented in Chapter 2 and will be dealt with again in Chapter 5. A good decision-making process such as the process presented in Chapter 1 attempts to do the following:

- Find all of the reasonably attractive alternatives.

- Define clearly the objectives by which the decision maker should select the preferred alternative.

- Find the best or a really good alternative by examining trade-offs across these criteria, across time periods, and across risk positions.

- Evaluate the value of postponing the decision to collect more information.

Before describing decision structures, we are going to consider the issue of how to deal with decisions that are related and occur across a period of time. The first perspective is a systems view (Figure 4-3) that adds a monitoring process to the elements of Figure 4-2. The point of this figure is that as we move from one decision to another we need to have a monitoring process in place in order to determine whether the outcomes we desire for previous decisions are occurring. If not, we must address these issues as part of our implementation plan or revisit our earlier decisions and make adjustments to the extent possible—or we must adjust our later decisions.

We can extend our time horizon even further and take a meta-systems view that includes trying to learn from our past. There is a vast literature now on learning organizations and projects (Matheson and Matheson 1998). Figure 4-4 depicts the role of learning in the process of achieving good outcomes as part of decision-making. A good learning process should affect our monitoring activities, implementation efforts, and future decisions. This learning will not only affect what alternatives we prefer in the future but also the meta-decision process that leads us to decide which decisions are most appropriate to consider.

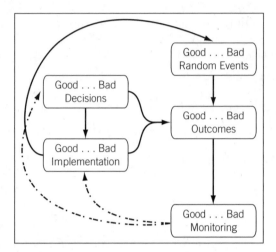

**FIGURE 4-3:** A Systems View of the Factors Affecting Good Outcomes

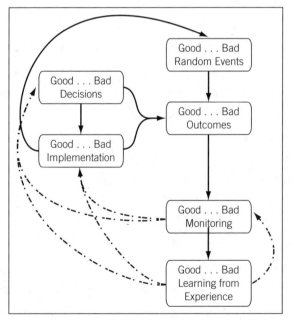

**FIGURE 4-4:** A Meta-Systems View of the Factors Affecting Good Outcomes

# History of Decision-Making

The history of human decision-making is as long as human life. The next three figures present highlights from the history of decision-making based upon publications by Buchanan and O'Connell (2006) and Smith and von Winterfeldt (2004). Figure 4-5 shows the history prior to the Industrial Age, beginning with voting in Athens and critical military decisions. The development of probability concepts and theories began near the end of this period. A famous quote from Napoleon in 1804 ends this period.

---

5th century BC—male citizens in Athens vote
4th century BC—Plato (discovers truth through senses) and Aristotle (values information gain and deductive reasoning)
333 BC—Alexander the Great cuts Gordian knot
49 BC—Julius Caesar decides to cross the Rubicon
14th century AD—English friar proposes "Occam's razor" (best theory is the simplest)
1641—Rene Descartes proposes reason to be superior to experience
1657—Christian Huygens publishes *On Reasoning in Games of Chance*
1660—Pascal proposes a wager on the existence of God, focusing on consequences rather than likelihood
1738—Daniel Bernoulli examines risk and risk aversion
1739–40—David Hume proposes the "is-ought" gap. The descriptive problem of "what is" is different from the prescriptive decision problem of "what ought to be."
1804—Napoleon publishes *Maxims,* in which he states, "Nothing is more difficult, and therefore more precious, than to be able to decide"

---

**FIGURE 4-5:** Highlights in the History of Decision-Making: 5th Century BC–1804

Figure 4-6 presents highlights from the history of decision-making from after the Industrial Age began through the eight-year period after World War II. Early developments in this period were by economists. Before, during, and after World War II, the advances came from the integration of probability theory and economic theories related to value and risk.

1881—Edgeworth defines indifference curves for commodity bundles
1907—Irving Fisher (economist) introduces net present value for decision-making
1921—Frank Knight defines risk (outcome probabilities can be known) and uncertainty (outcome probabilities cannot be known)
1931—Ramsey explains the inference of probabilities and utilities from preference among gambles
1938—Chester Barnard distinguishes personal and organizational decision-making
1944—von Neumann and Morgenstern define mathematical bases for game theory and rational economic decision-making
1947—Herbern Simon argues for bounded rationality and selecting "good enough" decisions (satisficing)
1948—RAND Corporation is formed to perform analyses for government decision makers
1952—Harry Markowitz provides mathematical methods for diversifying a stock portfolio to achieve consistent returns
1954—Savage extends rational economic decision-making to subjective expected utility
1954—Edwards initiates the descriptive study of how humans make decisions

**FIGURE 4-6:** Highlights in the History of Decision-Making: 1881–1954

Highlights from the history of decision-making during the transition from the Industrial Age through the Information Age are shown in Figure 4-7. The work since the middle 1950s has focused on quantitative methods for analyzing decisions, including value trade-offs, risk and time trade-offs, and uncertainty. This book does not focus on this material but provides insights for decision-making based on much of this work and related psychological research about the problems real decision makers have.

1966—Ronald Howard defines *decision analysis* to be a practical implementation of decision theory using value and probability assessments of decision makers and experts
1967—Peter Scott Morton's Ph.D. dissertation begins the research on and use of decision support systems
1968—Raiffa writes an introductory text for decision analysis
1968—First consultants practice decision analysis
1972—Irving Janis defines "groupthink" for flawed group decision-making; Cohen, March and Olsen publish "A Garbage Can Model for Organizational Choice"
1973—Black & Scholes, and Merlon develop methods for valuing "options"; Mintzberg describes several types of decision-making styles
1976—Keeney and Raiffa define mathematics for value and utility functions
1978—Peterson creates Decision Conference as a means for delivering decision analysis for participative decision makers
1978–1980—First commercially available decision analysis software
1979—Kahneman and Tversky describe heuristics and biases associated with human decision-making
1989—Recognition-primed decision-making gets started
1992—Keeney proposes value-focused thinking

**FIGURE 4-7:** Highlights in the History of Decision-Making: 1966–1992

## Approaches to Decision-Making

Many decisions are simple, preprogrammed, or already made. For example, project managers do take a considerable amount of time to think long and hard about what software to use to schedule project tasks. Many other decisions are not as structured and are more strategic in nature, such as choosing whether to invest in a particular project. Scholars of decision-making have long differentiated between structured and unstructured decisions. Structured decisions are those decisions for which the decision maker or an organization has a decision process. Examples include new product development (for firms in the product development business) and buying a new car or house. Unstructured decisions are those that are made without using any defined process, such as how to deal with a sudden illness or how to react to a new product that was unexpectedly introduced by an unexpected competitor. Mintzberg et al. (1976) proposed a process for unstructured decisions. Buede and Ferrell (1993) compared several such processes in Table 4-1. Interestingly, by defining a process for unstructured decisions, Dewey (1933), Simon (1965), Mintzberg et al. (1976), and Buede and Ferrell (1993) are, in fact, turning unstructured decisions into structured decisions, at least within the confines of the table.

**TABLE 4-1:** Processes for Unstructured Decisions

| Dewey (1933) | Simon (1965) | Mintzberg et al. (1976) | Buede and Ferrell (1993) |
|---|---|---|---|
| Suggestion—The mind leaps to a possible solution | Intelligence— Collection of information | Identification— Decision recognition and diagnosis | Problem Definition— Goal formation, problem structuring, and information processing |
| Intellectualization— Formation of a problem or question | | | |
| Development of Hypotheses | Design— Development of options | Development— Search and design | Decision Recommendations— Problem structuring, information processing, and analysis |
| Reasoning— Analysis of hypotheses | Choice— Evaluation of options | Solution—Screening and evaluation and choice | Choice—Analysis and option selection |
| Testing of Hypotheses | | | Implementation |

Dennis Buede and David Ferrell, "Convergence in Problem Solving: A Prelude to Quantitative Analysis," *IEEE Transactions on Systems, Man and Cybernetics* 23.3: 746–765. Copyright © 1993 by IEEE. Reprinted with permission.

Mintzberg and Westley (2001) suggest three ways to approach a decision: "Thinking first," "Seeing first," and "Doing first." "Thinking first" is the traditionally analytical process: Define the problem, diagnose its causes, identify objectives, brainstorm solution alternatives, perform an analysis, and decide.

"Seeing first" is described as a four-step creative discovery process: preparation >> incubation >> illumination >> verification. This description of "seeing first" suggests that the problem has been defined and diagnosed, and that the perceptual discovery of a solution that is clearly good enough completes the process. This description of "seeing first" suggests that the problem has been defined and diagnosed, and that the perceptual discovery of a solution that is clearly good enough completes the process.

However, the workshops described by Mintzberg and Westley include drawing a collage for the issue as an implementation of "seeing first." This collage combines defining the problem, diagnosing the problem, and examining several solutions. This description suggests an analytical process focused on the visual rather than thinking. This drawing-oriented visual process emphasizes communication and obtaining buy-in. Mintzberg and Westley provide summaries of the three approaches as consistent with this last description of "seeing first" (Table 4-2).

"Doing first" involves trial and error or experimentation. This experimentation is best when we do not feel sure about the pros and cons of each alternative, so we select one or several actions and try them out, gaining information about how well each one works. This information then allows us to transition to the thinking or seeing approach.

Table 4-2 provides a comparison of the three approaches of Mintzberg and Westley (2001).

**TABLE 4-2:** Comparison of "Thinking, Seeing, and Doing First"

| "Thinking First" qualities | "Seeing First" qualities | "Doing First" qualities |
|---|---|---|
| Science | Art | Craft |
| Planning, programming | Visioning, imagining | Venturing, learning |
| The verbal | The visual | The visceral |
| Facts | Ideas | Experiences |

Table 4-3 summarizes these three approaches (Mintzberg and Westley 2001).

**TABLE 4-3:** Summary of "Thinking, Seeing, and Doing First"

| "Thinking First" works best when | "Seeing First" works best when | "Doing First" works best when |
|---|---|---|
| The issue is clear | Many elements have to be combined into creative solutions | The situation is novel and confusing |
| The data are reliable | Commitment to those solutions is key | Complicated specifications would get in the way |
| The context is structured Thoughts can be pinned down Discipline can be applied | Communication across boundaries is essential | A few simple relationship rules can help |
| e.g., an established production process | e.g., new product development | e.g., facing a disruptive technology |

An example of a "seeing first" decision process is the use of *cognitive maps,* as proposed by Axelrod (1976). A cognitive map is a directed graph (nodes and arcs) that shows concepts or ideas as nodes. The arcs then signify some kind of relationships between the nodes. The relationships can be based on relationships or sequential timing or some deeper concept such as causation or implication. Figure 4-8 provides a cognitive map-based on some concepts from systems engineering (Buede 2000). Cognitive maps can be a significant augmentation to the communication process. The

Observe – Orient – Decide – Act (OODA) loop process presented in two figures in the next section are also examples of a concept map.

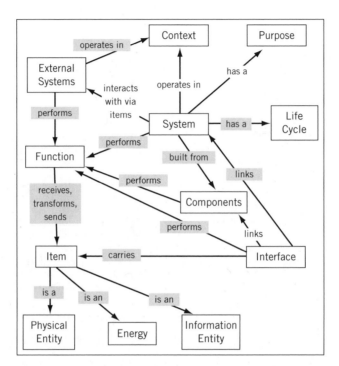

Dennis M. Buede, *The Engineering Design of Systems: Models and Methods* (Hoboken, NJ: John Wiley & Sons, Inc., 2000). Copyright © 2000 by John Wiley & Sons, Inc. Reprinted with permission.

**FIGURE 4-8:** Concept Map from Systems Engineering

## Decision-Making Structures for "Thinking First" Tasks

Decisions that permit reflection by the project manager should be made by means of some cognitive process. Such a process should consist of steps by which the possible alternatives are reviewed, objectives are outlined, and careful consideration of trade-offs is completed. Some decisions that can be made over hours or longer time frames are made once and never revisited; other decisions are made periodically based upon new information. Table 4-4 illustrates some simple and complex decisions in each of these two categories.

**TABLE 4-4:** Sample "Thinking First" Decisions

|  | Simple | Complex |
|---|---|---|
| **One-Time Decision** | Buying basic IT hardware and software<br>Hiring a new employee<br>Deciding who should be sent to training<br>Deciding the project organization | Selecting an architecture design for a new product<br>Deciding what research or risk mitigation efforts should be funded<br>Buying advanced technology for IT support<br>Hiring a senior member of the project staff during a crisis situation |
| **Sequential Decision** | Deciding whether to accept the current work product or pass it back for improvement<br>Deciding project risk<br>Deciding how the project will be managed | Deciding on yearly planning/budgeting<br>Determining a project development strategy<br>Revisiting early project termination<br>Proceeding to the next phase |

A truly great example of "thinking first" was created by Colonel John Boyd of the U.S. Air Force, who developed an action selection strategy that was first applied to air-to-air combat in the Korean War. This strategy was to be implemented by U.S. pilots, who were informed that enemy pilots were using a similar strategy. Actions included shooting and employing maneuvers that would be deceptive and provide ambiguous cues to the enemy, thus making the enemy's decision process more difficult. Information was valuable throughout this process in that the decision was to be based on a clear view of the situation or context. Boyd called this process the OODA loop. Boyd and others later realized that the OODA loop was a general decision-making process that is as relevant to business activities in government and industry as it is to warfare (Richards 2002 and 2004).

Boyd's action selection strategy included the following: "Observe" means to look for and gather *relevant* information. "Orient" means to make sense of the information and establish the context for the decision; this is often called situation awareness today. Included in "Orient" is addressing the meta-decision. "Decide" means making a decision using a process of evaluating the alternatives with respect to the objectives in light of the facts and existing uncertainties. "Act" means to implement the decision, including setting up a monitoring process that determines what information would be the most valuable to collect. This process would be repeated as often as necessary (Figure 4-9). Other similar cycles exist, such as the Plan-Do-Check-Act (often called the Shewhart or Deming cycle). That cycle dates back to the 1920s with Shewhart (1939) and the 1950s with Deming.

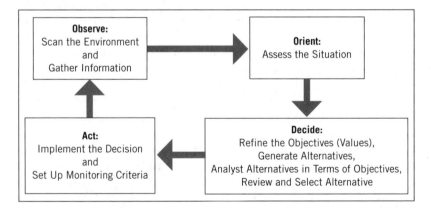

**FIGURE 4-9:** Simple Representation of the OODA Loop

Figure 4-10 provides a more detailed view of the OODA loop, showing (1) three generic types of information that feed the decision maker's observations, (2) five elements of the situation that must be addressed, and (3) feedback loops from three sources (the decision, the action, and interactions between the decision maker and the rest of the world).

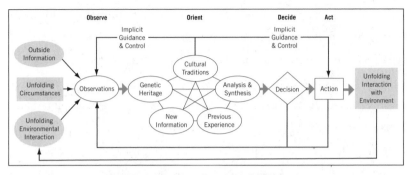

**FIGURE 4-10:** More Detailed OODA Loop

The three categories of information, which are shown on the left side of Figure 4-10 and feed the observation process, are quite carefully crafted. By carefully crafted we mean they nicely represent all possible types of information available to a decision maker. The top two categories (outside information and unfolding circumstances) come from outside the decision process. Outside information includes the information that provides context to the decision, such as what is going on in other decision contexts that might be relevant to this particular decision context. Information about unfolding circumstances captures information from outside sources that is directly related to this decision situation, such as available resources that were expected to arrive. The most obvious category is information related to the implementation of the selected action and its interaction with the world. In air-to-air combat, this information would include sensor reports about other aircraft in the area. For a project manager, this information includes reports from the appropriate organizations about cost, schedule, and performance; reports from other personnel about cost, schedule, and performance; and other reports about the budgets and expected performance parameters desired by management.

The second category, unfolding circumstances, includes technology developments and associated reports, changes in the marketplace associated with the focus of the project that might affect what the project should be doing, and changes in the organization responsible for the project. Consider the following case study.

## CASE STUDY

### Iridium

"Iridium" was the name of a product created by a consortium of companies from around the world in 1990 to create a mobile phone that would enable its owner to talk to anyone anywhere in the world, at any time. By the time the product was ready, a large portion of the world's population had mobile phones that were less capable but much more usable and less expensive. A $5 billion investment was sold for $25 million in 2001 because the company could not find customers willing to pay $3,000 for the brick-like phone and $7 per minute for calls.

The changing marketplace faced by the Iridium project was completely ignored by the project manager and the firms contributing money to the project. This project illustrates the importance of paying close attention to unfolding circumstances.

The last category of outside information could include reports from experts associated with activities not associated with the unfolding interaction.

Boyd stressed the importance of the "Orient" step in the OODA loop to shape or interpret the information coming from the "Observe" step. The purpose of the "Orient" step is to get the decision maker to review the project manager's current status, the most important, current objectives, and the most operationally relevant strategy. Most project managers are familiar with SWOT analysis—strengths, weaknesses, opportunities, and threats. Strengths and weaknesses are internally focused; opportunities and threats are externally focused. A SWOT analysis is the type of activity that should be undertaken during the "Orient" step. Currently, many people talk about doing "situation assessment" and achieving "situation awareness," which is also part of "Orient."

We discussed the importance of addressing the meta-decision when we addressed Figure 4-1—deciding what decision to address. This meta-decision analysis also fits here. Payne, Bettman, and Johnson (1993) address the importance of orientation, situation awareness, and meta-decisions in *The Adaptive Decision Maker*. Consider the following case study (Sculley and Byrne 1987).

## CASE STUDY

### Pepsi

An example of a meta-decision is that faced by Pepsi when its management was trying to gain market share on Coca Cola. According to Sculley (CEO of Pepsi at the time), Coca Cola had a tremendous advantage in market share that could be largely traced to the shape of the Coca Cola bottle. Pepsi tried to counter the bottle disadvantage but to no avail. It was not until they did an experiment involving how much soda consumers would consume that they realized they could package Pepsi in larger containers and consumers would purchase these larger containers. The larger containers overcame the advantage of the shape of the Coca Cola bottle.

Here we must caution the reader about the overwhelming tendency people have to deceive themselves about reality. There has been a great deal of research dealing with human biases and heuristics in decision-making and other judgmental tasks; we review this material in Chapter 8. Some of these important biases that are relevant for consideration within the OODA loop follow:

- **Selective search for evidence:** People generally seek information that will confirm their beliefs rather than seeking evidence that will prove themselves wrong. Science teaches us that we can never prove a proposition by accumulating more and more positive examples that it is true, but we can disprove a proposition by finding one instance where it is false. Disconfirming evidence is therefore much more valuable than confirming evidence and should have the effect of reducing our overconfidence.

- **Anchoring and adjustment:** People will often start with an initial value and adjust away from it to obtain related values. In general, such adjustments are insufficient, being biased toward the starting value.

- **Availability:** People tend to attach higher probability to events that they recall readily. Recent events, or those that are more salient to the individual, impact the individual's perception of the frequency of such events. How readily an event can be imagined can also be a factor. For example, accidents that make the news are judged more likely to occur than accidents that are just as likely but do not tend to make the news. Specifically, a death by a person shooting a gun is about as likely as a death by accidental falling (in 2003); however, most people think the former is much more likely than the latter because shootings appear in the news more often.

As discussed in Chapter 2, three elements are always present in a decision situation: (1) the alternatives, (2) the values associated with the objectives, and (3) knowledge about the world now and in the future. This third element clearly comes from the "Orient" stage, which is derived from the "Observe" stage. In fact, the alternatives also are derived from the "Orient" stage.

Some key points Boyd made in his many briefings (some as long as 15 hours) and points made by others are:

- Use as many information sources as possible, but recognize the limits of each information source and the possibility of deception by others, which could corrupt the information. Project managers have to be concerned about the credibility of their information sources as well as the possibility that one or more sources might be deceptive.

- Place the information that is available into the context of the situation ("Orient"), because the same information in different contexts can have dramatically different meanings.

- Examine the trade-offs among the multiple objectives available because these trade-offs can change with time due to the changing context. Clarify these trade-offs with the current context and make sure that others involved in the decision also understand the trade-offs.

- Include in the implementation of your decision a monitoring program that uses available information-gathering resources so that the success or failure of the decision and its implementation can be tracked over time as part of the "Orient" step. Follow-up decisions can modify this implementation or change it entirely.

## Decision-Making Structures for "Seeing First" Tasks

There are many situations in life in which one must make a split-second (or instinctive) decision based on the demands of the situation. Klein (1998) has studied many of these cases and termed the quick (or "seeing") decision process *recognition-primed decision* (often called RPD). Figure 4-11 presents a process model for RPD (Klein 1998). The figure begins with the context and situation as background. Something happens. For a project manager, this can be a crisis or an opportunity that needs a reaction quickly. While not life-threatening, as were situations for the firefighters or law enforcement officers studied by Klein, these kinds of situations can be project-threatening or opportunities for success.

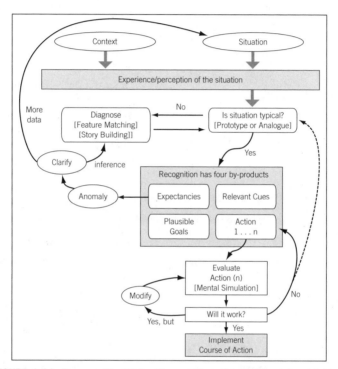

**FIGURE 4-11:** Process Model for Recognition-Primed Decision-Making

The decision maker uses a set of cues and expectancies to recognize the context and the situation. If the situation is familiar to the project manager (follow the right side of Figure 4-11 from top to bottom with no side loops), the preferred choice will be found by a process of evaluating a short list of possible options based on the project goals. As stated early in this chapter, Simon (1955) called this *satisficing*. A last check is made to ensure that the selected reaction will work; if so, implementation begins.

Now what happens if recognition does not occur initially? The project manager moves to the left of Figure 4-11 after deciding that the situation is not typical. A diagnosis phase is initiated with an attempt to use features of the situation to try to recognize or find an analogy that can aid recognition. The decision maker then builds a story around this recognition. If successful, the project manager moves back to the recognition and option selection process.

If there is a problem with recognition after the recognition and option selection process has been entered, the anomaly is defined and the project manager moves back to diagnosis or even reverts to reassessing the situation.

Finally, if the project manager has selected an action but later determines that it might not work, options not selected can be revisited and attempts to find the next best one can be made. This is repeated until the option that the project manager believes will work is found.

## Decision-Making Structures for "Doing First" Tasks

The concept of "doing first" involves experimentation for the purposes of gathering information for learning and iterating toward a good decision solution. We have already described the "thinking first" and "seeing first" processes. "Doing first" can result from either one and is typically not initiated without first being part of either "thinking first" or "seeing first" For example, if the decision maker is thinking about competing alternatives and weighing their pros and cons, "doing first" might be selected because there is not enough information to define pros and cons. By selecting "doing first" as an alternative, the decision maker is gathering information about one or more of the possible alternatives so that a better decision can be made later. Similarly, during a "seeing first" decision process, the decision maker might recollect that "doing first" worked very well in a similar situation and select it as the alternative course of action. Thus, our suggestion is to decide whether "doing first" makes sense within either a cognitive or a perceptive process and then use the appropriate process.

## Decision-Making Methods and Aids

People tend to rely upon heuristics or "rules of thumb" to make decisions; however, not all decisions can be made that simply because too many variables and factors exist along with the uncertainty that characterizes most project management decisions. Heuristics are simplification strategies (they save time and effort) and in many cases work reasonably well, but sometimes they can inject faulty judgment or cognitive bias into the process. Some biases are the straightforward product of laziness and inattentiveness, and although heuristics typically yield accurate judgments, they can produce biased and erroneous judgments also.

In addition to a decision process, there are many useful methods that help a decision maker in making the best decision. All methods can be categorized as *qualitative* (making decisions based on concepts or aggregated comparisons, such as good or poor), or *quantitative* (making decisions based on numerical inputs and numerical comparisons). Some decision makers prefer qualitative methods, while others prefer quantitative methods. Individuals without mathematical backgrounds might prefer a qualitative approach, but a qualitative approach should never be the default. In many cases, a quantitative approach is preferred.

Decision-making aids help stakeholders as well as project managers understand difficult choices and trade-offs. Decision trees incorporate risk and uncertainty. Decision matrices and tables screen solutions. Other aids include (1) decision hierarchies, (2) influence diagrams, (3) spreadsheets, (4) tornado diagrams, (5) risk profiles, and (6) sensitivity analyses. Not all aids apply to project management, and the ones chosen should be appropriate for project managers. The essential objective of a decision aid is to help communicate decisions to stakeholders and to help the project meet cost, schedule, and product expectations. Decisions trees are no stranger to project management. An explanation of decision trees, tornado diagrams, and risk profiles is presented in Appendix C.

## Implementing the Decision

The implementation of a decision is perhaps the most important task for the project manager. Managers are sometimes more interested in making a decision and then evaluating the result to determine if the decision achieved the stated purpose than they are in implementing it. There is often an obsession with making decisions and leaving the implementation to the lower levels in the organization. Decisions often require interpretation by management to be adequately implemented; if management doesn't do that, the decision can be improperly implemented and can fail. Implementing a decision requires as much planning and management oversight as planning the decision and making it. Project managers must account for whether the decision was implemented or if the decision changed during implementation—a result that can create a difference between what was decided and what was implemented.

The real value of a decision becomes apparent only after implementation, and yet implementation cannot begin until goals have been set, the decision has been approved, personnel have been assigned, and funds have been allocated. People often think that after decisions are made, implementation is quite straightforward and requires no guidance. In practice, however, both the decision and implementation of the decision must be planned—and should be planned *concurrently*. In addition, the implementation of the decision should be evaluated to determine if (1) the stated purpose of the decision was achieved, (2) the stated purpose of the decision was not achieved, or (3) improper implementation methods have resulted in a need for an extended completion time.

General rules for implementation are:

1. Verify that the decision you have chosen is a good decision.

2. Work out how to implement your decision.

3. Work out how to monitor its effectiveness.

4. Commit yourself to your decision and act on it.

## Avoiding Failure during Implementation

In project management, it is not enough to select the best decision alternative. If the decision is not implemented successfully, a favorable outcome is unlikely. After a decision has been made, appropriate action must be taken to ensure that the decision will be carried out as planned. Decisions have routinely failed to be implemented due to a lack of resources, such as necessary funds, space, or staff, or some other failure, such as inadequate supervision of subordinates and employees (Harrison 1987). Proper planning can effectively eliminate such failures.

Implementing the decision is a complex function and the one in which most project errors occur. Alexander H. Cornell captures the complexity of this function (Harrison 1987):

> Constraints surface in the Implementation Phase, constraints of a physical, administrative, distributional fairness and political nature, in addition to the ever-present financial and other resource constraints . . . . The "adversary process" is triggered and if care is not taken, a good [decision] can be negated by those who attack it . . . . This can be an agonizing period for one who may have devoted his or her very best to the [decision], but it is the real world.
>
> Then, too, it is during the phases of implementation . . . that other unforeseen effects appear. Things that were believed measurable may prove not to be so; unknowns and uncertainties appear which require adjustments . . . —all of which are designed to *reduce* the amount of uncertainty and to make known the unknown; to treat side effects and spillovers which may not have been foreseen, especially the important external ones.

There are thus many obstacles to the successful implementation of managerial decisions. Some are known and others appear during implementation. Chief among these obstacles are (1) the perception of the reduced importance of a decision after it has been made and implemented, (2) the control of the outcome of a decision by those who were not involved in its making, and (3) the development of new situations and problems affecting the quality of the implementation that command the attention of the decision makers after the choice has been implemented (Harrison 1987). Another main obstacle is the lack of planning for implementation early in the decision-making process. It is often the case that implementation is not considered until after the choice has been made. When this occurs, the project can absorb unnecessary amounts of time and valuable resources as the project manager hurriedly tries to arrange for implementation.

## Monitoring, Assessment, and Control

Outcomes rarely occur as planners have envisioned them. Thus, a follow-up and control process should be established to ensure the project remains on track during implementation. This process should consist of three steps: (1) monitoring, (2) assessment, and (3) control. These steps make up the closed-loop process shown in Figure 4-12. The purpose of this process is to provide continuous testing of actual results to determine if managerial objectives defined early in the decision-making process have been achieved. This process becomes the sanity check for the project during the implementation function.

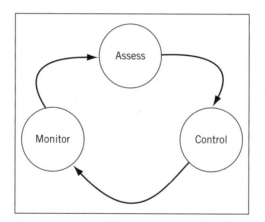

**FIGURE 4-12:** Monitoring-Assessments-Control loop

*Monitoring* is the collecting, recording, and reporting of project information that is important to the project manager and other relevant stakeholders (Mantel, Meredith, Shafer, and Sutton 2001). The purpose of monitoring is to ensure that all team members have the information and resources required to exercise control over the project. The key to designing a monitoring system is identifying the special characteristics of performance, cost, and schedule that need to be controlled to achieve project objectives. All decisions will affect the performance, cost, and schedule elements of the project. In addition to designing a monitoring system, the exact boundaries within which these characteristics should be controlled must be determined.

*Assessments* are critical in monitoring outcomes in order to determine what changes are warranted throughout the implementation function. Assessing is the evaluation of monitored data and information to determine whether the project is progressing according to schedule, budget, and required performance. This step should occur repeatedly. The information gained in this step is referred to as *feedback*. Feedback is used to compare actual performance to expected performance. When the actual performance does not align with the expected performance, there can be many reasons: the decision itself, poor implementation, or a lack of resources. If the decision itself is the problem, it might be necessary to consider a new decision.

*Control* is the use of the monitored data and assessment information to develop actions to bring actual project performance into agreement with planned performance (Mantel, Meredith, Shafer, and Sutton 2001). The process of control begins with a clear view of the project objectives. Criteria are defined to reflect more specific aspects of project objectives. Performance measures are then developed for each criterion. The performance measures become the control standards to determine whether the project is healthy. If the project is unhealthy, controls are necessary to correct deviations from the standard that is expected. Corrective action can include (1) reordering operations, (2) redirecting personnel, or (3) resetting the managerial objectives (Harrison 1987).

This chapter began with defining a decision as the selection of one or more alternatives from many, based on one's preferences over a set of objectives and given what is known at the time. Knowing one's objectives and searching for information that will help differentiate alternatives are important aspects of making a decision. Finding the best set of possible alternatives is also very critical. Several literary perspectives on decision-making and important decisions made by people in the past were presented to set the stage for further discussion.

We concentrated on what good decision-making means: *Good decisions must be based on the process that was used, not the outcome that was obtained.* It is easy to fall into the trap of evaluating a decision based on the outcome, but the decision maker seldom has control of the outcome. Besides focusing on finding good alternatives, knowing one's objectives and values, and collecting information that differentiates alternatives, there are other aspects of decision-making that must be considered, such as checking to determine if there is easily collected information that could change the decision, making sure the decision being made is the most appropriate decision to make at this time, and considering the impact this decision is likely to have on other related decisions.

Decision makers can be too relaxed about their decisions—waiting to see what happens. Good decision makers must be aware of what people and events can be influenced and must use their time to "sell" their desired solution to the problem. Of course, this desired solution is the decision problem that must be thoughtfully considered in light of the decision maker's values and knowledge about the state of the world. This chapter also related the concepts of "implementation" and "random events" to the previous concepts of "good ... bad decisions" and "good ... bad outcomes." Building a monitoring system and learning from experience were also added as key decision-making concepts. We expressed the belief that many students of decision-making have adopted—*good decision-making processes will generate a higher percentage of good outcomes than will poor decision-making processes.*

A short history of the many topics associated with decision-making was presented to give the reader the sense that this is a topic that has been addressed in many thoughtful ways by many people over the centuries.

There are at least three major approaches to decision-making: "thinking first," "seeing first," and "doing first." Each of these is appropriate for specific situations. Knowing when to use each one is part of good decision-making.

The OODA loop was described for "thinking first" decisions. Key points here were understanding available information sources, integrating the information into a situational assessment so as to affect the meta-decision and decision processes, continually balancing the key trade-offs needed with the search for more information so that an appropriate decision is made on a timely basis, and following through with implementation and monitoring activities.

A process called RPD was described for "seeing first" (quick-response) decisions. The use of either the OODA loop or RPD was recommended for "doing first" decisions.

Near the end of the chapter, we provided a quick overview of the many types of decision aids that are available to decision makers. Some of the qualitative aids will be described in the remainder of the book. References were provided for the other types of aids.

Finally, the implementation of decisions was addressed.

In Chapter 5, we identify the hundreds of decisions that are required to successfully manage projects. The decisions we identify are presented as part of a decision structure that represents both the product system and the development system.

# Project Management Decisions

W e have already established the fact that success is the primary objective in project management and decisions are the "yellow brick road" that leads to success. In other words, decisions provide a framework for project managers to guide and control events during product development. Unfortunately, the sequence of decisions and associated choices available to the development team at the beginning of development has a nearly uncountable number of paths.

Krishnan and Ulrich's (2001) concept of a *decision framework* refers to the conceptualization of how product development is executed. Krishnan and Ulrich were able to identify about 30 major decisions made within organizations during the development of physical goods at the project level. They found that although different organizations make different choices and might use different methods, all of them make decisions about a collection of issues such as the product concept, architecture, configuration, procurement arrangements, distribution arrangements, and project schedule. Their view of product development is comparable to a deliberate business process involving hundreds of decisions, which has been termed the *decision perspective*.

The decision perspective is a synthesis of four common perspectives (marketing, organizations, engineering design, and operations management) that cut across the project life cycle; it includes decisions for the product system, the principal organization, and the development or management system that manages product development. This perspective does not focus on how decisions are made; it focuses on what the decisions *are* and is comprehensive.

In this chapter, we refer to the hundreds of decisions required to successfully manage projects. The decisions apply to uncertain, complex, and changing projects that are affected by the dynamics of the environment, technology, or markets. Such decisions are intended to handle the uncertainty, complexity, and flexibility inherent in project management.

This chapter presents the following sections:

- A Project Management Decision Structure

- Decisions for Project Management

- Product (Operational) System Decisions

- Development (Project Management Organization) System Decisions.

## A Project Management Decision Structure

A project management decision perspective enables effective decision-making—determining the quality of the outcome in accordance with the choices, information, and preferences of the project manager in the presence of uncertainties and known/unknown risks. The decision perspective guides the construction of a model for all decisions made that permits use of the same kind of checking, testing, and problem elimination activities that systems engineering and software engineering use.

Because the project manager is the person responsible for managing the project and making decisions that support the outcome of the project, if the project manager does not make decisions, the decisions might not be made at all. True project management requires an active manager, not a reactive one.

Four activities are used to manage the schedule, cost, and product performance of the product or system being managed:

- Planning
- Organizing
- Directing
- Monitoring

The first activity and the major responsibility or task of the project manager within the decision perspective is planning—the beginning stage. The planning activity encompasses creating the project plan and creating a plan for handling special problems. Clearly, a great deal of emphasis must be placed on planning because the decisions made about planning will have a direct impact on decisions made in subsequent activities performed by the project manager. Planning requires that project managers plan hundreds of decisions that support the project management process. Planning must take place only when the project manager has a complete view of the entire project and a full understanding of the total project life cycle.

The second activity is organizing the decisions. The project manager must decide how to organize the project and must allocate resources to tasks. In the directing activity, the project manager oversees the day-to-day execution of the project or directs the execution of the decisions. In the monitoring activity, the project manager ensures that the actual progress of the project keeps pace with the estimated progress and determines whether the project should be terminated.

Besides the four activities (e.g., planning and organizing) in the decision perspective, four elements are considered and described in more detail below:

- Decision levels—the management level at which the decision is made

- Decision types—the part of the development process impacted by the decision (such as needs analysis and test planning)

- Decision order—the order in which a group of related decisions should be made

- Interdependency—the effects of one decision on one or more other decisions.

## Decision Levels

A *decision level* is the level of management at which specific decisions are made. Most organizations function according to three levels of management: upper, middle, and lower. We refer to the upper level as the level at which strategic decisions are made, the middle level as the level at which operational decisions are made, and the lower level as the level at which tactical decisions are made. The level at which decisions are made was described in Chapter 2 and will be revisited briefly now.

Strategic decisions are decisions that affect the entire organization relative to the management of projects. These decisions are generally administrative in nature. Operational decisions are decisions about resource use. These decisions have an impact on tactical decisions and support strategic decisions. Tactical decisions are day-to-day decisions that directly affect a project and the product or system managed. Each level deals with a unique set of decisions. The program manager makes decisions at the strategic level. The project manager makes decisions at the operational level. Selected leaders of the project team make decisions at the tactical level.

## Decision Types

A decision type is a category of similar decisions—or a topic category. An efficient way to organize or group decisions is by type. When this occurs, the decision-making process is made simpler. A primary advantage is that, after grouping, decisions can be arranged in the order in which they need to occur. Topic categories, as stated, describe the various types of decisions and tell what the decision is about. Examples of topic categories, which will be introduced later in this chapter, include (1) needs analysis, (2) life-cycle requirements, (3) management structure, (4) product system design, and (5) test planning. Table 5-1 provides an overview of the topics and subtopics addressed here. The two rows of column headings are the topics. The subtopics are the entries in each for the four main columns.

**TABLE 5-1:** Decision Topics and Subtopics

| Product System | | | Development System (Project Management Organization) |
|---|---|---|---|
| **Definition and Design** | **Integration and Qualification** | **Life-Cycle Planning** | **Development** |
| Needs Analysis<br>• Problem Definition<br>• Problem Validation<br><br>Product System Analysis and Concept Design<br>• Concept Definition<br>• Concept Evaluation<br>• Concept Validation<br><br>Product System, Product Subsystem, and Component Requirements and Design<br>• Requirements Definition<br>• Design Definition<br>• Test Definition<br>• Validation Definition<br><br>Test Planning<br><br>Product System, Product Subsystem, and Component | Product System, Product Subsystem, and Component Test<br>• Integration<br>• Verification<br>• Product System Validation | Life-Cycle Requirements and Architecture<br><br>Stakeholder Role in Determining Life-Cycle Requirements<br><br>Manufacturing<br><br>Operation, Support, Maintenance, and Upgrades | Management Structure<br>• Project Definition<br>• Stakeholder System<br>• Project Manager Construction<br>• Team Development<br><br>Project Management Planning<br>• Information Definition and Validation<br>• Resource Definition and Validation<br>• Control Structure Definition and Validation<br><br>Development System Construction<br>• Organizational Structure<br>• Role Definition<br>• Makeup<br>• Resources<br>• Evaluation<br>• Validation<br>• Location<br>• Training |

Topic categories are developed at each level and are intended to make the decision-making process more efficient. The topic is the label for the category and describes the types of decisions that must be made. The decisions presented in this chapter target the project organization and the product or service being managed.

## Decision Order

*Decision order* refers to the sequence in which decisions are made. The design of an automobile, aircraft, or computer involves hundreds of decisions. The decision-making task is rendered significantly more difficult when many design tasks and decisions are interdependent. However, this can work to the advantage of a project manager because analyzing complex relationships among design decisions facilitates better organization of the design tasks, improves coordination among the designers, and facilitates faster and better product development (Eppinger et al. 1990). Future decisions typically depend on the outcome of earlier decisions. In managing projects, this is also true. Making decisions randomly will likely bring disaster to any project. Decisions must be planned, as far as possible, in an order that prevents schedule delays, cost overruns, or failure to attain product performance objectives. More important, early decisions cannot be put off until later; later decisions should not usually be made before their time.

Figure 5-1 shows a sequence of decisions. Although this is the natural order in which decisions are made, not all decisions are sequential. Decision-making can also occur concurrently, meaning that many decisions can be made simultaneously with other decisions.

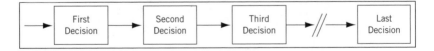

**FIGURE 5-1:** Sequential Decisions

*Problem definition* and *project definition* decisions are examples of decisions that should be made early in the project management process.

Problem definition is the determination of what problem really needs to be solved by the product or system. Project definition is the determination of what product is going to be developed and how the project is going to be organized to enable this development. Both of these should occur early because these decisions provide information and data for a majority of later decisions. If these decisions are not made, made poorly, or made too late, the biggest mistakes made in a project are likely to occur—mistakes that have rippling effects throughout the project. The decision to select stakeholders should also be identified as early as possible because stakeholders are used to assist in all phases of product or system development. As stated earlier, stakeholders assist in defining the need, clarifying requirements and specifications, and testing. Project managers should be selected after the project requirements are defined but before other team members are selected. The project organization should be defined after product and system requirements have been defined.

In most cases, all decisions that need to get made will eventually be made. The problem is that we do not make the right decisions as expeditiously as we ought, or we make decisions too early that are best left for later. The decision to terminate a project typically comes too late—after valuable resources have already been wasted. When untimely decisions are made, projects stand a greater risk of failure—product development fails, and there are missed organizational objectives.

## Interdependency

Decisions are interdependent and must be planned using a comprehensive view of the project. For this to occur, the project manager must be able to envision all phases of the project simultaneously when planning the project. Interdependency among decisions occurs when structured, social, or economic determinants of one decision influence other decisions. Most decisions evidence important elements of interdependence with other decisions. Most decisions are linked to other decisions.

For example, a decision on project organization is likely to be made jointly with a decision about project location. The realization that decisions are interdependent typically leads to a significantly narrowed set of realistic decision options. This is particularly advantageous because some options will make little sense when combined. More important, when decisions are linked, the project manager must plan ahead by effectively coordinating current and future decisions.

Whether a decision maker is making several interdependent decisions serially or concurrently, the project manager needs to consider later decisions when making early decisions.

## Decisions for Project Management

Decision-making, the basis for the design—the creation of requirements, architecture, and blueprints—and qualification—testing to verify that a product meets its requirement and to validate that it is the right product—of both the product and the development system during the product development process, uses decisions. Examples of key decisions for project management include those dealing with (1) the organizational structure for doing engineering, (2) the time sequence of skills and resources on hand, (3) the architecture selection, which affects the ability to handle the product's cost, schedule, and performance when design changes have to be made, (4) new technology used in the design, and (5) the validation tools or mechanisms to be employed.

Making good decisions for both the product and the development system is in essence a self-evident approach to designing (Suh 2001). In project management, the project manager should be concerned with both the product and development system when developing products and when seeking to meet organizational objectives.

## Product (Operational) System Decisions

The product system, the product to be released to customers (users), contains elements and features related to satisfying stakeholder needs. These needs are defined in documents such as a mission statement and concept of operations. Later, requirements documents such as the originating requirements document, system requirements document, and various specifications documents are developed.

The performance, cost, and schedule of the product are affected by decisions that influence physical, functional, and interface elements of the product. Decisions for the product system support (1) definition and design, (2) integration and qualification, and (3) life-cycle planning. The types of product system decisions are introduced and discussed in the following sections; however, all decisions are presented in Appendix B.

### Definition and Design Decisions

*Needs analysis* includes problem definition and problem validation— the beginning activities of the product development process. These activities are foundational to the initiation of the project management process and to the successful execution of the design and qualification of both the product and development systems (project management organizations). *Problem definition* and *problem validation* represent a definition of stakeholder needs, the mission requirement, and the context of the need, and they also validate the need according to stakeholder input. These activities are critical because as the need or the problem comes into focus, the functionality that the user expects in the product system flows down to the component level of the product system.

A clear definition of the need initiates *product system analysis and concept design,* which include *concept definition, concept evaluation,* and *concept validation.* This activity includes making decisions related to defining the technology and its feasibility, and for selecting and validating suitable concepts for product system development that meet stakeholder needs. Here, it is important that information about the stakeholder needs converges with information about technical capabilities. As all of this information is collected and processed, items related to performance and cost will roll into the stakeholder requirements. This activity helps to establish top-level product system functions, which are the primary prerequisite for the establishment of performance requirements.

*Product system, product subsystem and component requirements and design* includes *requirements definition, design definition, test definition,* and *validation definition.* The requirements definition activity includes making decisions that relate to defining detailed operational requirements that support product design and development. Requirements evolve during the requirements definition activity as information is gained through continual stakeholder interaction; however, during test definition and validation definition, requirements can be added, refined, constrained, or even deleted based on the output.

*Test planning* includes testing and evaluation planning for the *product system, product subsystem,* and *component* levels. An early decision related to this activity is how to prove that the system will meet its key performance targets and perform its intended functions. This is one of many decisions that should be made early because it affects the design of the product system. Another decision that should be made during this activity is how the pieces are going to physically fit together. This decision will also affect the design of the product system and the work to be performed by the development system (project management organization). Initial planning for product system integration and verification, and validation activities, begins in the test planning decision activity for execution during the actual decision activity.

## Integration and Qualification Decisions

The *product system, product subsystem,* and *component test* includes *integration, verification,* and *product system validation* activities. Product system integration and verification results as the product system is assembled from the component level up to the system level and undergoes verification that the product system has been built correctly, according to requirements and specifications. This activity includes those decisions related to proving that the system has been built correctly.

System validation occurs when all requirements have been verified and the product system has been validated as meeting its objective (Jackson 1997). The product system validation activity includes those decisions related to proving that the right system has been built.

## Life-Cycle Planning Decisions

Important life-cycle planning decisions include *requirements and architecture; stakeholder roles in determining life-cycle requirements; manufacturing; and operation, support, maintenance, and upgrades.*

Life cycle-focused design is responsive to customer needs as well as design, as is designing both the product system and the development system (project management organization), which supports development of an operational product. Life cycle-focused design is also responsive to life-cycle outcomes. Blanchard and Fabrycky (1998) propose that life cycle-focused design should consider operational outcomes expressed as producibility, reliability, training, maintainability, supportability, serviceability, refinement, and disposability. Specifically during product design, consideration should be given to a product's production, which gives rise to a parallel life cycle for bringing a manufacturing capability into being. The product system, product subsystem, and component requirements and design activity not only help to design and develop the product but also help to develop the requirements for the manufacturing process that follows. Understanding other life-cycle system requirements early in the product development process contributes to attaining success in the engineering of the total product system.

Problem definition and project definition decisions are examples of decisions that should be made early in the project management process. As indicated, these decisions provide information and data for all other functions throughout the development process, and they facilitate an exchange of information between the product and development systems (project management organizations). Decisions made during problem definition, problem validation, concept definition, evaluation and validation, and program management planning are early decisions essential to initiating any project. These decisions represent the biggest mistakes if decisions are not made, made poorly, or made too late.

The decision to develop the test plan should be made prior to and not during the actual test activity. The test planning activity should actually begin as part of the advance system planning during concept definition, evaluation, and validation (Blanchard and Fabrycky 1998). There must be a way to evaluate the product system to ensure that requirements have been met; therefore, testing considerations are required at an early point in time.

Decisions associated with life-cycle planning should also begin during concept definition, evaluation, and validation, but they should be made no later than at the time of requirements definition, design definition, test definition, and validation definition. In essence, they should be made throughout the development process.

## Development (Project Management Organization) System Decisions

The purpose of the development system (project management organization) is to provide the infrastructure necessary to design and qualify the product system. The project manager serves as the manager, but all elements of the development system are responsible for managing the processes and requirements that support product system development. The development system is foundational to all activities that support the product system and is divided into three areas: (1) *management structure,* (2) *project management planning,* and (3) *development system construction.* These three areas combined represent the resources, processes, and elements necessary for successful product system development. These areas are addressed in more detail in the sections that follow. The decisions for each of these areas are presented in Appendix B.

Decision-making in the area of the development system deals with planning conducted to design a product organization—its structure, in particular—and with organizing teams to facilitate communication and rapid decision-making. Development system construction describes the organizational structure, roles and responsibilities, team makeup, and necessary resources. The basis for team evaluation is also considered.

## Management Structure

This section includes those decisions related to defining the management structure of the development system—*project definition, stakeholder system, project manager construction,* and *team development.*

### *Project Definition*

The source of the initial information for the development system is the objectives for the project, which are defined by the *project definition activity.* Organizational objectives can also be considered in this activity. The project manager must understand the nature of the project in order to ensure that the objectives of the project can be met. The project will otherwise get off to a bad start. These goals often tie to organizational goals, as just stated. Ensuring that the right decisions are made can prevent starting a project badly. The nature of the project becomes the basis for all decisions that will follow. Unless the project is defined, it becomes a runaway train. User needs, combined with the project definition, provide critical information useful to the project manager and team, and ensure that project objectives are attained. Understanding the nature of the project also establishes the framework for carrying out the planning that is required. The problem definition activity of the product system also provides critical information useful in formulating the definition of the project.

### Stakeholder System

The success of the project management process hinges on the identification of every stakeholder as early as possible because they hold critical information that is needed to begin the product development process. The *stakeholder system* provides the engineers and project managers with the best opportunity to provide a system that accomplishes the primary objectives set by the stakeholders. Upon identification of stakeholders and their roles, the stakeholders should be involved throughout the management process in order to produce the best operational product or system. In addition, stakeholder roles should be defined. The inclusion of stakeholders early in the design process focuses on the "user requirements" element of concurrent engineering and mitigates the risk of numerous user-generated design changes later in the development process.

### Project Manager Construction

*Project manager construction* focuses on putting together an effective development team, beginning with identification of a project manager. Of all the decisions management makes in doing new product development, none can be more crucial to success than the choice of a project manager. The criteria for the project manager must be determined with respect to the requirements of designing and qualifying the product system. The project manager should be selected after the project requirements are defined but before other team members are selected. This component of the management structure defines the project manager criteria, role and authority, and required training.

### Team Development

Successful project management is only as good as the individuals and leaders who are managing the key functions (Kerzner 2006). The project manager uses individuals to manage the business, budget, and technical aspects of a project. Project team decisions focus initially on putting together the right team. The project manager focuses on the project objectives when determining the skills required to successfully complete the project.

Two key tasks in successful project management are designing a project team and organizing project teams in order to facilitate communication and rapid decision-making. Project team decisions focus on the organizational structure, roles and responsibilities, team makeup, and necessary resources (Powell 2002). Team evaluation should also be a part of project team decisions.

## Project Management Planning

This section includes those decisions related to defining the project management planning of the development system—*information definition and validation, resource definition and validation,* and *control structure definition and validation.*

Project management planning, a critical aspect of product system design, deals with the interaction and understanding of management elements involved in project development to enhance success; it is the glue that holds the entire project together and is programmatic in nature (Forsberg, Mooz, and Cotterman 2000). So in order to achieve the appropriate level of interaction and understanding, the planning process must address *information*. What information is going to be created or obtained from outside sources, by whom, distributed to whom under what circumstances, stored where and by whom, and validated or assessed as to accuracy by whom?

Resources need to be a central aspect of project management planning. The availability of funding for product development is often the critical resource and drives all planning schedules and performance estimates. However, other resources can be critical; examples include numbers and skills of people; office space and equipment; hardware and software systems; engineering, manufacturing, and testing facilities; and data. We should point out that one of the most critical resources available to the project manager is *time*. The planning process must therefore address how the expected availability of these resources matches their desired availability. Processes need to be put in place to monitor how many of each of these resources are expected and are in fact available at specific points in time.

Finally we address the definition and validation of control structures. As was stated earlier in this book, project management planning includes decisions that (1) relate to defining processes, activities, and events that have to be carried out to attain the objectives specified for the project, product, and organization; (2) reflect the overall management and discipline of the project; and (3) define the necessary resources for product development and resources for operation. This activity manages the integrity of the product development process and the quality of the product while *using decisions as the primary control structures*.

Before leaving this topic of project management planning, an important excursion is worthwhile. One of the most important aspects during project management planning is risk management. Risk management identifies many areas of program cost, schedule, and technical risk associated with important project *resources* and gives the project manager the *information* with which to make educated *decisions (control structures).* The risk management process provides a means of early warning of problems, a means for plan changes, and a means of deciding the best course of action. More important, it can increase management and stakeholder confidence (Jackson 1997).

## Development System Construction

This section includes those decisions related to defining the development system construction (e.g., project office) of the development system—*organizational structure, role definition, makeup, resources, evaluation, validation, location,* and *training.* The first element of development system construction is *organizational structure,* which addresses how the people who are part of the development system will be structured and how this will change over time. *Role definition* addresses the definition of the different kinds of positions that will exist in the project office and what the responsibilities and authorities will be for those positions. *Makeup* comprises a number of decisions relating to how the project office will be staffed over time by functional and skill levels.

*Resources* addresses the various types and constraints on monetary and infrastructure resources associated with the development system. *Evaluation* includes the bases, means of evaluation, and risks associated with the development system, not the project. *Validation* comprises the approaches to validating that the plan for the project office is adequate to the task. *Location* includes the physical layout of the project office, as well as the communication and technology assets associated with the project office. *Training* addresses the types and timing of training required for the people in the project office.

Stakeholders should be identified as early as possible because stakeholders are used to assist in all phases of development—to assist designers in defining the need, clarifying requirements and specifications—and in all phases of testing. This helps to ensure continual product validation because most critical product decisions will occur early in the project. If the customer is not involved before these decisions are made, momentum will make it unlikely that decisions can be reversed later as a result of customer input (Smith and Reinertsen 1998).

The project manager or team leader should be selected after the project requirements are defined but before other team members are selected (Forsberg et al. 2000).

The development system should be designed after the product system requirements have been established and understood. This is necessary because organizational teams must be tailored to the technical and acquisition phase that the program finds itself in. This leads to the decision of when team members should be added to the organizational team. Having more members than necessary at various points throughout the product development process results in unnecessary costs (Forsberg et al. 2000).

## CASE STUDY

### The Sidewinder Missile

We end this chapter with a case study of the Sidewinder missile—a successful project. Sample decisions that led to the project's success are highlighted in bold. This case clearly highlights the decisions responsible for project, product (the Sidewinder), and organizational success.

The Sidewinder missile, along with its physical characteristics, was the masterpiece of Dr. William Burdette McLean (1960, 1962), a gifted technologist and exceedingly gifted systems engineer. McLean served as the project manager and chief systems engineer throughout Sidewinder development, managing all aspects of systems design and development. The Special Projects Office, the program office under which McLean operated, was created to oversee the Fleet Ballistic Missile (FBM) Program for the U.S. Navy. The FBM program encompassed not only the Sidewinder missile program but also other military missile programs such as Polaris and Trident.

What began as a simple sketched concept of a guided air-to-air rocket in 1947 became a fully operational missile system in 1956. The Sidewinder, a Navy missile, evolved out of McLean's frustration with the limitations of unguided air-to-air rockets. He and his team were not commissioned to design the Sidewinder and therefore had no externally imposed specifications. **(What is the management strategy?)** Prior to arriving at China Lake, McLean saw the effectiveness of operating an organization outside of the formal bureaucracy and with little to no corporate regulations to get things done. This philosophy is known as "skunkworks." **(What is the system design strategy?)** McLean further believed that a better creative approach to the design of a system could be used in the absence of a set of definitive specifications. Specifications, in his view, tended to channel thinking along one approach. This philosophy realized the need for a *creative system development approach*—the use of goals in the design and development of the Sidewinder missile. This approach created more freedom to think and led to highly optimized solutions.

**(What are the user needs?)** The objective of the Sidewinder project was to "produce a system that was simple, reliable, and effective." Ultimately, the system needed to respond to user needs. **(What is the source and method for determining product requirements?)** To be responsive to user needs, the decision was made for the designer to maintain contact with users throughout the project life cycle (design, development, and testing). **(Who are the users?)** The users were aircraft pilots who would carry the missile into combat. This was a key management decision for arriving at the best solution to meet user need. McLean said (Westrum 1999):

If our designer is to be truly successful, he must have a more direct contact with this consumer than can ever be provided by a set of written specifications. His first task is therefore to get out in the field and get clearly in mind the functions that the consumer would like to perform. . . . The designer who does not take the trouble to try to broaden his specifications by understanding the basic problem will seldom deliver an outstanding product. . . . It is essential for the designer to question his specifications and to go back to primary sources in order to develop a real understanding of his problem, and the basis for the need, if he is to create a successful product.

The advantage of this decision was that it resulted in fewer communication hurdles and greater team member alignment. The users also assisted in defining the need, in clarifying requirements and specifications, and in validating the product system.

A number of additional key decisions contributed to the success of the Sidewinder. **(What is the system design approach?)** First and foremost, McLean did not believe in beginning product system development with a predefined set of requirements. The absence of formal requirements, in his view, allowed the best solution for the users in terms of what could be accomplished. Instead, he began with a goal. Only when laboratories could experiment freely did they arrive at the best solutions to technical problems.

This decision affected later decisions. For example, during research and development, two to three groups of laboratories were found working on common subsystem developments. The purpose was to provide the user with the best technical capability. This decision prevented the project from dying or being forced into a corner because it did not depend on a single technical solution from the beginning. **(What is the cost strategy?)** Another decision was made to conserve resources. Too much data was believed to be a waste of time and money. A minimal amount of data proved adequate to determine where to proceed next. Because formal requirements were not established in advance, there was no obligation to obtain a specified amount of data.

**(What are the information requirements?)** For this management approach to work, communication was required between every element involved in the development of the Sidewinder missile. As research and development proceeded, so would a dialogue with the users, to make sure the options the users chose were those that research and development could deliver. Deciding the best communication method among project team members also supported research and development efforts. The objective of these decisions was to reduce the number of upgrades, which would ultimately result in enormous cost savings throughout the life cycle of the missile.

This chapter covered a variety of decisions that must be considered when successfully managing a project. The decisions range from selecting a project to deciding when a project should be terminated. These decisions cannot be overlooked or dismissed if the project schedule, budget, and specifications are to be met. Although the primary objective of this chapter is the identification of decisions, just as important is the order in which decisions are made. In most cases, people are making concurrent decisions. The concurrency, which occurs during the project life cycle, promotes collaboration across both the product system and development system. This collaboration is necessary to product successful products.

The following specific points were made in this chapter:

- Because project managers make hundreds of decisions, decisions should not be made randomly but according to some structure. Random decisions increase the risk of project failure.

- Decisions must be planned, as far as possible, in an order that prevents schedule delays, cost overruns, and failure to attain product performance objectives.

- Early decisions must not be put off until later, and later decisions usually must not be made before their time.

- Product system decisions affect the product to be released to customers (users) and elements and features related to satisfying stakeholder needs.

- Development system (project management organization) decisions affect the infrastructure responsible for the design and qualification of the product system.

In Chapter 6, we introduce decision frames. Decision frames assist the project manager in documenting what is known, why the decision was important, what alternatives and objectives were considered, and why the chosen alternative was considered the best. A decision frame essentially defines the context for the decision and the elements that are part of the decision problem.

# CHAPTER 6

# Framing the Decision

A *decision frame* is a decision aid that can be used while making a decision to capture important information, and it presents a snapshot view of critical elements the project manager should consider in making a decision. A decision frame defines the context for the decision and the elements (alternatives, objectives, uncertainties) that are part of the decision situation. Most decisions made by people are based on a few seconds (or less) of thought. The idea of creating a conscious decision frame or documenting the decision frame for most decisions is not even an afterthought. For those decisions that can be scrutinized by management, auditors, an Inspector General, regulators, or a court, however, it is becoming clear to many people that creating some sort of audit trail for decisions is a wise thing to do.

A decision frame is such an audit trail because it documents what is known, why the decision is important, what alternatives and objectives are being considered, and why the chosen alternative is considered the best. Some explicit consideration of the decision frame just makes sense for the most important decisions made by project managers.

This chapter presents the following sections:

- The Importance of Decision Frames
- A Suggested Frame
- Suggested Decision Frame Format for Project Management.

## The Importance of Decision Frames

Decision frames have been shown to exist in people's heads in psychological experiments; these same experiments have shown that the choice of a decision frame can dramatically affect how a person thinks about a decision and shapes the decision that is made.

Consider the two choices provided by Tversky and Kahneman (1981) in an experimental setting:

A: A sure gain of $240

B: A 25 percent chance to gain $1,000 and a 75 percent chance of getting nothing.

84 percent of 86 people chose the more certain A.

Next, the same people were offered a choice of C or D.

C: A sure loss of $750

D: A 75 percent chance of losing $1,000 and a 25 percent chance to lose nothing.

87 percent of those same 86 people preferred D (the gamble).

The framing of the question in this experiment was critical. Note that the expected value of B is:

$250 (0.25 * $1,000 + 0.75 * $0), which compares favorably to but is not significantly better than the sure $240 in A. The expected loss in D is $750, the same as the sure loss in C.

In a follow-up question, the experimenters asked the same subjects to choose between E and F:

E: A 25 percent chance to win $240 and a 75 percent chance to lose $760.

F: A 25 percent chance to win $250 and a 75 percent chance to lose $750.

In this case everyone chose F because it dominates E (the probabilities are the same but the outcomes in F are always better than the outcomes in E). However, if we add A and D together (the preferred choices of most people), we get E (the dominated choice). Similarly, if we add the less attractive choices B and C above, we get the dominating choice F.

The lesson of this experiment is that framing a choice in terms of gain pushes people toward the certain decision, while framing the choice in terms of a loss pushes people to choose to gamble. Yet most people are risk averse and prefer to avoid gambles.

Different people commonly view the same decision through different lenses. The optimist says a glass half full and half empty is "half full," the pessimist says it is "half empty," and the engineer says "the glass is twice as big as it needs to be." Russo and Schoemaker (2002) point out the following:

Training employees can be viewed as a cost or as an investment.

A negotiation can be viewed as a competition (win-lose) or as joint problem-solving (win-win).

What is important to keep in mind here is that there are many ways to think about how to make a decision, sometimes called the "meta-view" of a decision situation. Selecting one way to think about the decision, e.g., expenditure versus investment, can drastically affect the way the decision maker approaches a resolution. There is no "right" answer, but some answers can be much more productive than others. As a result, many successful people and researchers recommend trying multiple meta-views or frames for a specific decision situation before selecting one view to use in approaching the decision.

It is often useful from the perspective of creativity to view the decision being faced from a different perspective. Fairhurst and Sarr (1996) described the following framing techniques:

- Metaphor: Gives a decision a new meaning by comparing it to something else.

  - A metaphor for a decision to invest in researching a new technology could be either an insurance policy or a gamble.

  - A metaphor for a decision to replace the current chief engineer could be replacing an old automobile with a station wagon, a sedan, or a sports car.

  - A metaphor for the system architecture is either the blueprint file for a house or an artist's sketch of a new subdivision.

- Story (myths and legends): Frames a decision by anecdote in a vivid and memorable way.

- Slogan, jargon, and catchphrase: Frames a decision in a memorable and familiar fashion.

- Contrast: Describes a decision in terms of what it is not.

  - Documenting the requirements for a system is not carving the requirements in stone.

  - Implementing a cut in the budget is not extending the project to meet new needs of stakeholders.

- Spin: Talks about a concept so as to give it a positive or negative connotation.

## A Suggested Frame

Figure 6-1 displays a *metaphor decision frame,* conceived around building a house, for any decision. After discussing this metaphor frame, we will particularize it to a project management context. The decision frame identifies the context in which the decision is being made, including the stakeholders, resource constraints, relevant environment, broad objectives, and some operational use cases for defining success and failure. The stakeholders for a new house are (1) the person or family paying for the building of the house, and (2) the company that is going to build the house. Other stakeholders that might be relevant include the neighbors and community in which the house is being built. Other stakeholders might include extended family members and guests who will be visiting and environmental activists who might be worried or delighted about the construction process or end result.

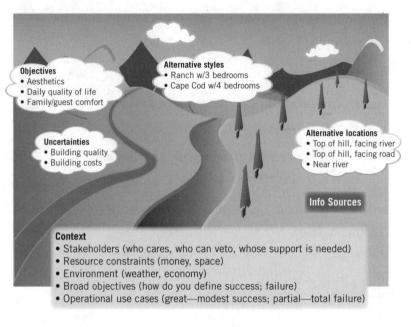

**FIGURE 6-1:** Metaphor Decision Frame—Building a House

Resource constraints include money and perhaps available land and types of equipment that can be used. If there are many trees or scarce plant or animal life on the land, resource constraints might include their protection.

The environment in this case is the water on or near the land, the road network, the relation of the sunrise and sunset to the site, and the average and extreme high and low temperatures. Broad objectives include living a comfortable, protected life and achieving financial goals.

Some use cases might be:

**Great success:** Over a 20-year period, the house had been easy to build and was affordable, there was plenty of room and comfort for a growing family, no loss of life or damage was caused by environmental emergencies (e.g., floods), many happy guests visited over many years, and a 500 percent growth in investment was obtained upon the sale of the house.

**Modest success:** Over a 20-year period, there was a need to expand the house or sell it due to growth of the family, minor damage was done to the house by an environmental emergency, some guests had to stay at nearby hotels due to lack of space, and there was a 200 percent growth in investment upon the sale of the house.

**Modest failure:** The house cost 20 percent more than was expected to build or an environmental emergency made extensive repair to the house necessary.

**Major failure:** The builder cannot complete the house for an affordable price, the family decides it is not comfortable in the house and has to sell it, or an unforeseeable environmental emergency destroys the house.

Based upon the broad objectives and the use cases, it is clear that there should be some fundamental objectives for the decision about building the house that relate to the cost of building the house, the daily quality of life (e.g., comfort, sufficient space), protection against environmental emergencies, potential costs to repair the house due to environmental emergencies, and resale value. Further reflection might yield additional fundamental objectives such as the aesthetics of the house, the monthly operating costs for the house if the cost of energy increases dramatically, and the ability of interested family members to grow a garden.

The alternatives for building the house might include two major issues: what style and size of house to build and where to build the house on the lot (including the orientation of the house relative to the road, the river, and the sun). Example style and size alternatives are shown in the middle of Figure 6-1. Similarly, examples of the location and orientation of the house are shown on the right side of Figure 6-1. *Note that the selection of a specific alternative for one issue (Cape Cod with four bedrooms) can influence which alternatives in another issue (such as the location and orientation of the house) should be selected. It is sometimes not possible to make decisions in one category independently of those in another category.*

Uncertainties can affect the quality of the decision dramatically in that some decision alternatives are designed to be low risk by being robust in the face of uncertain consequences. Other alternatives are more aggressive or risky in the face of these alternatives, requiring more energy during implementation and operation, as well as some cash reserves for fallback options in case the unexpected occurs. For the house metaphor, the uncertainties might include the financial position and experience of the builder, the likelihood of specific environmental emergencies, the zoning and growth potential of the nearby town, and the likely growth and interests of the family. So the location and orientation of the house is relatively low risk with respect to the risk issues just mentioned. However, it may be that some builders are not experienced at building a Cape Cod style house, but other house styles might have problems with zoning or environmental problems. So the selection of house type might be higher risk.

Finally, most decisions involve gathering and processing information. Some, but not most, of this information might already be in a database. Some information might come from experts or trusted colleagues. Some information might need to be obtained from people who are not as well known or trusted as we would like. Finally, some information is available from other sources and must be collected or purchased. Knowing as much as possible about what information is available and what is not, and what form the available information is in, will be quite helpful as the decision process proceeds.

## Suggested Decision Frame Format for Project Management

Table 6-1 shows a Generic Decision Frame for Project Management, which is a data collection form for project managers to use in capturing the decision frame for important decisions they face. This generic decision frame is used in several cases studies throughout the remainder of the book.

**TABLE 6-1:** Generic Decision Frame for Project Management Decisions

| Context for Decision |
| --- |
| **Stakeholders:** |
| **Resource Constraints:** |
| **Environment:** <br> *Social:* <br> *Organizational:* <br> *Legal:* <br> *Natural:* |
| **Broad Objectives:** |
| **Use Cases:** |

| Fundamental Objectives for Decision | Alternatives for Decision |
|---|---|
| **Programmatic Objectives:** | **Programmatic Alternatives:** |
| *Cost Objectives:* | |
| *Schedule Objectives:* | |
| *Performance Objectives:* | |
| **System/Product Objectives:** | **System/Product Alternatives:** |
| *Cost Objectives:* | |
| *Schedule Objectives:* | |
| *Performance Objectives:* | |
| **Supportability/Life Cycle Objectives:** | **Supportability/Life Cycle Alternatives:** |
| *Cost Objectives:* | |
| *Schedule Objectives:* | |
| *Performance Objectives:* | |
| **Uncertainties:** | **Information Sources:** |
| *Programmatic Uncertainties:* | *Data:* |
| *System/Product Uncertainties:* | *Experts:* |
| *Supportability/Life Cycle Uncertainties:* | *Other Sources:* |

The beginning of the decision frame helps define the context of the decision. Who is involved as a stakeholder? That is, who is making the decision, who might be affected by the decision, and who might be able to affect the decision? Are there any resource constraints? If so, what resources are involved and how significant are the constraints? What is the environment in terms of social, organizational, legal, and natural constraints or possibilities? What broad objectives should be considered in defining the objectives for this specific decision? Finally, what are some use cases—from complete success to complete failure—that might result from the decision? The elements of these use cases often provide information about the objectives and alternatives that need to be documented in other sections of the decision frame.

The Fundamental Objectives for Decision section addresses the fundamental objectives for this specific decision, and the Alternatives for Decision section addresses specific alternatives of the decision. The objectives are segmented in terms of the programmatic, the product or system of the project, and the life cycle of the product. In most cases, not all three parts of the life cycle will be relevant, but they are included to remind you that they might be more relevant than you initially think. Each of the categories of objectives is further divided into cost, schedule, and performance.

The Uncertainties section of the decision frame provides the decision maker with the opportunity to identify key uncertainties, and the Information Sources section addresses important information sources. Uncertainties will change as the decision situation evolves. Generally speaking, high-level managers and most project managers report that there is little relevant data for most of their decisions and that experts must be relied upon for their judgments to make up for that missing data.

An example of a decision frame for the Sidewinder case study, which was presented in Chapter 5, is shown in Table 6-2. The decision being addressed in this decision frame is how the Sidewinder design team should go about establishing the needs of the Sidewinder stakeholders at the beginning of the development process. (Note that this is just one of thousands of decisions made by the Sidewinder project manager, William McLean, who also served as chief systems engineer.)

**TABLE 6-2:** Sidewinder Missile Decision Frame

| Context for Decision |
|---|
| **Stakeholders:** actual pilots, test pilots, crew members aboard ships carrying the Sidewinder; Sidewinder design team; Department of Defense |
| **Resource Constraints:** very limited early budget because the program was not legally established, limited technology, and limited materials and equipment |
| **Environment:**<br>*Social:* freedom to think; commitment to project success<br>*Organizational:* limited political bureaucracy; little to no regulations; loose organizational structure<br>*Legal:* little by today's standards<br>*Natural:* blue water ocean |
| **Broad Objectives:** design a simple and reliable product on a shoestring budget; create a new missile technology |
| **Use Cases:** (1) operate under a skunkworks organizational design, adopt a nontraditional design approach, create multiple project sub-teams to create multiple technical solutions, design product system to goals instead of requirements with the use of proven technology; (2) operate as a major program within the Navy, meet with everyone associated with operating a Sidewinder missile to obtain formal feedback about their needs, document these needs and submit them for formal approval, build to these need statements or requirements |

| Fundamental Objectives for Decision | Alternatives for Decision |
|---|---|
| **Programmatic Objectives:** | **Programmatic Alternatives:** |
| *Cost Objectives:* limited money for collecting data | (1) Create a single laboratory team that meets with pilots, ship's crew members, and technologists to establish a documented set of needs or requirements up front; early contact with users only<br>(2) Use multiple teams to simultaneously study alternative design solutions to common subsystems based on an overall understanding of performance and operational constraints; continual dialogue with users |
| *Schedule Objectives:* time was unconstrained | |
| *Performance Objectives:* high commitment to mission success | |
| **System/Product Objectives:** | **System/Product Alternatives:** |
| *Cost Objectives:* minimal cost; utilize existing technology | (1) Build the Sidewinder based upon an architecture that best meets the requirements<br>(2) Design the product via a "build a little, test a little" approach with the freedom to dramatically change the design architecture at any time; formalize the requirements that were met by the design at the end |
| *Schedule Objectives:* still unconstrained | |
| *Performance Objectives:* fire control in the missile; simple, reliable, and effective system | |
| **Supportability/Life Cycle Objectives:** | **Supportability/Life Cycle Alternatives:** |
| *Cost Objectives:* life-cycle cost focus | (1) Ensure the designed missile can be stored and operated within normal shipboard operations<br>(2) Ensure the designed missile can be fired as needed by the pilot as the mission changes |
| *Schedule Objectives:* none | |
| *Performance Objectives:* operate in shipboard environment with high reliability | |

| Uncertainties: | Information Sources: |
|---|---|
| *Programmatic Uncertainties:*<br>(1) Support and interest of DoD<br>(2) Adequate funding | *Data:*<br>(1) DoD leadership<br>(2) Test data |
| *System/Product Uncertainties:*<br>(1) Whether missile concept will be<br>    accepted by DoD<br>(2) Refusal of test pilots to participate in test<br>(3) Concept risks | *Experts:*<br>(1) Team members<br>(2) Feedback from pilots<br>(3) Physical tests |
| *Supportability/Life Cycle Uncertainties:*<br>(1) Competitive missiles | *Other Sources:*<br>(1) Research, development, and test<br>    facilities |

The Sidewinder was the first air-to-air missile developed for use by U.S. Navy fighter pilots. The program was initially unfunded and was started without formal permission by William McLean. He adopted a skunk-works approach (see the first use case in the decision frame in Table 6-2) at China Lake, an isolated Navy base in the California desert. A competing Air Force program called the Falcon took the opposite approach (see the second use case in the decision frame in Table 6-2).

The programmatic and system/product alternatives adopted by McLean are shown in italics on the right side of the decision frame. This approach was consistent with the skunkworks approach that he used because a funded program for the Sidewinder had not been initially approved. However, after the Sidewinder program was approved by the Navy, McLean kept to this skunkworks approach ("build a little, test a little") throughout the entire program. The design team was able to inter-act with ship personnel and pilots as they rotated through assignments at China Lake. The China Lake team was able to design and perform a wide range of tests that focused on successful missile performance rather than programmatic success.

A great many uncertainties were associated with the new technologies employed in the Sidewinder missile. These technologies included a passive infrared homing system using proportional navigation that was built from vacuum tubes, the use of Canards (forward guidance fins) rather than tail-based control fins to maneuver the missile based on the seeker's information, the use of "rollerons" to limit the roll rate of the missile during flight (by serving as gyroscopes), and a fragmentation warhead triggered by a passive infrared proximity fuse. Data to reduce the uncertainties and other data were collected by test programs at China Lake and competing contractor design teams scattered throughout the United States. McLean went after the best contract talent he could obtain after the Sidewinder became a funded program. He kept these contract teams competing with each other until the final design was formally fixed so that they were motivated to do their best.

This chapter presented the concept of a decision frame for defining and structuring the context of the decision, the alternatives, the objectives, and the associated uncertainties of the decision situation. A decision frame is a way of defining the problem or the opportunity being addressed as a decision.

The importance of the decision frame chosen by a decision maker has been documented by many researchers. Research has shown that different decision frames for the same topic result in significantly different alternatives being considered and in the ultimately selected alternative. As a result, project managers would do well to consider multiple possible frames as part of any significant decision. Even for simple decisions, sketching out relevant portions of the decision frame that we have provided might well prove to be a highly cost-effective use of time.

Some problems are really opportunities and should be viewed that way. For example, many companies are saving money and making more profits by adopting "green" technology. Other companies are resisting the trend to consider the environment in their decision-making. Each of these approaches might be the correct approach for specific situations, but which situation is relevant for the situation you might be part of?

This chapter also presented a metaphor of a decision frame for building a house and adapted that metaphor to a generic decision frame for project managers to use for any decision they face. An extension to the Sidewinder case study presented in the last chapter was provided in this chapter to demonstrate how the decision frame might prove useful to a project manager. Additional examples are provided in the chapters that follow in order to demonstrate how decision frames can be used to help make decisions.

The generic decision frame presented in this chapter produces a set of decision alternatives that push people toward a specific decision. The best decision is reached when decision alternatives exist that have the potential to satisfy project objectives. Chapter 6 covered the following points:

- We must be careful how we frame our decisions because we are subconsciously guided toward specific alternatives based on how we have characterized the decision in our own head and to other people.

- We should try out several frames for very important decisions to see if we come to the same selected alternative with each frame. If we do not have a robust selected alternative, we should consider what influence the different frames are having and consider which frame makes the most sense.

- A decision tool called a Generic Decision Frame has been provided for use on important decisions so that we can record many of the important considerations in one place for quick review and careful consideration. The decision tool prompts us to think of many issues that we might otherwise overlook. The Sidewinder case study from the previous chapter was recast in this format.

In Chapter 7 we present several techniques for generating decision alternatives. Early in Chapter 7 stakeholder and value analysis are presented. Then several creativity techniques are described. The Cuban Missile Crisis and the development of Windows NT by Microsoft are cast in the decision frame format.

# CHAPTER 7

# Generating Decision Alternatives

When only one course of action is possible (and action must be taken), there are no decision alternatives to compare. Additionally, the best decision cannot be made when there are too few alternatives. The best decisions usually result when many decision alternatives are considered and a strategy exists for arriving at the best decision. An effective strategy consists of three tasks. The first task is to generate a sufficient number of unique alternatives. In the second task, alternatives must be evaluated by defining how well each does on a set of objectives and making value trade-offs for their differences. Having the right information is critical to this task. Task three consists of searching for newer alternatives that provide higher value in meeting objectives than a previously selected alternative under task two. Project managers can increase their chances of arriving at the single best decision alternative by using this strategy. When no strategy exists, not only are important alternatives overlooked but a bad decision can be the result.

This chapter describes searching for alternatives and trades between alternatives and addresses when more information and analysis is needed in order to generate additional alternatives that produce higher value in reaching managerial objectives. How to apply the decision frame in dealing with decision alternatives is also presented.

This chapter presents the following sections:

- The Problem Definition Process

- Searching for Alternatives

- Using All Alternatives to Find Additional Alternatives

- Determining the Need for More Information and Analysis

- Alternatives and Decision Frames—The Cuban Missile Crisis.

## The Problem Definition Process

In this chapter, the focus is on generating *decision alternatives*. This is a new term being introduced to the project management community. We do not find this terminology in the *PMBOK® Guide,* in project management training, or in project management organizations. We define a decision alternative as a feasible or candidate solution that has the potential to satisfy stakeholder needs, wants, and desires.

Stakeholder needs, wants, and desires are expressed as functions, objectives, and values that exist for the project management organization and for the product or system being developed by the organization. To develop good decision alternatives, project managers need information that will aid them in understanding the needs, wants, and desires of every stakeholder relevant to the project. How do project managers gather this information? The need is initially defined by a designated stakeholder and is revised through a process we call *problem definition.*

Every project begins with a problem; the problem must be fully defined before appropriate solutions can be developed. In project management, the project has a problem, the product has a problem, and the organization has a problem. The project must meet cost, schedule, and product performance objectives. The product must satisfy client needs, wants, and desires. The organization must satisfy business objectives. Identification of a problem results in identification of an objective. Problems can be separate and distinct, but in project management objectives are often interdependent.

Project managers cannot perform their functions without organizational support, the product cannot realize its objectives without management and organizational support, and the organization cannot realize its objectives without a successful product. The problem definition process helps stakeholders define their problem before an attempt is made to develop feasible solutions that satisfy objectives. Two examples—the BMW Z3 and the Walkman by Sony—are presented in Appendix A. Each begins with identification of a problem. Organizational and product objectives that address the problem are defined. Project decisions that result in overall project success are made, enabling organizational and product objectives to be met.

The *problem definition* process consists of three key tasks: stakeholder analysis, functional analysis, and value analysis. As already stated, project managers are concerned with three problem definitions: (1) one for the project, (2) one for the product or service being performed, and (3) one for the project organization. The problem or need is defined by analyzing the stakeholders involved, analyzing the functions of the organization and of the product or services to be provided, and understanding decision-maker values for both the organization and the product.

## Stakeholder Analysis

Stakeholder analysis assists the project manager in identifying stakeholders and in identifying their needs, wants, and desires relative to the problem. Stakeholders can include decision makers, consumers, users, clients, owners, bill payers, regulatory agencies, sponsors, project managers, project team members, manufacturers, and marketers.

The project manager must be concerned with the needs, wants, and desires of both the project organization and end users. This can be achieved by performing a literature review of relevant laws, organizational policies, applicable studies previously performed, and pertinent discipline-specific principles and by consulting with every stakeholder relevant to the project. Interviews, focus groups, and surveys are other methods that can be used to gain an understanding of the problem. The output of the stakeholder analysis is a clear definition of the problem, which is negotiated between the decision maker or client and the engineer and project manager.

## Functional Analysis

*Functional analysis* is the second task. It assists the project manager in identifying the key functions and objectives that the selected decision alternative must satisfy. A *function* is defined as "a characteristic task, action, or activity that must be performed to achieve a desired outcome" (Trainor and Parnell 2008). For the project, a sample function can be "meet cost." For a product (e.g., an automobile), a sample function might be "conserve gas." For a company, a sample function might be "generate profit." Functions are usually identified during the stakeholder analysis process through interviews, focus groups, and surveys. Decision makers or their designated representatives are responsible for validating the functions required to meet project objectives, product objectives, and organizational objectives. The output of the functional analysis process is a *functional hierarchy.*

A functional hierarchy is a hierarchical display of the functions and sub-functions that are necessary and sufficient to achieve the system objectives (Trainor and Parnell 2008); it is represented by a fundamental objective, functions, and objectives, as shown in Figure 7-1. The fundamental objective is defined by the problem. Objectives support functions, unless sub-functions exist. When sub-functions exist, objectives directly support sub-functions. Functions are represented as verb object phrases, and objectives are represented as "Minimize," "Maximize," or "Optimize."

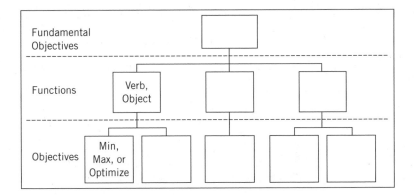

**FIGURE 7-1:** Functional Hierarchy

## Value Analysis

In *value analysis,* we are evaluating the future value of the decision alternative based on how well it supports project, product, and organizational objectives. This future value of each decision alternative can be described qualitatively or characterized quantitatively or both. (We will discuss each approach in later sections of this book.) We use information available from stakeholder and functional analysis to create these *values* that can be used to evaluate decision alternatives. Most, but not all, of the values are defined by stakeholders. In most cases, values are defined by owners, users, and consumers. In the design and development of an automobile, we would be concerned about the values of the maintenance technician (owner), the user (driver), and the consumer (also the driver). In this example, passengers are also considered consumers. Within the project organization, values are likely defined by a number of decision authorities in addition to the stakeholders (the CEO, the CFO, the CIO, accountants, financial analysts, the program manager, the project manager, and the project team).

The output of the value analysis process is a *qualitative value hierarchy.* A qualitative value hierarchy is a functional hierarchy that includes a *value measure* for each objective. Examples of a qualitative value hierarchy are shown for a generic project in Figure 7-2 and for the design and development of a vehicle (product) in Figure 7-3. Upon development of a qualitative value hierarchy, a *value measure range* is developed for each value measure.

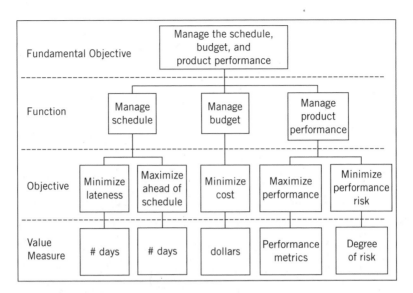

**FIGURE 7-2:** Project Management Value Hierarchy

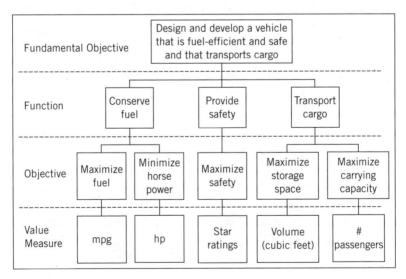

**FIGURE 7-3:** Vehicle Design Value Hierarchy

The value measure range is a scale that is used to assess how well each decision alternative satisfies objectives contained in the hierarchy. The range interval begins with a minimal acceptable value and ends with a maximal acceptable value. Value measure ranges are defined by stakeholders.

Using the example in Figure 7-3, stakeholders (users/consumers) might define the value measure range for "mpg" as 20 mpg–35 mpg. In this example, 20 mpg is of minimal value (0), and 35 mpg is of maximal value (1, 10, or 100). Decision alternatives take values of 0 to, perhaps, 100, depending on the miles per gallon attained. This is represented in the table and graph shown in Chapter 8, in Figure 8-5. The decision alternative that best satisfies the fundamental objective based on the value that it provides across all value measures (miles per gallon, horsepower, dollars, cubic feet, and passengers) becomes the *decision solution*. Projects, products, and organizations can have many functions and objectives. A qualitative value hierarchy presents functions and objectives in an easy-to-read format that makes the assessment of decision alternatives simpler. Value analysis marks the end of the problem definition process.

We view the problem definition process as the most difficult process in project management and perhaps the most important; the wrong problem will most likely produce the wrong solution. At the completion of the problem definition process, project managers should expect to have:

- A well-defined problem that meets the approval of key stakeholders

- A set of organizational functions and objectives

- Defined organizational values used to measure success

- A set of product or system functions and objectives

- Defined product or system values used to measure performance

- A well-defined trade space, the difference between the key alternatives on the value objectives being used to evaluate the alternatives

- An initial risk analysis

- Definition and development of the required decisions and the decision solutions based on the problem definition.

At this point, we can begin the search for decision alternatives or solutions that satisfy functions, objectives, and values for both the organization and the product or service managed by the project manager.

## Searching for Alternatives

Every successful organization has a clearly defined set of managerial objectives. Every successful organization also has an effective strategy for meeting or exceeding its objectives. The strategy is not rocket science nor is it the best-kept secret. The key is making and implementing the right decision solution.

The first step in making a decision is to ensure that information is gathered about every possible decision alternative. For example, information must be gathered on the project location, the type of project organization, resource allocation, and project member skills. Every alternative that is generated is then evaluated based on how each performs in satisfying cost, schedule, and performance objectives. Because each alternative carries with it some degree of uncertainty and risk, the decision solution must also consider techniques to reduce these.

Although there are many techniques for searching for alternatives, certain key elements should be present during the search process (Leigh 1983):

1.  **Fluency:** The production of a large number of ideas

2.  **Flexibility:** The production of a large variety of ideas

3.  **Elaboration:** The development, embellishment, or filling out of an idea

4.  **Originality:** The use of ideas that are not obvious, banal, or common in the statistical sense.

Techniques that embrace these elements will produce a sufficient number of alternatives relevant to managerial objectives. A basic model for generating alternatives is shown in Figure 7-4. We begin with generating ideas and then we refine those ideas. Refined ideas turn into alternatives. In the final step, we screen or evaluate those alternatives against how well they meet project objectives. This model allows for feedback and iteration.

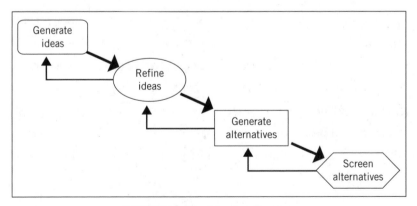

**FIGURE 7-4:** The Ideation Process

The remainder of this section outlines various methods or creative techniques that have been found useful for creating and developing alternatives, including brainstorming, brainwriting, and groupware. Some are used best by individuals while others are best suited to group use.

## Brainstorming

Brainstorming is a *group* creativity technique designed to generate a large number of ideas or alternatives for the solution to a problem. Brainstorming is a lateral thinking process in which groups of 8 to 12 people come up with ideas and thoughts that are uncensored and in very rough form—they may even seem at first to be a bit shocking, or perhaps "wild and crazy." The environment should be relaxed and should include a facilitator who leads the brainstorming session, encouraging participation and writing ideas down as they are contributed orally by group members. During the brainstorming process, preliminary ideas that have been offered by the group are then modified by the group, led by the facilitator, and by the end of the session, those changed ideas have been transformed into useful ideas that can often be stunningly original. This popular technique was developed over 65 years ago and is based on five basic rules (West 2008):

1.  **No criticism of ideas:** All judgment of ideas is deferred, and participants feel free to voice all ideas without fear of judgment of the idea or themselves. Ideas should be evaluated only at the end of the brainstorming session.

2.  **Encourage wild and exaggerated ideas:** "Wild and crazy" ideas often contain nuggets of unique insight that can be built upon. Such ideas will be refined and filtered during later concept evaluation.

3. **Seek large quantities of ideas:** Brainstorming sessions are fast-paced and spontaneous. Ideas produced in this fashion are not only useful in their own right but are frequently catalysts for other ideas from group members.

4. **Build on each other's ideas.** Ideas offered from one person's perspective often trigger wholly new ideas from others.

5. **Focus on quantity:** This rule is a means of enhancing divergent production, aiming to facilitate problem solving through the quantity of ideas. The assumption is that the greater the number of ideas generated, the greater the chance of producing a radical solution that is effective.

The sole product of a brainstorming session is a list of ideas. Nothing is rejected or criticized in the early stages; however, one disadvantage of brainstorming is the dominance of the group by one or more individuals. In later stages, ideas are evaluated, forged, and modified for acceptance based on their feasibility of meeting managerial objectives.

## Brainwriting

Brainwriting is brainstorming in silence, and it is particularly useful with a group of people who are somewhat reticent and would be unlikely to offer many ideas in an open group session like brainstorming. The objective in using brainwriting is to eliminate the influence of dominant individuals and vocal majorities. There are two variations of brainwriting. In structured brainwriting, ideas are written on a piece of paper that is passed from member to member. Ideas are added to the list or existing ideas on the list (made by others) are developed further. In unstructured brainwriting, ideas are written on note cards and collected in a central location. The project manager can sift through the lists generated and make a selection of feasible alternatives.

## Groupware

Groupware is term that refers to software that allows geographically dispersed people to collaborate. It has become a popular tool for use in conducting brainstorming sessions and other types of collaboration. A main advantage of groupware over other techniques is that it allows people to work together remotely. Another advantage over traditional in-person brainstorming is that groupware emphasizes anonymity.

Some of the more common reasons people want to use groupware include:

- To facilitate communication
- To enable communication where it would not otherwise be possible
- To reduce travel costs
- To bring together multiple perspectives and expertise
- To form groups with common interests where it would not be possible to gather a sufficient number of people face-to-face
- To save time and cost in coordinating group work
- To facilitate group problem solving

Examples of groupware tools include GroupSystems®, email, newsgroups, shared whiteboards, teleconferencing, and video-teleconferencing.

Other valuable techniques exist, but these three techniques are most commonly used in generating alternatives for projects. Another technique, morphological analysis, is presented in the next section.

## Using All Alternatives to Find Additional Alternatives

Morphological analysis is a comprehensive way of listing and examining the total set of possible combinations that might be useful in solving a given problem. Current alternatives are laid out in a manner that produces additional alternatives. The process is conducted in five steps (West 2008):

1. Concisely formulate the problem to be solved.

2. Localize all parameters that might be important for the solution (decision).

3. Construct a multidimensional matrix containing all possible solutions (decision alternatives).

4. Assess all solutions against the purposes to be achieved.

5. Select suitable solutions for application or iterative morphological study.

Table 7-1 provides an example of a project design using morphological analysis. Morphological analysis breaks an alternative down into characteristics or components. Several possibilities are defined for each characteristic, enabling many alternatives to be identified as a combination of one or more possibilities from each of the characteristics. Table 7-1 provides a simple example for identifying alternatives for setting up the project office. The first column simply counts the number of possibilities in the other columns. The second through fourth columns are labeled with the characteristic names. The cells in a particular column associated with a characteristic are filled in with possible solutions for that characteristic. So for project organization the possible solutions are pure, matrix, functional, and mixed. It is important to note that there need not be the same number of possibilities in each column, but there do need to be at least two possibilities in each column or that characteristic is not worth including. Empty cells in Table 7-1 have been shaded.

When we have adopted the rule that an alternative must include one and only one possibility from each characteristic, the total number of alternatives is the product of the number of possibilities for each characteristic. In Table 7-1 there are 72 possible combinations (4 x 3 x 2 x 3).

**TABLE 7-1:** Project Design Morphological Box

| Possibilities | Project Organization | Project Location | Project Budgeting | Data Reporting Method |
|---|---|---|---|---|
| One | Pure | Onsite | Top-down | Reports |
| Two | Matrix | Virtual | Bottom-up | Meetings |
| Three | Functional | Satellite | | Virtual reports |
| Four | Mixed | | | |

# Determining the Need for More Information and Analysis

Information is necessary to fashion alternatives that are relevant to the managerial objectives. When a sufficient number of feasible alternatives are generated, they are analyzed and evaluated to determine a satisfactory solution. Until this happens, additional information might be required. However, because project managers will never have enough information, they must seek a balance in their search activity among

(1) the cost of additional information, (2) the amount of the perceived payoffs, and (3) the amount of time they have to devote to gathering additional information.

At some point, additional information becomes increasingly difficult to obtain, but the cost climbs exponentially (Harrison 1987). And as the cost climbs, marginal value begins to decrease. Only a limited amount of effort should be devoted to the search activity to prevent a cost/payoff imbalance from occurring. Additionally, no matter how much time and money are spent in pursuit of additional information that can be formulated into alternatives, the search can never obtain *all* the information related to a particular objective (Harrison 1987). The project manager must keep the project on track and operate within the budget for this phase of the project. Do your best—make the best of what you have and move the project forward.

## Alternatives and Decision Frames— The Cuban Missile Crisis

As mentioned in Chapter 6, decision frames can help in the task of analyzing decisions. The decision frame captures important information and presents a snapshot view of critical elements that the project manager should consider in making a decision. The limitation of the decision frame is that it provides only the context for the decision. A decision aid, such as those covered in the next chapter and in Appendix C, is needed to make a choice from the alternatives. The case of the Cuban Missile Crisis is presented here to demonstrate how to apply a *decision matrix* when dealing with alternatives. A decision matrix considers the decision frame in arriving at the best decision alternative to satisfy the problem.

## Background

In 1962, President John F. Kennedy was faced with deciding what action to take in response to the Soviet missile buildup in Cuba. The Soviet move began in the spring of 1962. The presence of missiles was revealed on October 14, 1962, when they were nearly operational. The problem with this was the danger of nuclear war. The positioning of long-range nuclear missiles in Cuba placed the Soviets in a position that threatened U.S. security in the Western Hemisphere.

The background of this project defines the context for the decision.

| Cuban Missile Crisis Decision Frame for Responsive Action |
|---|
| **Context for Decision:** |
| **Stakeholders:** Cuba, Soviets, China, US citizens |
| **Resource Constraints:** Time |
| **Environment:**<br>*Social:* good relations with Soviets, worldview<br>*Organizational:* none<br>*Legal:* use of nuclear weapons against other nations<br>*Natural:* impact of radioactive fallout |
| **Broad Objectives:** destroy missile threat |
| **Use Cases:** |

## The Fundamental Objectives, Uncertainties, and Decision Alternatives

Several objectives that would provide the framework for the decision were identified. Because cost was not a factor, there were no cost objectives. However, time was an important objective. Project success was based on several performance objectives. The United States wanted Soviet removal of the missiles, world support for its position, and a weakening of the Sino-Soviet relationship.

Because of the potential for nuclear war, there was a great deal of uncertainty surrounding the selection of a particular alternative. This was indeed a very sensitive situation. How would the Soviets react to the action taken? What was the possibility of a nuclear war? How would the United States be viewed by the world? These were some of the uncertainties that the United States had to consider when deciding how to act. In search of alternatives, the Executive Committee of the National Security Council was primarily constrained by limited information. This lack of information made it difficult to determine for certain a particular outcome, regardless of the alternative chosen. To meet the overall and fundamental objectives of the project, seven alternatives were defined. The first objective was the movement of missiles out of Cuba. Second, a shifting of world power was intolerable. Third, the defense of the Western Hemisphere had to be preserved. Fourth, a U.S. response should not sway world opinion in support of the Soviets. Fifth, a U.S. response should retain the favor of public opinion in the U.S. Sixth, a U.S. response should not strengthen the relationship between the Soviets and the Communist Chinese. Finally, a U.S. response should not result in a permanent rupture in U.S. relations with the Soviets.

The remaining aspects of the decision frame are presented next.

| Fundamental Objectives for Decision | Alternatives for Decision |
|---|---|
| **Programmatic Objectives:** | **Programmatic Alternatives:** |
| *Cost Objectives:* none | (1) Do nothing<br>(2) Invasion |
| *Schedule Objectives:*<br>(1) as soon as possible | (3) Diplomatic approach<br>(4) Air strike |
| *Performance Objectives:*<br>(1) willful removal of missiles<br>(2) US and world support<br>(3) weakened Sino-Soviet relationship | (5) Blockade |

| System/Product Objectives: | System/Product Alternatives: N/A |
|---|---|
| *Cost Objectives:* N/A | |
| *Schedule Objectives:* N/A | |
| *Performance Objectives:* N/A | |
| **Supportability/Life Cycle Objectives:** | **Supportability/Life Cycle Alternatives:** |
| *Cost Objectives:* none | (1) sustain good relations with allied countries |
| *Schedule Objectives:* none | (2) damage relations with allied countries |
| *Performance Objectives:*<br>(1) weakened relations between Soviets and China<br>(2) tainted worldview of Soviets | |
| **Uncertainties:** | **Information Sources:** |
| *Programmatic Uncertainties:*<br>(1) Soviet reaction<br>(2) Nuclear destruction | *Data:*<br>(1) Intelligence |
| *System/Product Uncertainties:* N/A | Experts: |
| *Supportability/Life Cycle Uncertainties:*<br>(1) Future relations with other countries | *Other Sources:* |

## The Comparison and Evaluation of Alternatives

Although equipped with limited information, the Executive Committee continued its search for feasible alternatives. Its efforts resulted in the following six decision alternatives: (1) do nothing, (2) diplomatic approach to Castro, (3) diplomatic pressure, (4) invasion, (5) surgical air strikes, and (6) blockade. Using a decision matrix, each of the six alternatives was evaluated on how well it satisfied each of the seven objectives.

Jumping ahead of our approach to decision-making, we present an analysis of these alternatives that was published by Harrison (1987). Remember, the ultimate or overall objective is to "destroy the missile threat." The decision matrix for these alternatives is shown in Table 7-2. The number at the intersection of each alternative and an objective represents the payoff or value to the United States if that alternative were chosen. The scale used is zero to ten. The higher the value of the payoff, the more favorable the outcome to the United States The last column represents the total payoff for each alternative. Because the objectives are equally weighted, the total point value is the sum of payoff for each objective. As noted in Table 7-2, the Blockade alternative receives the highest score in meeting project objectives (Harrison 1987).

**TABLE 7-2:** Decision Matrix: The Cuban Missile Crisis

| | Objectives | | | | | | | |
| --- | --- | --- | --- | --- | --- | --- | --- | --- |
| | (1) Missiles are removed | (2) U.S. retains balance of power | (3) U.S. hemispheric defenses are preserved | (4) Favorable world opinion | (5) U.S. opinion remains favorable | (6) Chinese-Soviet relationship is not strengthened | (7) U.S. relationship with Soviets is preserved | Total Point Value |
| **Weight** | 10 | 10 | 10 | 10 | 10 | 10 | 10 | |
| **Alternatives** | | | | | | | | |
| 1. Do nothing | 0 | 1 | 1 | 4 | 2 | 5 | 2 | 15 |
| 2. Diplomatic approach to Castro | 2 | 4 | 1 | 2 | 2 | 5 | 4 | 20 |
| 3. Diplomatic pressures | 2 | 2 | 2 | 4 | 3 | 5 | 4 | 22 |
| 4. Invasion | 8 | 8 | 8 | 0 | 2 | 2 | 0 | 28 |
| 5. Air strikes | 8 | 8 | 8 | 2 | 2 | 2 | 0 | 30 |
| 6. Blockade | 4 | 6 | 8 | 8 | 10 | 8 | 6 | 50 |

E. Frank Harrison, Table 12.1, *The Managerial Decision-Making Process,* Third Edition (Boston: Houghton Mifflin Company): 402–403. Copyright © 1987 Houghton Mifflin Company. Reprinted with permission.

This same approach can easily be taken to make decisions necessary to achieve project management success. All management projects have a set of defined objectives; decisions have to be made to meet the objectives. The decisions required are used by the project team to generate decision alternatives, and the choice is made based on information available to the project. Project managers might not always use a decision aid to make the decision. A decision aid assists the project manager in making the best decision. These tools are valuable, yet the use of these tools alone is inadequate. Project managers must remain aware that using a tool does not necessarily mean the project will be managed better. Knowledge of the tool and the quality of the information required for the use of the tool is important.

## The Choice

The best choice is usually not the best choice because it is free of risk. The best choice is made based on how well it meets managerial objectives in the face of apparent risk and uncertainty. The Blockade alternative is the best choice given the risk and uncertainty identified in the decision frame. Every course of action will contain some risk. In this case, although a blockade could potentially precipitate Soviet retaliation in Berlin, the benefit would be that it would signify firmness of intention to attack but would not be as extreme as an air strike would be (Harrison 1987). The project manager will do well to understand the risk posed by each alternative as each alternative is evaluated. The decision frame helps to identify all risks and provides additional information required to make a well-informed decision.

# CASE STUDY

## Microsoft's Windows NT

In 1988, Bill Gates reached a decision to make a clean break from the work that had been started on the Windows 3 operating system and its predecessor DOS. He hired Dave Cutler from Digital Equipment Corporation (DEC) to begin the design of what became known as Windows NT; NT stood for New Technology. The Windows NT project started in November 1988 with the goal of delivering the finished product by 1991; the end of March 1991 was set as the official target in October 1989. The driving factors for Windows NT were to take advantage of the new RISC chips that were being developed, to be a UNIX-killer, and to be compatible with OS/2. Early design goals were easy portability to other 32-bit architectures, scalability and multiprocessing support, support for distributed computing (shared resources among multiple computers), support for application programming interfaces (APIs) required by POSIX, and the security features needed to meet U.S. Government Class 2 (C2) capabilities. When the Golden Master for Windows NT was finally delivered in May 1993, the primary design factors had changed to compatibility with the Intel 386 (RISC had never become a driving force); compatibility with OS/2, DOS, and Windows; and a new file system that increased reliability.

Dave Cutler served in the roles of project manager and senior designer (software/systems engineer) even though several project managers had been appointed to run the project. These short-lived project managers could not interject themselves successfully between Cutler and Steve Ballmer, who served as the interface between the project and Bill Gates. Cutler had led the design of the VMS operating system for DEC's VAX computer prior to joining Microsoft. The key architecture elements of NT were the kernel, the graphical user interface, and the networking components. The kernel (called HAL by Cutler) is the core of the operating system that separates the hardware from the rest of the operating system. So the kernel talks to the hardware but not to the application software. The non-kernel portion of the operating system talks to the application software and kernel but not to the hardware.

As project manager and senior designer, Cutler had key people create high-level specs for the major elements of Windows NT and then instituted a very decentralized network of small design teams (3–5 people) to create the software modules that were integrated into the components for which the specs had been written. Adopting this approach was consistent with Cutler's beliefs about how to get the most productivity and quality from a large group of programmers—over 250 on the NT project. So Cutler did not consciously evaluate alternative organization structures for the NT staff. However, there are some clear trade-offs for organization structures that many project managers consider when setting up their organizations.

Two of the key design issues that had to be reworked in the last two years of NT development were security and the file system. Networking was a rapidly growing realm of computers in the late 1980s and early 1990s. As networking became more important, security became a bigger and bigger issue. Cutler and his team did not initially appreciate how important security would become and how difficult it was to design security into the operating system. So early in the design process, security was treated as a feature for Windows NT and was not addressed seriously until the fall of 1991. The two key elements of the security architecture that were adopted were "trusted domains with pass-through authentication" and "flexible administration." The first of these two elements is a very common approach when the bigger network can be secured effectively. However, when people are connected to the Internet (which could not have been foreseen during the design of NT), the approach of trusted domains can be a problem. Then, the concept of flexible administration led to local and global domains with lots of special code and many security holes. This approach also has some performance penalties.

Windows NT has been quite a success in the sense that every release of the Windows operating system from July 1993 to the beginning of 2007 has been based on the NT architecture, as shown in Table 7-3. The latest Windows version, Vista, is the first to take a radically different approach to security by considering how to design security into the architecture from the beginning.

**TABLE 7-3:** Legacy of Success for the Windows NT Architecture

| Ver | Marketing Name | Editions | Release Date | RTM Build |
|-----|----------------|----------|--------------|-----------|
| NT 3.1 | Windows NT 3.1 | Workstation (named just *Windows NT*), Advanced Server | July 27, 1993 | 528 |
| NT 3.5 | Windows NT 3.5 | Workstation, Server | Sept. 21, 1994 | 807 |
| NT 3.51 | Windows NT 3.51 | Workstation, Server | May 30, 1995 | 1057 |
| NT 4.0 | Windows NT 4.0 | Workstation, Server, Server Enterprise Edition, Terminal Server, Embedded | July 29, 1996 | 1381 |
| NT 5.0 | Windows 2000 | Professional, Server, Advanced Server, Datacenter Server | Feb. 17, 2000 | 2195 |
| NT 5.1 | Windows XP | Home, Professional, Media Center (2002, 2003, 2004 & 2005), Tablet PC, Starter, Embedded | October 25, 2001 | 2600 |
| NT 5.2 | Windows Server 2003 | Standard, Enterprise, Datacenter, Web, Small Business Server, Computer Cluster | April 24, 2003 | 3790 |
| NT 5.2 | Windows XP (x64) | Professional x64 Edition | April 25, 2005 | 3790 |
| NT 6.0 | Windows Vista | Starter, Home Basic, Home Premium, Business, Enterprise, Ultimate, N editions for Home Basic and Business, x64 editions for all expert for Starter | Business: 30 Nov 2006 Consumer: 30 Jan 2007 | 6000 |

**TABLE 7-4:** Windows NT Decision Frame for the Project Organization

| |
|---|
| **Context for Decision:** |
| **Stakeholders:** Users, Microsoft design team, Microsoft stockholders |
| **Resource Constraints:** limited programming and testing support with many other demands on their availability |
| **Environment:**<br>*Social:* jealousies among programmers (inside and outside the design team)<br>*Organizational:* communication via Steve Ballmer for direction and to keep Bill Gates informed<br>*Legal:* none<br>*Natural:* none |
| **Broad Objectives:** get to market quickly with a product that most users will accept; maintain Microsoft's dominance in the market |
| **Use Cases (Alternatives):** (1) adopt a strong hierarchical structure for the project organization and maintain clear flow down of requirements, (2) create a half dozen to dozen high-level specs for the major NT components and adopt a flexible organization structure with small teams (3–5 people) to program modules of each component, (3) adopt a matrix organization to staff programming teams on an as-needed basis. |

| Fundamental Objectives for Decision | Alternatives for Decision |
|---|---|
| **Programmatic Objectives:** | **Programmatic Alternatives:** |
| *Cost Objectives:* budget for about 200 people | Structure program using a matrix organization |
| *Schedule Objectives:* deliver product in 1991 | *Structure program with a large number of small teams (3–5 people) working within a flexible hierarchical structure with little middle management* |
| *Performance Objectives:* low turnover of staff based on high interest level and belief that programmers "own" product | Structure program with a rigid hierarchical structure with 5–7 person teams and a manager at the bottom |
| **System/Product Objectives:** | **System/Product Alternatives:** |
| *Cost Objectives:* minimal cost; utilize existing technology | Adopt a client-server architecture to minimize crashes and enhance application personality and portability |
| *Schedule Objectives:* still unconstrained | Use a more traditional layered architecture that has faster performance but suffers in portability |
| *Performance Objectives:* high reliability (less crashing), high portability across chip sets, enable the "personalities" of applications to shine through, maintain downward compatibility with applications; impose limited performance penalties on users | *Adopt a client-server framework but use a layered approach in the kernel and application subsystems* |
| **Supportability/Life Cycle Objectives:** | **Supportability/Life Cycle Alternatives:** |
| *Cost Objectives:* life cycle cost focus | |
| *Schedule Objectives:* none | |
| *Performance Objectives:* achieve a platform for the design of future Windows products; | |
| **Uncertainties:** | **Information Sources:** |
| *Programmatic Uncertainties:*<br>Support and interest of Bill Gates and Steve Ballmer<br>Productivity of programmers | *Data:*<br>Test data |
| *System/Product Uncertainties:*<br>Current trends in PC industry<br>Desire among users for high compatibility with existing applications | *Experts:*<br>Frequent feedback from Ballmer<br>Several conversations with Gates<br>Programmers judgments<br>Industry experts |
| *Supportability/Life Cycle Uncertainties:*<br>Future trends in PC industry<br>Future trends of PC users<br>Emergence of other operating systems and hardware | *Other Sources:* |

This chapter addressed the generation of decision alternatives. However, we emphasized the fact that before a decision alternative can be generated, the problem must be defined. We first laid out the problem definition process and the results of that process. We then described four useful techniques that can be used to generate decision alternatives. Afterwards, we presented the four key elements in each technique that help to make the process easier. We described why more information and analysis might be needed when the first generation process does not produce a sufficient number of feasible decision alternatives; however, the decision to obtain more information must be based on (1) the cost to obtain additional information, (2) the time required to obtain additional information and (3) the amount of perceived payoff. After a sufficient number of decision alternatives have been generated, a decision frame can be used to incorporate project information into a format that will make decision-making easier.

The following specific points were made in this chapter:

- A good problem definition is needed before a good decision solution can be found.

- Stakeholder analysis is useful in identifying the problem.

- Functional analysis is useful in defining project and product functions and objectives.

- Value analysis is useful in developing stakeholder values.

- The best decision cannot be made when there are too few decision alternatives.

■ A three-step approach is taken when generating decision alternatives. In step one, a sufficient set of unique feasible decision alternatives are generated. In step two, alternatives are evaluated according to how well they satisfy project objectives. In step three, additional alternatives that add to project value are generated.

■ Information is necessary in order to fashion alternatives that are relevant to the managerial objectives. When a sufficient number of feasible alternatives are generated, the alternatives are analyzed and evaluated to determine a satisfactory solution. Until this happens, additional information might be required.

■ Alternative generation techniques include (1) brainstorming, (2) brainwriting, (3) groupware and (4) morphological analysis.

■ During the process of searching for alternatives, four key elements should be present: (1) fluency, (2) flexibility, (3) elaboration, and (4) originality.

■ A decision frame is a decision aid that captures important information and presents snapshot views of artificial elements that the project manager should consider in making a decision.

■ An effective decision solution is one that satisfies the values articulated by the key stakeholders.

As mentioned, the decisions required and the candidate decision solutions are defined and developed based on the problem definition. After the problem has been adequately defined and decision alternatives have been generated, we are now ready to analyze the decision alternatives according to how well they satisfy product and management objectives.

In Chapter 8, we introduce techniques for analyzing decision alternatives and discuss the pros and cons of each technique. We also address the cognitive biases that relate to decision-making.

# CHAPTER 8

# Analyzing the Alternatives in Terms of Values and Uncertainty

A s Chapter 6 discussed, a key task is to recognize you have a decision and to frame it properly in terms of alternatives, values (either qualitatively or quantitatively defined), and information. It is often a very difficult task to evaluate the alternatives in light of the values and the limited information available in order to arrive at a proper selection of the "best" alternative given the current situation; remember the difference between the good decision and the good outcome—good decisions do not necessarily ensure good outcomes. Recognizing and framing the decision are part, but only part, of a good decision. You must take the next step, shown in Figure 8-1, and conduct some kind of analytic comparison of the alternatives on the objectives using the information currently available in order to project the choice of each alternative out into the future.

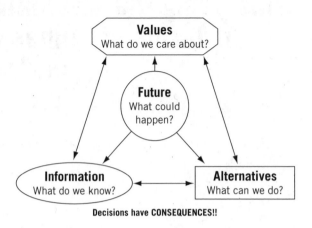

**FIGURE 8-1:** Key Elements of a Decision

This chapter presents several qualitative approaches to analyzing alternatives in light of our values and uncertainty. Aspects of quantitative approaches are presented as well. Cognitive biases that limit our ability to perform these analyses are discussed. Finally the cardinal issues of good decisions are summarized.

The chapter presents the following sections:

- Qualitative Approaches

- Quantitative Approaches

- Dealing with Biases and Heuristics

- Requirements for Good Decisions.

## Qualitative Approaches

Several qualitative approaches are available for use as tools in reviewing alternatives for a particular decision and recommending one of them. This section discusses five such approaches: list of pros and cons for each alternative, development of a fundamental objectives hierarchy with a qualitative assessment of each alternative on the fundamental objectives, consequence table, Pugh matrix, and Even Swaps.

### Pros and Cons

The most famous approach is that described by Benjamin Franklin in a letter written to Joseph Priestley in 1772 (Bell and Labaree 1956). Priestley had recently been offered a new position in London that would increase his pay and prestige but delay the scientific experiments that he was conducting in chemistry. Priestley had written to Franklin to inquire whether he should move from Leeds, where he was well established, to London. Franklin was facing a similar problem himself; he greatly enjoyed London and all of the stimulation provided by the culture, science, and sophistication in London. But Franklin also missed his family and friends, and the opportunities to contribute to the growing rebellion in what was to become the United States. Here is the letter that Franklin wrote Priestley (Bell and Labaree 1956):

To Joseph Priestley

London, September 19, 1772

Dear Sir,

In the Affair of so much Importance to you, wherein you ask my Advice, I cannot for want of sufficient Premises, advise you what to determine, but if you please I will tell you how.

When these difficult Cases occur, they are difficult chiefly because while we have them under Consideration all the Reasons pro and con are not present to the Mind at the same time; but sometimes one Set present themselves, and at other times another, the first being out of Sight. Hence the various Purposes or Inclinations that alternately prevail, and the Uncertainty that perplexes us.

To get over this, my Way is, to divide half a Sheet of Paper by a Line into two Columns, writing over the one Pro, and over the other Con. Then during three or four Days Consideration I put down under the different Heads short Hints of the different Motives that at different Times occur to me for or against the Measure. When I have thus got them all together in one View, I endeavor to estimate their respective Weights; and where I find two, one on each side, that seem equal, I strike them both out: If I find a Reason pro equal to some two Reasons con, I strike out the three. If I judge some two Reasons con equal to some three Reasons pro, I strike out the five; and thus proceeding I find at length where the Balance lies; and if after a Day or two of farther Consideration nothing new that is of Importance occurs on either side, I come to a Determination accordingly.

And tho' the Weight of Reasons cannot be taken with the Precision of Algebraic Quantities, yet when each is thus considered separately and comparatively, and the whole lies before me, I think I can judge better, and am less likely to take a rash Step; and in fact I have found great Advantage from this kind of Equation, in what may be called Moral or Prudential Algebra. Wishing sincerely that you may determine for the best, I am ever, my dear Friend,

Yours most affectionately,

B. Franklin

Franklin did not return to his home in Philadelphia until 1774, when his wife died. Priestley stayed in Leeds until 1780, when he moved to Birmingham. Priestley did move to London later in life and then to the United States.

The key point of Franklin's list of pros and cons is that identifying aspects of each alternative as they relate to your value structure (objectives) is a way of being able to differentiate between the alternatives. An incomplete example of a pros and cons matrix is presented in Table 8-1. The decision represented in Table 8-1 is the type of transportation that should be implemented in order to move a defined set of people and equipment from point A to point B when there is a river between points A and B. What other entries would you add to this table?

**TABLE 8-1:** Example of a Pros and Cons Matrix

| Alternatives | Pros | Cons |
| --- | --- | --- |
| Build bridge | • Low operating cost | • High up-front cost<br>• Susceptible to damage |
| Use ferries | • Flexible costs<br>• Flexible capacity<br>• Quick start | • Not likely to meet peak demand<br>• Susceptible to strikes |
| Build tunnel | • Low operating cost<br>• Less impact due to weather | • Very high up-front cost<br>• Fixed capacity |
| Use helicopters | • Flexible costs<br>• Flexible capacity<br>• Quick start | • Not likely to meet peak demand<br>• High operating cost |

This approach does a good job of stimulating the decision maker to generate differences between the options. But the result is not a systematic approach to organizing the pros and cons, or differences between the alternatives, into a coherent set of objectives, as discussed in the decision frame section of the previous chapter.

## Fundamental Objectives Hierarchy

Keeney (1992) makes a strong case for value-focused thinking in his book by that name. Whether our values are defined qualitatively or quantitatively, the key concept in value-focused thinking is developing a comprehensive set of well-defined objectives early in the decision process and using those objectives to develop more and better alternatives and then evaluating the alternatives. These objectives should be (1) consistent with the current decision context and (2) not means-oriented for the current decision. Recall that this was part of the process for defining the decision frame. Means-oriented criteria are tied to the alternatives being made.

For example, if the project manager needs to decrease the budget for the next year, some undesired, means-oriented objectives would be reducing the staff operations, reducing contract support, and reducing travel. An example of fundamental objectives for this decision are (1) reducing monetary expenditures over the next year, (2) maintaining quality of operations, and (3) keeping all activities on schedule. Not all of these fundamental objectives are possible simultaneously, so the decision involves how to balance across all three while meeting the demands of the situation.

Project managers usually think in terms of three key fundamental objectives: cost, schedule, and performance. One way to segment each of these is to focus on the life cycle of the product or system: development, testing, production, deployment, training, etc. Often the costs for these segments of the life cycle come from different budgets; if this is the case, then having this type of cost breakout in the fundamental objectives hierarchy makes sense. However, if the various cost elements come from the same budget, then they are not really separate fundamental objectives because a dollar is a dollar.

Figure 8-2 shows an objectives hierarchy that was used to evaluate alternative architecture designs by the U.S. Defense Communications Agency (now the Defense Information Systems Agency) in 1980. The alternatives were differentiated by their reliance on commercial resources, facility hardening, switch capabilities and capacities, encryption, and use of satellites and mobile assets. The objectives hierarchy in Figure 8-2 has performance issues on the left and issues related to risk, cost, and schedule on the right. The risk objectives addressed cost, schedule, and product performance.

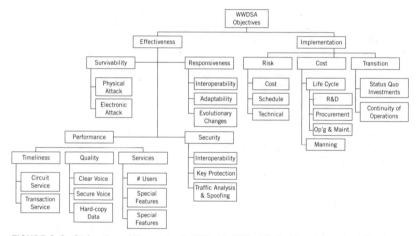

**FIGURE 8-2:** Objectives Hierarchy for World Wide Digital Systems Architecture (circa 1980)

<u>P</u>roblem, <u>O</u>bjectives, <u>A</u>lternatives, <u>C</u>onsequences, and <u>T</u>radeoffs (PrOACT) (1999) is a process developed by three well-known decision researchers: Ken Hammond, Ralph Keeney, and Howard Raiffa (1999). Problem definition within PrOACT is similar to the decision frame

definition discussed in Chapter 6. The PrOACT process for defining objectives is:

- Write down your concerns associated with the decision.

- Convert your concerns into well-defined, succinct objectives.

- Separate ends from means in order to create ends-oriented (fundamental) objectives.

- Define what you mean by each objective so that others will understand them.

- Test your objectives to ensure they completely capture your interests.

The biggest mistake commonly made in defining objectives is that some important objectives are left out. A recent research paper reported a finding that people often leave as many as half of the relevant objectives out of a list that they have been asked to create. These forgotten objectives are not the least critical ones either.

Recall that our fundamental objectives must capture all of the differences between the alternatives that will be considered. The objectives should also be different from each other; there should be no overlap in their definitions.

After the fundamental objectives are defined, the decision maker can employ either a qualitative or quantitative analysis process. A qualitative analysis process would adopt a categorical rating scheme for each alternative on each objective. A simple, commonly used approach is to create three (sometimes more) categories that go from best to worst: "great," "average," or "poor" for all objectives. Without quantifying these ratings, it is often easy to discern that one alternative is better than or tied with the others on most objectives. If this is the case, then that one alternative can be selected without more detailed analysis. If several alternatives are better than the others on 10–30 percent of the objectives, the decision will be harder to justify and some more detailed analysis might be warranted. Often it is not possible to determine the best alternative but it is possible to find alternatives that are worse than other alternatives on all (or nearly all) of the objectives, making these alternatives candidates for elimination.

## Consequence Table

An increased level of sophistication in qualitative analysis beyond that just described (labeling each alternative as "great," "average," or "poor" on each objective) can be achieved by using the objectives hierarchy just discussed and a *consequence table*. The consequence table contains a row for each bottom-level objective and a column for each alternative. Now, instead of just writing "great," "average," or "poor" in each cell, the decision maker writes a few words or phrases that describe the consequences of having selected the alternative (in the column) on the objective (in the row). There might be some cells in the table for which there is great uncertainty; if so, this uncertainty should be noted.

After completing the table, the decision maker could review each objective (row) and should rank order which alternative performs best to worst on that objective. Here, we recommend giving the best alternative a high number (seven if there are seven alternatives) and giving the worst alternative a one. It is important to emphasize here that these numbers are called an ordinal scale and it is not theoretically correct to take averages and do multiplications with numbers on an ordinal scale.

The advantage of creating this rank ordering of alternatives for each objective is that we can review the table (as we did in the section above with the labels "great," "average," and "poor") and determine whether any of the alternatives is worse than another alternative on all objectives. If so, this alternative is called "dominated" and can be removed from the analysis. Consider Table 8-2. In this table, alternatives *A, B,* and *C* each have a few rankings of "5," which is the best. Only alternative *B* has no rankings of 1. More careful inspection of the table shows that the ranking of *B* is always greater than the ranking of *D,* so *D* is dominated by *B* on every objective and can be eliminated. Note that it is possible to show ties in such a table; alternatives *A* and *D* are ranked 1(2) on objective 9, indicating a tie.

**TABLE 8-2:** An Example of a Dominated Alternative

| Objectives | Alternatives | | | | |
|---|---|---|---|---|---|
| | A | B | C | D | E |
| Objective 1 | 5 | 3 | 2 | 1 | 4 |
| Objective 2 | 4 | 5 | 2 | 3 | 1 |
| Objective 3 | 3 | 4 | 5 | 1 | 2 |
| Objective 4 | 4 | 3 | 5 | 2 | 1 |
| Objective 5 | 1 | 5 | 3 | 4 | 2 |
| Objective 6 | 3 | 5 | 1 | 4 | 2 |
| Objective 7 | 5 | 3 | 4 | 1 | 2 |
| Objective 8 | 1 | 4 | 5 | 2 | 3 |
| Objective 9 | 1 (2) | 4 | 5 | 1 (2) | 3 |
| Objective 10 | 5 | 4 | 1 | 3 | 2 |

There is a common tendency with a table like Table 8-2 to add the ranks of each alternative and pick the alternative with the largest number. This is very risky. First, doing this assumes that the objectives are equal in importance and variation, but they almost never are. By variation, we mean that the ranks for one objective might be very close together (almost tied) and for another objective the ranks might indicate a huge swing in variation (the worst-ranked alternative is nearly unacceptable and the best-ranked alternative is near perfection).

It might be possible to get some insight from these sums, however; for example, if the sum of ranks for one alternative is nearly twice the sum of each of the other alternatives, then that one alternative might be the best no matter what more detailed analysis was done. In Table 8-2, the column sums are 32, 40, 33, 22, and 22. On the basis of these sums, it would be hard to rule out any of the first three alternatives.

Note that these sums do not give us any indication of whether there is a dominated alternative. Alternatives $D$ and $E$ have the same sum. While $D$ is dominated by $B$, $E$ is not dominated by any of the other alternatives.

## Pugh Matrix

The Pugh matrix (Pugh 1991) takes a similar tack to the consequence table. An example of a Pugh matrix is shown in Figure 8-3. The Pugh matrix uses a three-point ordinal scale: + (superior), S (acceptable or satisfactory), and – (inferior). This approach can be used to find dominated alternatives but should not be used to maintain that one alternative is better than the others unless the evidence (+'s) is overwhelming for that alternative. Note that the Pugh matrix assumes all of the objectives have equal importance and variation.

| Objectives | Alternatives | | | | |
|---|---|---|---|---|---|
| | A | B | C | D | E |
| Objective 1 | + | − | + | − | + |
| Objective 2 | + | S | + | S | − |
| Objective 3 | − | + | − | − | S |
| Objective 4 | − | + | + | − | S |
| Objective 5 | + | − | + | − | S |
| Σ + | 3 | 2 | 4 | 0 | 1 |
| Σ − | 2 | 2 | 1 | 4 | 1 |
| Σ S | 0 | 1 | 0 | 1 | 3 |

**FIGURE 8-3:** Pugh Matrix Example

## Even Swaps

A more advanced technique called Even Swaps is described by Hammond et al. (1999). This technique involves creating a consequence table and then making adjustments to some of the entries in the table in order to neutralize differences in the table. For example, suppose you were buying a used car and wanted a Ford Mustang. You found two good candidates manufactured in the same year that are equivalent on all but three dimensions. One Mustang costs $20,000, is blue, and has 40,000 miles on it. A second Mustang costs $15,000, is red, and has 50,000 miles.

An example of an Even Swap is to conclude that you prefer red to blue and would be willing to pay $2,000 to turn a blue car red. (Note that we are not talking about how much it would actually cost to get the Mustang painted red. There is an important difference between what you are willing to pay (a preference) and what it would actually cost.) So we could now say you were indifferent between the first Mustang ($20,000; blue; and 40,000 miles) and a hypothetical Mustang that cost $22,000, was red, and had 40,000 miles. This hypothetical Mustang is now more similar to the second Mustang, making the comparison easier because the two cars differ on only two dimensions rather than three.

Carrying this Even Swaps example to conclusion, suppose you are now willing to pay $4,000 to reduce the mileage of the second car from 50,000 to 40,000 miles. (Note that in this case it is impossible to reduce the mileage on the Mustang in the real world. But it is still possible to talk about how much you would be willing to pay if it were possible.) The second Mustang ($15,000; red; 50,000 miles) is now equivalent to a $19,000 red Mustang with 40,000 miles. As compared to the equivalent of the first Mustang ($22,000, red, and 40,000 miles), the Even Swaps approach concludes that you are $3,000 better off with the second Mustang (the $15,000 red Mustang with 50,000 miles).

Finally, it is important to note that you could consider a third alternative: buying the blue Mustang for $20,000 and paying to get it painted red. Suppose it cost only $1,000 to get a really good red paint-job on the Mustang? The third alternative now costs $21,000 for a red Mustang with 40,000 miles. Should you prefer this third alternative to the second alternative ($19,000 red Mustang with 40,000)?

For complex problems involving four or more alternatives and ten or more objectives, this Even Swaps approach can get quite complicated.

## Quantitative Approaches

There are several sophisticated and theoretically justified approaches to performing quantitative analyses of alternatives across multiple objectives. It is beyond the scope of this book to get into the details of these approaches, but we do provide an introduction to some important issues to address and some cautions. Belton and Stewart (2002) and Kirkwood (1997) provide summaries and discussions of such approaches.

## The Basics

The *decision analysis approach* is the approach recommended by the authors of this book. This approach provides for dealing with multiple conflicting objectives in a theoretically correct manner. The *quantitative value model* is intended to evaluate only feasible decision solutions after alternatives that are deemed unacceptable due to insufficient value on one or more value measures have been screened out. The model has three parts: (1) value functions that translate measures on dimensions such as purchase cost, miles per gallon, and safety into a unit-less value dimension; (2) "swing" weights that capture the importance of the measures and the degree of difference among the value space being considered on the measures and value on different dimensions into a unified value measure that spans all the measures; and (3) a mathematical equation to do the math.

Academics and practitioners have proposed many value equations that could be used. However, only a few value equations are rigorous in the sense that there is an underlying theory for why the value function makes sense from a decision-making perspective. The simplest possible such mathematical expression for the quantitative value model is given by:

(8-1) $$v(x) = \sum_{i=1}^{n} w_1 v_1(x_1)$$

where $v(x)$ is the total value of a feasible decision alternative. For $i = 1$ to $n$ (for the number of value measures), $x_i$ is the score of the feasible decision alternative on the $i$ th value measure, $v_i(x_i)$ is the single dimensional value of the feasible decision alternative on the $i$ th value measure, and $w_i$ is the swing weight of the $i$ th value measure. The saving weights are typically normalized so they sum to $1.0 - \sum_{i=1}^{n} w_1 = 1$ —but this is not a requirement (Kirkwood 1997). This equation is most intuitive and has been used by many practitioners who did not even know there was an underlying theoretical justification for its use. This theoretical justification is the most restrictive of all such theoretically justified equations and relies in practice on using fundamental objectives rather than means objectives.

The three steps in this method are:

1.  Define value scales for one or more metrics that quantify each objective. These value scales should have an interval-scale property, which is defined so that the worst possible result is a 0 and the best possible result is a 100. An interval scale means a value difference of 10 on one part of the scale is the same size value difference as any other difference quantified as a 10. Fahrenheit and Celcius temperature scales are interval scales for temperature. Note that we cannot say that 100 degrees F is twice as hot as 50 degrees F, but we can say that the interval between 50 and 100 is equal in heat gained to the difference between 25 and 75 degrees F.

2.  Capture "swing" weights for each objective. These swing weights represent the relative value to the decision maker of going from the bottom to the top of the various value scales. These weights must be on a ratio scale, meaning that a difference in value swing that is twice as important as another difference in value swing should

have a weight that is twice as large. It is not enough to just capture the importance of the objectives, because the range of consideration across the alternatives for the objectives might be uneven. We have found that many arguments about the weights boil down to differences in this "swing." It is also common for people to not accurately gauge the ratios correctly and have them too close together.

3. Score each alternative on each metric using the interval value scale defined in step 1.

After these three steps have been completed, a weighted average of value scores can be computed and reliably used to support a project manager in choosing between alternatives (see Figure 8-1).

## Value Functions

Value functions contain both an $x$ axis and a $y$ axis. The $x$ axis represents the range of a measure on which value is to be addressed. The $y$ axis represents values that a decision alternative receives relative to the score of each decision alternative for that measure. A value function should be developed for each value measure $i$. This value function transforms a measure such as purchase cost in dollars, fuel economy in miles per gallon, or safety based on a 5-star metric into a value measure that is scaled from 0 to 1. This value function must be an interval scale, meaning that equal intervals in value dimension ($y$ axis) have equal value differences no matter where they are. The value function can be discrete or continuous. Continuous functions typically follow the four basic shapes shown in Figure 8-4 (Parnell and Driscoll 2008). $x_i^0$ represents the worst value of $x_i$ on the value function. $x_i^*$ represents the best value of $x_i$ on the value function. The curves on the left are monotonically increasing, and the curves on the right are monotonically decreasing from a minimum to a maximum level of the value measure. The decision maker is responsible for describing the shape of the curve for each value measure based on a specific incremental increase in the measure scale.

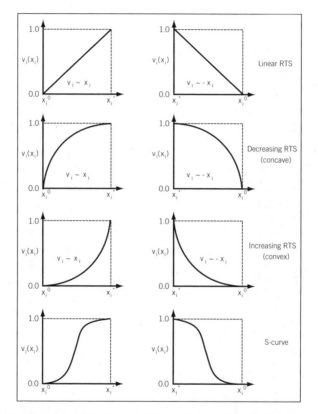

Gregory S. Parnell, Patrick J. Driscoll, and Dale J. Henderson, editors. *Decision Making in Systems Engineering and Management.* Copyright © 2008 by John Wiley & Sons, Inc. Reprinted with permission.

**FIGURE 8-4:** Typical Shapes of Value Function

We illustrate the development of a value function using the value measure miles per gallon (mpg). The minimal acceptable value to the stakeholder is 20 mpg, and the maximum acceptable value is 40 mpg.

The incremental increase from 20 to 25 mpg is 5 units and from 25 to 30 mpg, 20 units. The other judgments are shown in the table at the top left of Figure 8-5. As the values increase from 20 mpg to 40 mpg, the curve reflects an S-curve as shown to the right in Figure 8-5.

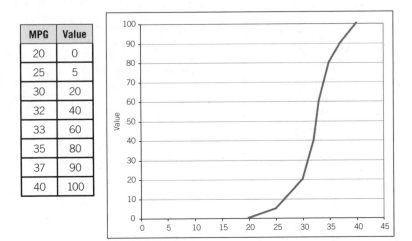

| MPG | Value |
|-----|-------|
| 20  | 0     |
| 25  | 5     |
| 30  | 20    |
| 32  | 40    |
| 33  | 60    |
| 35  | 80    |
| 37  | 90    |
| 40  | 100   |

**FIGURE 8-5:** Value Function for Maximizing Miles per Gallon

We will demonstrate this for a Honda Odyssey that gets approximately 25 mpg ($x_i$). Using the value function shown in Figure 8-6, we see that 25 mpg gets a value of 5 ($v_i(x_i)$).

After summing all the weighted values across the value measures, we can calculate the total value $v(x)$ for a decision alternative. The decision alternative scoring the highest value may be chosen as the decision solution; however, that decision rests ultimately with the decision authority.

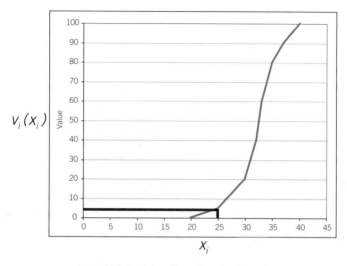

$$V_i(x_i)$$

**FIGURE 8-6:** Value Function for "mpg"

## Swing Weights

We now turn our attention to weighting the value model. It is possible to derive equation 8-1 from the axioms of decision analysis, so it is clear that the weights in that equation have to account for the relative importance of the "swings" from the bottom to the top of the value functions being used. Using the weights to reflect just the raw importance of the measures might lead to poor decisions. When the bottom or top of the value function is adjusted, the weights also need to be adjusted.

This topic of capturing the swing in value as part of the value weights is the least understood and more important part of quantitative decision-making methods. (See the discussion about changing from a blue to a red Mustang in the Even Swaps section earlier in this chapter.) In the case of the Mustangs there were only two alternatives, and the value function can adopt the actual values of the two alternatives on each measure. We need not talk about green or black Mustangs until one of them becomes a viable alternative. The amount of money the decision maker was willing to pay to change from the blue to the red Mustang or the 50,000-mile to 40,000-mile Mustang was a discussion about swing weights for these two dimensions. Because the fictional person in the example was willing to pay $2,000 for the color change and $4,000 for the mileage change, his swing weight for mileage should be twice as large as his swing weight for color.

Using the example value hierarchy from Chapter 7 shown in Figure 8-7, we begin determining weights by probing the stakeholder about the relative importance of each value measure as compared to all other measures. The first step is to get the stakeholder to rank order the importance of the swings in value measures from the bottom to the top of the value scales. Table 8-4 shows these swings. Note that the full range of values for each measure does not need to be considered if the alternatives do not include those values. Because there are no two-passenger cars or 5-star-safety cars in consideration, these values are not included in the feasible swing for the value functions.

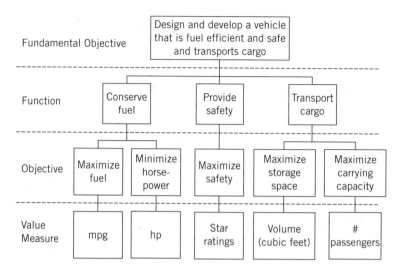

**FIGURE 8-7:** Vehicle Design Value Hierarchy

**TABLE 8-3:** Swings on Value Measures

|  | Fuel economy (miles per gallon) | Horsepower (hp) | Safety (Star rating) | Storage Space (cubic feet) | Carrying Capacity (# passengers) |
|---|---|---|---|---|---|
| Worst value on the measure | 20 | 200 | 3 stars | 5 | 4 |
| Best value on the measure | 40 | 400 | 4 stars | 35 | 5 |

The stakeholder for this problem ranks the value measures as follows: (1) safety, (2) miles per gallon, (3) horsepower, (4) storage space, and (5) passenger capacity. Note that if the safety swing is considered important to the decision maker, safety can still be the highest-weighted measure, even though its swing is small.

The second step is to get the stakeholder to assess the relative value of the swing in importance of each value measure relative to the carrying capacity of passengers. There are many ways to capture these judgments of the decision maker; see Kirkwood (1997) and Buede (2000). For this example, we use the most direct approach of asking for ratio judgments of value with respect to the swing in carrying capacity. The stakeholder identifies (1) safety as three times more important than carrying capacity (3x), (2) miles per gallon as three times more important (3x), (3) horsepower as two times more important (2x), and (4) volume as equally important (1x). The carrying capacity value measure receives a factor of (1x), indicating its relative importance as equal to value measure (4), volume. The importance is represented by the mathematical expression, which is an un-normalized weight. The mathematical expression for the normalized weight is given by:

$$w_i = \frac{p_i}{\sum_{i=1}^{n} p_i} \text{, such that } \sum_{i=1}^{n} w_i = 1 \qquad (8\text{-}2)$$

Using equation 8-2, our weights for the value measures in Figure 8-7 are (1) 0.3, (2) 0.3, (3) 0.2, (4) 0.1, and (5) 0.1, respectively. We can now calculate the value $(v_i(x_i))$ of each decision alternative for each value measure to determine the decision solution that best satisfies stakeholder needs.

A recent swing weighting value assessment tool developed by Parnell (2007) is called a *swing weight matrix*. Figure 8-8 shows a swing weight matrix for the car purchase decision discussed in this section. The columns represent three segmentations (critical, moderate, nice to have) of the intrinsic importance of the measures to the decision in question. The rows represent three segmentations of the variation permitted on the measures, from unconstrained to significant constraints. Each measure is then placed into the appropriate cell in the three-by-three matrix. (Some swing weight matrices might have four or five segmentations of the rows or columns.) The measures in the top right corner cell must have the highest swing weight. The measures in the bottom left cell must have the lowest swing weight. As we move to the right in a row, the swing weights must increase. As we move from the bottom to the top cell in a column, the swing weights must also increase.

| Swing Weight Matrix | | Level of Importance | | |
|---|---|---|---|---|
| | | Nice to Have | Moderate | Critical |
| Permitted Variability on Measures | Unconstrained | Horsepower (2) | Fuel Economy (3) | |
| | Some Constraints | Storage Space (1) | | |
| | Significant Constraints | | Carrying Capacity (1) | Safety (3) |

**FIGURE 8-8:** Swing Weight Matrix

In this example, the safety measure is highly constrained (only 3- and 4-star ratings), so it would have to be in the bottom row. Because it is so high in priority, it must be critical to the decision maker. Fuel economy, on the other hand, is relatively unconstrained, so it should be in the top row. Its relative high priority means it must be at least moderate in importance. If it were critical in importance, it would have to have a higher weight than safety.

Because fuel economy is in a higher row but a column to the left of the column for safety, the swing weight for fuel economy could be greater than, equal to, or less than the swing weight for safety. In our example, the decision maker said "equal to." The variation of horsepower was also relatively unconstrained, so it should be placed in the top row. Given its priority, the decision maker must have felt it was relatively nice to have. The placement of storage space and carrying capacity is left to the reader to determine.

## Some Cautions

Because numbers for our values have been introduced, various forms of sensitivity analysis and "what-if" analysis can be performed to determine how sensitive the recommended decision is to small changes in the numbers. Several commercial software packages can be used to support this type of quantitative decision; many people use their favorite spreadsheet software package for these computations.

One caution is most important: An approach that quantifies the value of one alternative on one objective/metric so that it is affected by the value of another alternative on the same objective/metric is subject to a phenomenon called "rank reversal." This means that if we conduct an analysis and then delete an alternative because it is dominated, the rank order of the remaining alternatives might change. Be careful in using methods that have this "feature." A common operation that causes this problem is "normalizing" the value scores on each objective/metric so they sum to 1.0.

Some complexities that can impact these decisions are uncertainty and risk. Often it will be hard to guess correctly how well a particular alternative might perform on a metric associated with an objective. Simple analytic techniques involve specifying a probability distribution for the performance of the alternative in question on that metric. However, often a string of uncertain factors are causing this uncertainty, and specifying a single probability distribution to cover all of these factors is difficult, unreliable, or both. In this case, more formal probability modeling techniques might be applied for the most important high-impact decisions. (See Buede 2000 and Paté-Cornell 1996).

When uncertainty exists, we must consider whether the project manager is risk-averse. For high-stakes decisions, using expected value does not capture the risk-averseness of many project managers. There is much in the literature on risk aversion and how to model it. (See Buede 2000, Howard and Abbas 2007, and Schuyler 2001).

A final caution is to avoid approaches that quantify weights and scores using rank orders. There is a well-known example (Pariseau and Oswalt 1994) of a Navy procurement that involved seven proposals being evaluated on 17 objectives or criteria (Figure 8-9). The evaluation team rank ordered each criterion on the basis of importance without regard to the swing; the most important criterion got a score of "1" and the least important got a "17." Then the seven proposals were rank ordered, criterion by criterion, with the best proposal getting a rank of "1" and the worst a rank of "7." To determine the best proposal, the weight ranks were multiplied by the score ranks for a given proposal and summed, yielding the weighted sum of ranks in the bottom row of Figure 8-9.

| Proposed Alternatives | Weights | Design Options | | | | | | |
|---|---|---|---|---|---|---|---|---|
| | | A | B | C | D | E | F | G |
| AC | 15 | 1 | 2 | 6 | 4 | 5 | 3 | 7 |
| AL | 5 | 1 | 2 | 6 | 4 | 5 | 3 | 7 |
| EN | 11 | 1 | 7 | 4 | 3 | 5 | 2 | 6 |
| CR | 6 | 5 | 7 | 3 | 2 | 4 | 6 | 1 |
| MA | 3 | 3 | 4 | 5 | 1 | 6 | 2 | 7 |
| DO | 1 | 1 | 3 | 5 | 4 | 6 | 2 | 7 |
| ON | 8 | 6 | 5 | 3 | 2 | 7 | 4 | 1 |
| CN | 7 | 1 | 3 | 5 | 3 | 6 | 2 | 7 |
| MR | 14 | 7 | 6 | 2 | 4 | 3 | 5 | 1 |
| EF | 2 | 1 | 2 | 6 | 4 | 5 | 3 | 7 |
| AD | 17 | 1 | 2 | 5 | 4 | 6 | 3 | 7 |
| SA | 12 | 1 | 2 | 5 | 4 | 6 | 3 | 7 |
| RE | 9 | 1 | 7 | 4 | 3 | 5 | 2 | 6 |
| OF | 10 | 7 | 6 | 3 | 4 | 2 | 5 | 1 |
| LU | 13 | 1 | 2 | 6 | 5 | 7 | 4 | 3 |
| DC | 4 | 7 | 2 | 5 | 4 | 3 | 6 | 1 |
| DS | 16 | 6 | 7 | 3 | 4 | 2 | 5 | 1 |
| Total | | 471 | 642 | 658 | 568 | 727 | 559 | 651 |

**FIGURE 8-9:** Improper Use of Rank Order Scales

There are several problems with this approach, which was successfully protested by one of the losing bidders. First, it is not legitimate to sum ranks or sum weighted ranks because ranks are an ordinal scale with no differentiation of the distance (in value in this case) between different rank orders. It is also not legitimate to multiply one rank order times another rank order for the same reason. Finally, this approach of giving the most important criterion a "1" and the least important a "17" and then multiplying makes the least important criterion far more important in determining the best proposal than the most important criterion is.

There is a spread of 7 for the proposals on the most important criterion and a spread of 119 (7 times 17 minus 7 times 1) on the least important criterion.

## Dealing with Biases and Heuristics

Cognitive biases have been defined in many ways:

- "[M]ental errors caused by our simplified information processing strategies" that are "consistent and predictable."

- Distortion in the way people perceive reality.

- Similar to optical illusions in that the error remains compelling even when one is fully aware of its nature. Awareness of the bias, by itself, does not produce a more accurate perception.

- Resulting from subconscious mental procedures for processing information.

- Not resulting from any cultural, emotional, organizational, or intellectual predisposition toward a certain judgment

The key biases that relate directly to decision-making are:

- **Information bias:** Seeking information for the sole reason that more information will certainly help in the decision process, without regard to finding that information that could affect which decision should be taken. Seeking information is the first step for most decision makers and is consistent with this bias. One key message of this book is that it is best to think through the decision first and then seek information that would help determine which alternative is the best.

■ **Bandwagon effect:** Making decisions that many others are making because so many other people cannot be wrong. People have different value structures and find themselves in different situations, so making different choices is common.

■ **Status quo bias:** Preferring alternatives that keep things relatively the same.

■ **Loss aversion:** Avoiding losses is strongly preferred over acquiring gains. This leads to a status quo bias and very risk-averse behavior.

■ **Neglect of probability:** Disregarding probability when selecting an alternative from among several, each of which might have a very different chance of success. If some alternatives have greater chances of success than others, that fact should be considered.

■ **Planning fallacy:** Underestimating task-completion times. This is a well-known risk factor (DeMarco and Lister 2003).

Researchers in the field of intelligence analysis have been studying the effect that human cognitive biases can have on errors of judgment that result in mistaking non-causal relations for causal relations. Heuer (1999), one of the key researchers in this field, described six such biases, which are relevant to decision-making in any domain, including project management:

■ **Bias in favor of causal explanations:** A tendency to develop causal explanations of observations and to ignore the possibility that perceived links are due to random factors.

■ **Bias favoring perception of centralized direction:** Tendency to attribute actions of an organization to centralized direction or planning.

- **Similarity of cause and effect:** Belief that causes and effects are similar in magnitude or other attributes.

- **Internal vs. external causes of behavior:** A tendency to overestimate the role of internal factors and underestimate the role of external factors in determining behavior.

- **Overestimating our own importance:** Tendency for people to overestimate the extent to which they can successfully influence the behavior of others.

- **Illusory correlation:** A tendency to infer correlation between events from co-occurrence without considering the frequencies of the other possible patterns of these events.

Psychologists have studied errors that people make in estimating the probability that a future event might happen. Here are some of the results:

- **Availability rule:** This heuristic refers to the tendency to judge the likelihood of an event by the ease with which examples can be remembered or imagined. So dying from an airplane crash is thought to be more likely than dying from an accidental gunshot, but based on data from the National Safety Council, the lifetime odds for a U.S. resident dying from these two causes were nearly equal in 2003.

- **Anchoring:** The tendency to estimate a probability by adjusting from a previous estimate or anchor point. Typically, adjustments from the anchor point are too small.

- **Expressions of probability:** Verbal expressions of uncertainty—such as "possible," "unlikely," and "could"—have long been recognized as sources of ambiguity and misunderstanding.

■ **Base-rate fallacy:** This bias refers to a tendency to focus on explicit indicators for an event and ignore the statistical base rate of the event. For example, we often ignore the base rate of a disease and assume that a positive test result means we positively have the disease. Many unneeded operations are performed each year because of this fallacy.

■ **Assessing probability of a scenario:** The assessed probability of a scenario is related to the amount of detail in its description, rather than its actual likelihood. A more detailed scenario (losing one's house due to a flood caused by a hurricane) is judged more likely than a less-detailed scenario (losing one's house due to a flood), even though the opposite is true.

## Requirements for Good Decisions

Yates (2003) maintains that a decision requires the resolution of ten fundamental issues, which are the need; the people (or mode); the resources for making the decision; the options or alternatives; the possibilities, consequences, or objectives; the probabilities that certain possibilities might occur; the values associated with the possibilities and objectives; the trade-off values among objectives; the process of getting the decision makers to an acceptable selection of an alternative; and the implementation of that alternative. The following discussion of Yates' ten fundamental issues provides project management examples of each of the ten issues.

**Need:** Deciding whether a decision should be made.

A company receives a request for a bid on a large project.

A competitor releases an upgraded product.

Customers increasingly complain about poor service.

Companies constantly are confronted with events like these—problems to address and opportunities to exploit. Successful decision managers vigilantly monitor the business landscape so they can see these events unfolding and determine whether, when, and how to initiate a decision-making effort.

**Mode:** Who will make this decision? How will they decide?

Should a particular decision be made by a senior executive or delegated?

Is a consultant's expertise needed?

Should a committee be convened?

If so, who should serve on it and what process should they follow?

Managers must understand the numerous means of making decisions and carefully apply them to specific issues.

**Investment:** What resources will be invested in decision-making? Decision makers must weigh the material resources needed to make a decision—direct expenses and staff time, for example—as well as the emotional costs, including stress, conflict, and uncertainty in the organization.

**Options:** What are the potential responses to a particular problem or opportunity? The goal here is to assemble and evaluate options in a way that:

Unearths the ideal solution (or one close to it).

Wastes minimal resources.

Methods for gathering potential choices include soliciting ideas from staff, seeking input from a consultant, brainstorming, and evaluating how other organizations have responded to a similar issue.

**Possibilities:** What could happen as a result of a particular course of action? Managers must foresee outcomes that are likely to be important to beneficiaries and stakeholders in the decision. Many decisions fail when these parties—including employees, customers, and neighbors—are blindsided by adverse outcomes the decision makers failed to even consider.

**Judgment:** Which of the things that could happen would happen? Decisions are shaped by predictions, opinions, and projections; it's important to evaluate their accuracy and determine how much weight to give them. The quality of these judgments improves markedly as the number of people participating in the process increases—particularly when the participants provide a variety of viewpoints.

**Value:** How much would beneficiaries care, positively or negatively, if a particular outcome were realized? Different stakeholders may have dramatically different values regarding an action and its outcomes. The intensity of these values determines whether they will take action supporting or opposing the decision.

**Trade-offs:** Every prospective action has strengths and weaknesses; how should they be evaluated? There are formal "trade-off tools" that can help with complex decisions. In most cases, when this issue is resolved, the decision is made.

**Acceptability:** How can we get stakeholders to agree to this decision and the procedure that created it? It's critical to identify groups that might object to a decision, why they feel that way, whether they can derail the decision, and how to preclude such trouble.

**Implementation:** The decision has been made. How can we ensure it will be carried out? A decision that is not implemented is a failure. It's important to recognize, and prevent, circumstances that can cause this to happen. Such circumstances include failure to allocate adequate resources to the initiative, failure to assign a senior manager to champion the project, and failure to provide incentives that ensure staffers will make implementation a high priority among their responsibilities.

In this chapter we have discussed many ways to achieve resolution on the fundamental issues Yates summarized. Five qualitative approaches for decision-making were presented, moving from the simple to the more complex. The pros and cons matrix of Ben Franklin began to establish the differences among the alternatives, providing grist for an objectives hierarchy. We then presented an approach for creating a fundamental objectives hierarchy for doing a qualitative assessment using adjectives such as "great," "fair," and "poor." The third approach was a consequences table using rank orders for the alternatives on each objective. *Here we cautioned to avoid the nearly inescapable tendency to use these ranks of improper mathematics.* Instead, these numbers should be used to find dominated alternatives that can be discarded. The Pugh matrix was presented as another approach, similar to the consequence table, that can aid in finding dominated alternatives. Finally, the Even Swaps approach was presented for comparing a few alternatives on a few objectives to determine which might be best. The Even Swaps approach can help you create hypothetical alternatives that get closer to real alternatives but enable you to determine which is the preferred one.

Next, we summarized some of the essential characteristics of quantitative approaches and provided references to key resources for these approaches. Many quantitative approaches in the literature are masquerading as rational but in fact have major flaws that no rational approach would adopt. An example of one such case was provided. We then presented many of the biases that people exhibit in decision-making, strengthening our case for systematic, rational decision-making even more. We ended the chapter with Yates's cardinal decision issues.

The following specific points were made in this chapter:

- There are both qualitative and quantitative approaches to evaluating the alternatives we face in light of our values or objectives.

- The qualitative approaches can range from creating lists of pros and cons and making holistic choice to approaches that are nearly quantitative by involving rank orders. But please be careful of rank orders: They may be numbers, but they should not be used as numbers unless there is overwhelming evidence that one alternative does much better than the rest. If this is the case, the decision was an easy one anyway.

- The process of quantifying our values requires careful thought. This is a good thing because it causes us to question assumptions and define our terms carefully. But quantification of our values requires more time and should be reserved for hard, important decisions.

- Quantification of our values should be more defensible and reliable as a decision-making process.

In Chapter 9, we address the impacts of uncertainty and risk on making a decision. Uncertainty and risk should be understood as important issues to project managers and clearly can impact our selection of the preferred alternative.

# CHAPTER 9

# Handling Risk and Uncertainty

All projects experience a degree of risk and uncertainty. Projects are not predictable or certain—most are complex and changing, and are strongly affected by the dynamics of the environment, technology, and markets. The extent of unpredictability, contingency, and change will be different for different kinds of projects (Shenhar and Dvir 2007). Risk and uncertainty are the necessary evils in every project. No matter how much we plan, we cannot plan away risk and uncertainty. Because projects involve such a great deal of risk and uncertainty, they must be managed in a flexible manner. As a result, decisions cannot be rigid, fixed, or shaped once and for all but need to be viewed as adjustable and changing as the project moves forward.

Risk and uncertainty should not always be viewed as negative, as we will see in this chapter. They can frequently help project managers to make better decisions. This chapter presents sections on risk, project management risk, managing risk, developing a risk management plan, monitoring risk, understanding uncertainty, and dealing with uncertainty.

This chapter presents the following sections:

- Risk

- Project Management Risks

- How to Address Risk

- Developing a Risk Management Plan

- Continuing Risk Management

- What Is Uncertainty?

- How Do People Address Uncertainty?

## Risk

Decision-making involves risk and is very well covered in most decision-making texts. Project management involves risk, yet not much attention has been given to it. The reason for this is that the traditional approach to project management is based on a predictable, fixed, and relatively simple model. In that model, the project plan sets the objectives for the project and is used to manage the project from beginning to end. After the project is launched, progress and performance are assessed against the plan. Changes to the plan should be rare and, if possible, avoided (Shenhar and Dvir 2007). In a world where risk and uncertainty exist, this is not a realistic approach. The conditions that were present when the project plan was established are certain to change. Changes are certain to occur within the project organization and in the business environment over a multiple-year project.

Project organizations are in the business of generating profit and thus must expect and plan for risk. Before going any further, we define *risk* as the chance that an undesired event might occur. Risk appears in many forms:

- Schedule risk (Will the project exceed schedule?)

- Cost risks (Will the budget be exceeded)

- Technical risk (Will the technology work?)

- Programmatic risk (Will project resources be available when needed?)

- Business risk (Is the project financially feasible?)

- Market risk (Is there a profitable market for the product? Recall the Iridium example from Chapter 4.)

- Implementation risk (Can the product be put into action to deliver value?)

*More important, there is decision risk. (Is there a sufficient amount of accurate information to make critical decisions?)* There are highly probable risks and low probable risks. Highly probable risks have a high probability or likelihood of occurring. Low probable risks have a low probability or likelihood of occurring. The consequences of these risks can be negligible (a team member quits) to very serious (the project exceeds the budget by $1 million). Extremely serious risks have very significant consequences regardless of their probability of occurrence. The occurrence of a risk might not necessarily be bad, because risk can sometimes cause an individual or an organization to identify better ways of reaching an objective.

Risk is much like uncertainty in that it can never be eliminated. Risk can be mitigated, but it can never be eliminated because one can never attain certainty. We never know for certain what the future holds. Risk, therefore, constitutes a lack of knowledge of future events. To understand risks that require attention and risks that do not, several things must occur. When making managerial decisions, project managers must (1) identify potential risks, (2) determine their probability of occurrence, (3) determine their consequences to the project, and (4) decide which risks they will respond to and which they will ignore. These four tasks should be included in a risk management plan and should be updated as the project progresses.

## Project Management Risks

Project managers are responsible for monitoring, measuring, and mitigating all risks during the project life cycle. Project management risks traditionally fall into four categories: (1) schedule risks, (2) cost risks, (3) technical risks, and (4) programmatic risks. A *schedule risk* is the possibility that the program falls short of reaching a key milestone date. When this occurs, the overall project schedule and delivery date are affected.

A *cost risk* is the possibility of exceeding the project budget. Each life-cycle stage within the project will have its own budget. When the budget is exceeded for one stage, there will be a potential effect on the budget for the overall project. Life-cycle costs must be closely monitored because they are less certain and more likely to vary as the project progresses into the future.

*Technical (or performance) risk* is the possibility that a requirement of the product or system will not be fully achieved. These three risks (cost, schedule, and technical) are often correlated in the sense that if one exists, the others are likely to exist, too, and they can be traded off (one decreased at the expense of an increase in one or both of the other two).

*Programmatic risk* is the possibility that the project manager will not be able to effectively manage the successful completion of the project due to events that cannot be controlled. Programmatic risks can affect issues of cost, technology, and schedule, as shown in Figure 9-1. The figure shows that by spending more money in the program (increasing the cost and schedule risk for the program) we can reduce the performance risk of the product during the operational phase of the life cycle.

Examples of programmatic risks fall into the following categories: administration, financial, management, strategic, political, environmental, subcontractor, and legal. Specific examples include personnel reassignments, unexpected managerial requirements, acts of nature, and increased requirements for critical suppliers.

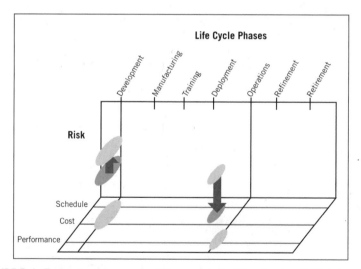

**FIGURE 9-1:** Example of Increasing Programmatic (Development) Risk to Decrease Operational Risk

## How to Address Risk

Managing decisions is essential to managing projects. Managing the risk that might be encountered in making decisions is also essential to managing projects. One of the most important aspects during project management planning is risk management. *Risk management* is the act or practice of dealing with risk, and proper risk management is proactive rather than reactive (Kerzner 2006).

Risk management identifies many areas of project cost, schedule, and product risk and gives the project manager the information with which to make educated decisions. The demands of project management are that all risk needs to be addressed and treated, because risk management can highlight areas of uncertainty or false confidence. Risk management helps project managers to decide the best course of action, to become aware of problems earlier rather than later, and to plan any necessary changes. Most importantly, it can increase management and stakeholder confidence (Jackson 1997).

When risk is not managed, it can wreak havoc on a project, as noted in the following case study.

## CASE STUDY

### The Financial Middleware Software Project

The client for this software project was an investment management company looking to lower its costs by creating a straightforward format for processing its customers' buy and sell orders. The traditional business process involved making investment decisions on behalf of clients, such as pension funds or wealthy individuals. The decisions to trade were made internally and involved three systems:

trading, accounting, and communication. The external process involved sending the trade details (stock name, quantity, price, and fee) to the respective bank within a prescribed amount of time. Before this project, most of these activities were performed by hand.

The company was a small organization that had no prior experience in monitoring complex software projects. The project was contracted to an external vendor, which claimed to have developed similar systems previously for the health care industry. The vendor suggested that this project would be a modification to its generic off-the-shelf middleware. At first, it appeared a perfect fit. The investment company needed a simple computerized platform, and the vendor was looking to expand its client base to financial institutions.

The new system consisted of three software components: middleware software to transfer trade information automatically, database software, and enrichment software, which receives the information from the database and sends it to an external bank.

All went well for the first four months; however, about midway through the project, things began to deteriorate. The modified systems did not function as expected, and the vendor had to allocate more resources to deal with the problems. When a first prototype was eventually delivered, the customer was unable to test it in due time. In the end, the vendor simply handed the source code to the customer and walked away. The investment firm was left to struggle with the software installation and testing on its own. The project was under constant review and change; deliverables were either altered or canceled. Finally, after long delays and additional cost, a workable version of the first mock-up was approved.

In retrospect, both parties miscalculated the extent of the risk and difficulty associated with this project. As it turned out, in comparison with medical systems, building a financial system containing complex business logic was a major leap. The customer did not possess the knowledge and expertise needed to manage or even define such a complex project. For its part, the vendor did not estimate the extent of change in the market that this product would introduce, assuming that it was simply an extension of a previous product for a different industry.

To manage risk, a risk management plan should be developed. Such a plan should inform management about potential events that could have an adverse impact on the project. A risk management plan is critical to decision-making. Risk management planning should specifically be done at the feasibility stage of the project—along with budgeting, scheduling, and product specification writing—and should continue well into the planning stage.

The project manager needs to know the risk profile for the project and what will have to be done to keep total risk under control before getting deeply committed to the project, just like whether the schedule, budget, and product specifications are achievable needs to be known (Smith and Reinertsen 1998).

Risk management includes (1) risk identification, (2) risk analysis, and (3) response to risk. A typical risk management process contains six steps, as depicted in Figure 9-2: identify the possible risks, analyze the risks, implement risk mitigation or watch strategies for selected risks, track those strategies to ensure success, control the strategies as needed, and communicate throughout the process to those who need the information.

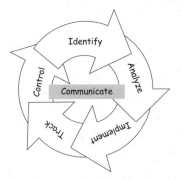

**FIGURE 9-2:** A Common Risk Management Process

Risk identification consists of a thorough study of all risks, including their sources and the situations under which they might occur. Because all risks will not be known at the beginning of the project life cycle, risk identification needs to continue as information becomes available and as each stage is encountered.

Scenario analysis and simulations are two methods for identifying risks. These two methods can model possible sequences of events, scenarios, and decisions and can provide insight on potential consequences. Another method is brainstorming. Testing is a very valuable method when assessing product or performance risk. Each method should include interaction with everyone involved in the project (e.g., project manager, project team, customer stakeholders, sponsors, contractors, subject matter experts) in order to gain critical information elements needed to develop comprehensive risk categories (Driscoll 2008). Risks and their sources can also be identified by interviewing project team members, stakeholders, or outside parties that might have previous experience in similar projects.

After the major risks have been identified, the following data should be obtained on each to facilitate risk analysis: (1) the probability of each risk event occurring, (2) the range of possible outcomes if it does occur, and (3) the probabilities of each outcome. Risk analysis should begin at the start of the project life cycle and continue right through all stages. During risk analysis, risks are categorized and prioritized in terms of their severity and probability. Risks, where possible, must be measured as to the extent of their threat to the program. Simply being aware of the potential risks is not enough for proper management of risk or control of its degree (Driscoll 2008). A thorough risk analysis enables the project manager to determine the consequences of each decision made (Mantel, Meredith, Shafer, and Sutton 2001):

The essence of risk analysis is to state the various outcomes of a decision as probability distributions and to use these distributions to evaluate the desirability of certain managerial decisions. The objective is to illustrate to the manager the distribution or risk profile of the outcomes (e.g., profits, completion dates, return on investment) . . . . These risk profiles are one factor to be considered when making the decision, along with many others such as intangibles, strategic concerns, behavioral issues, fit with the organization, and so on.

The value of performing a risk analysis is that it provides or should provide information on those risks that have the potential of crashing a project. As stated, not all risks require a response. More important, there are not enough resources to deal with all risks. Subsequently, project managers must be selective in choosing which risks to respond to with some sort of risk mitigation activity.

A risk profile can aid the project manager in determining which risks require attention. An example of a risk profile for a short project is shown in Table 9-1 (Driscoll 2008). The profile was developed for a generic project and includes information on the scale or severity of the risk, the probability of each risk event occurring, and the likely effect on schedule, cost, and product performance. Longer-term projects can have schedule impacts of months or years. Regardless of whether the risk is a schedule, cost, or performance risk, its impact is usually felt in at least two of the three project areas. For example, a schedule risk might impact schedule and cost. A performance risk usually impacts performance, schedule, and costs.

**TABLE 9-1:** Risk Profile

| | | | Impact on Project | | |
|---|---|---|---|---|---|
| | Scale | Probability | Schedule Delay | Cost Increase | Performance |
| **Value Ranges** | Very high | 20–30 percent | > 6 days | > 20 percent | Multiple major failures |
| | High | 5–10 percent | 3–5 days | 15–20 percent | Limited major failures |
| | Medium | 20–30 percent | 2–3 days | 10–15 percent | Single major failures |
| | Low | 10–20 percent | 1–2 days | 5–10 percent | Multiple minor failures |
| | Very low | 0.10 percent | < 1 day | < 5 percent | Limited minor failures |
| | Zero | 0 | 0 | 0 | None |

Gregory S. Parnell, Patrick Driscoll, and Dale L. Henderson, eds., *Decision Making in Systems Engineering and Management* (Hoboken, NJ: John Wiley & Sons, Inc., 2008): 72. Copyright © 2008 by John Wiley & Sons, Inc. Reprinted with permission.

A thorough analysis identifies risks that require a response. Risk response involves a decision about which risks to prepare for and which to ignore and simply accept as potential threats (Mantel, Meredith, Shafer, and Sutton 2001).

Risks thus need to be continuously tracked or monitored throughout the duration of the project life cycle. During risk response, mitigation strategies are developed to minimize the risks that can threaten the life of a project. Scenario analysis and simulations are two tools already mentioned that can be used to identify risk. These tools can also be used to analyze mitigating effects on risk. Because risk mitigation strategies often carry a degree of risk of their own, a risk contingency plan should be developed for the highest impact and most probable risks.

During the time that risk mitigation activities seem to be running into problems or are being perceived as successful, another step in the process should be performed. This step involves making adjustments or exerting control over how much risk mitigation to continue with and how.

Figure 9-2 illustrates the ongoing communication that must be present as the risk management process repeats itself on a weekly or monthly basis. Some of the most critical risks to find are ones that no one individual is completely aware of. It is only by comparing notes, doing scenario analysis, or joint brainstorming that these more complex risks can be identified. One person might be aware of the chance that an unexpected event can occur, but other people might better understand the full consequences if that event does occur.

There are inherent risks to every project. We show the case of the Hubble Space Telescope as an example of risks discovered after the project had been completed and investigate what risk mitigation strategies could have prevented the error. A decision frame is used to structure the analysis.

## CASE STUDY

### Hubble Telescope Testing Decisions

Three years late and many dollars over budget, the Hubble Space Telescope was ready to be launched in 1986. However, the explosion of the shuttle *Challenger* delayed the launch by four years. During this time, the Hubble project was given limited funds to finish the ground system. The Hubble was finally launched in April 1990 on the first shuttle flight after the *Challenger* explosion. On May 20, the Hubble took its first peek at the universe, and the scientists noticed a spherical aberration in the primary mirror that caused a severe distortion in the Hubble's sensors. The Hubble was providing a resolution of three times that available with telescopes on the ground, but the originating requirement for Hubble had been ten times that of Earth-based telescopes. In June 1993, the shuttle *Endeavor* carried a repair team to the Hubble. The astronauts took three days to install a corrective "contact lens," replace the original Wide-Field and Planetary Camera, and replace the original solar panels to eliminate the jitter that occurred twice in each orbit as the satellite moved from daylight to darkness.

The Hubble telescope is a two-mirror reflecting telescope, a special type of Cassegrain telescope called a Ritchey-Chrétien telescope. The primary mirror (2.4 meters in diameter) and secondary mirror were to be hyperbolic in shape; the manufacturing process was to grind the mirror as close as possible to this shape and then polish the mirror to achieve as smooth a surface as possible. During the grinding and polishing process, tests were conducted with a computer-controlled optical device, a reflective null corrector consisting of two small mirrors and a tiny lens. Unfortunately, the spacing between the lens and the mirrors was off by 1.3 millimeters and there was small chip in the black paint. The aberration, 0.001 arc seconds from the design specification, resulted in an error 100,000 times the size of the desired 1/50 the wavelength of light.

Lockheed Aerospace was awarded the prime contract for the support structure, including a task for systems integration. Eastman-Kodak and Perkin-Elmer competed for the job of the primary mirror. Perkin-Elmer provided a lower bid. Eastman-Kodak was given a contract to produce a backup primary minor, a risk mitigation strategy that could have been proven very insightful if the flaw in the Perkin-Elmer mirror had been detected.

Why was a mistake this large not detected? A knife-edge test was conducted on the main mirror. This sophisticated and complex test produced results showing there was a problem with the mirror and indicating that the null corrector must be flawed. Either Perkin-Elmer (the prime contractor) thought these results invalid and did not report them to NASA or NASA managers ignored them on the grounds that the knife-edge test results were not correct. Several other tests could have been conducted but were not. The two primary mirrors built by Perkin-Elmer and Eastman-Kodak could have been swapped and the null corrector tests rerun. A second test was an end-to-end test conducted on the assembled mirrors and other components. Perkin-Elmer was not contractually required to do this test; NASA investigated whether to conduct it but chose not to do so. After the flaw was found, NASA claimed this test would have cost more than $100 million but soon had to back down when independent estimates were ten times lower. Other tests were recommended to NASA by experts in the community.

This testing situation was caused and made worse by management conflicts and mistakes within NASA and by cost overruns. NASA had devised a management structure that included two centers, Goddard and Marshall. Marshall was given primary responsibility even though Goddard had more experience in systems of this type. During the course of the Phase C effort from 1977 to 1986, NASA had at least four program managers and three project managers.

Consider the decision situation faced by the project managers of Perkin-Elmer, Lockheed, and NASA. Time is running out in 1985 to get the telescope and support structure integrated with the data-capturing instruments and the solar panels. There has been no real test of the telescope, and Perkin-Elmer's contract does not call for a full system test. Lockheed is to perform testing as it integrates the various elements of what is known as the Hubble Space Telescope system. Should the NASA project manager insist on additional tests at Perkin-Elmer? Should the Lockheed project manager decide to forego some other tests in order to test the telescope? Should the Perkin-Elmer project manager decide more testing besides the failed knife-edge test is warranted? Should any of them insist on comparing the quality of the two primary mirrors before integration begins? There is no evidence, to our knowledge, that any of the project managers considered making this last decision, but it is hard to imagine that they would not have been curious and have thought it wise to investigate the question. The decision frame presented next deals with the decision of comparing the two primary mirrors with the thought that one might be considerably better than the other (Petersen and Brandt, 1995; Sinnott, 1990).

As can be seen from the decision frame for a comparison of primary mirrors (Table 9-2), it would not have been an easy decision to make. There are some significantly bad outcomes for each of the alternatives being considered. Many decision makers focus on the certain bad outcomes for an alternative that calls for actually doing something—something that might reveal any problems—and totally miss the uncertain bad outcomes of the alternative of doing nothing. Many philosophers and writers have termed this mistake an *error of omission* (not comparing the mirrors) with an *error of commission* (performing a comparison that dictates the use of scarce resources and a delay in time). In an error of omission, the error made in Hubble, we fail to take an action that could have minimized the risk of the absolute worst outcome.

**TABLE 9-2:** Hubble Decision Frame for Comparing the Two Primary Mirrors

| Context for Decision |
| --- |
| **Stakeholders:** Perkin-Elmer, Kodak, Lockheed, NASA, Scientists, Taxpayers |
| **Resource Constraints:** End of program (launch date) is close; there is not enough money to do everything that should be done; some testing facilities are not available |
| **Environment:**<br>*Social:* everyone wants a success, but no one wants to discover bad news at this late date<br>*Organizational:* there is some tension between the organizations and within the organizations to protect reputations; some of these tensions would push for achieving greater success potential and some would push against finding bad news; Perkin-Elmer clearly would not like to find out that Kodak's mirror is better; the scientific community was pushing for testing and comparison<br>*Legal:* there are no legal (contractual) requirements to make this comparison<br>*Natural:* find the best solution from those available |
| **Broad Objectives:** minimize changes that will cause schedule delays and cost increases |
| **Use Cases:** (1) find an appropriate means to perform a legitimate comparison and do so (outcomes include: no difference [waste of time and money], Perkin-Elmer mirror is better [waste of time and money], Kodak mirror is better [significant schedule delay and increased cost but superior performance and possible avoidance of major failure scenario], (2) try to find an appropriate means but fail to do so because of scarce resources [waste of small amount of time and money and ability to defend actions as having done everything possible], (3) continue without trying a comparison [no additional cost and schedule implications, but open to criticism for not conducting the obvious test] |

| Fundamental Objectives for Decision | Alternatives for Decision |
|---|---|
| **Programmatic Objectives:** | **Programmatic Alternatives:** |
| *Cost Objectives:* keep programmatic overrun as low as possible | Continue on plan and conduct no comparison |
| *Schedule Objectives:* achieve launch on shuttle in 1986 | Find a reasonable approach to conducting a comparison and do so (e.g., have the contractors test each other's mirrors with their own null correctors) |
| *Performance Objectives:* reduce risk of a programmatic failure | |
| **System/Product Objectives:** | **System/Product Alternatives:** |
| *Cost Objectives:* minimize the likelihood of a repair mission to fix a problem that could have been fixed on Earth | Operate the HST with whatever flaws it has once it is launched |
| *Schedule Objectives:* minimize the time to producing real scientific data with the HST | Send a repair mission to fix any serious flaws found after the HST begins operation |
| *Performance Objectives:* maximize the quality of the scientific data | |
| **Supportability/Life Cycle Objectives:** N/A | **Supportability/Life Cycle Alternatives:** N/A |
| *Cost Objectives:* | |
| *Schedule Objectives:* | |
| *Performance Objectives:* | |
| **Uncertainties:** | **Information Sources:** |
| *Programmatic Uncertainties:* Will more funds be available to continue if a serious flaw is found? | *Data:* Test data from mirror tests Sense of Congress for providing more funds |
| *System/Product Uncertainties:* How well will the telescope perform? How much difference is there between the two primary mirrors? | *Experts:* Engineers in industry and government who have worked on similar programs |
| *Supportability/Life Cycle Uncertainties:* Can a fix be found for a flaw in the primary mirror? | *Other Sources:* |

# Developing a Risk Management Plan

The goal of risk management is to take action to reduce the risk-induced variance on performance, cost, and schedule estimates over the project life cycle (Driscoll 2008). Figure 9-3 shows a graphical illustration of the spread or variance between worst-case and best-case estimates that is reduced early in the project life cycle (Driscoll 2008). Risk management efforts A and B yield more accurate estimates of total system costs, project completion, and project performance. The threat to project success was dramatically reduced when risk management was performed.

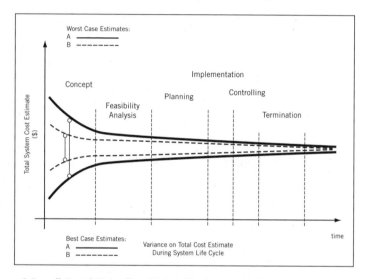

Gregory S. Parnell, Patrick Driscoll, and Dale L. Henderson, eds., *Decision Making in Systems Engineering and Management* (Hoboken, NJ: John Wiley & Sons, Inc., 2008): 71. Copyright © 2008 by John Wiley & Sons, Inc. Reprinted with permission.

**FIGURE 9-3:** Estimate of Project Variances over Life Cycle

A risk management plan has been traditionally used to identify, monitor, and treat uncertainties that can threaten a project. A good risk management plan includes (1) risk identification, (2) risk analysis, and (3) risk response and the answering of six questions (Driscoll 2008):

- What can go wrong?

- What is the likelihood of something going wrong?

- What are the consequences?

- What can be done and what options are available?

- What are the trade-offs in terms of risk, costs, and benefits?

- What are the impacts of current decisions on future options?

These questions are helpful when conducting scenario analysis, simulations, and brainstorming sessions. A comprehensive risk management plan will assist the project manager and the project team in ensuring that the project remains on track to meet project objectives. More specifically, a risk management plan identifies risk and follow-on actions for possibly reducing risk to the project. When a plan is absent, an unexpected event can occur and cause the project to terminate prior to completion, exceed budget or schedule, or miss product objectives. The risk management plan is an effective tool in managing risk, but handling risk is not quite as simple as developing a plan.

Risk is a difficult element to manage. Just when you think you have all bases covered, something else pops up. Negligible risks can easily become serious as the project progresses. An ongoing risk analysis is required. Not only can negligible risks become serious but new risks can emerge as the project gets under way due to environmental changes. Such changes are usually beyond the control of the team. Ongoing risk analysis engages in monitoring, measuring, and mitigating risks throughout the life of the project.

## Continuing Risk Management

The development of a risk management plan does not eliminate risk. The hard work has just begun. Now that the plan has been developed, it has to be implemented. This requires constant oversight during the project work to ensure that the risks and their effects do not change. In the controlling stage of a project, the project manager monitors and controls the project to ensure it continuously meets project objectives. Planned risks must also be managed during the monitoring and controlling process to ensure that the project remains on track to meet short-term, mid-term, and long-term objectives.

During the monitoring process, because there are risks to the plan, the project manager must be aware that conditions can change and might require development of additional risk-handling strategies. Updating existing risk-handling strategies and analyzing known risks again might also be required. If new risks are identified, the project manager must be prepared to revise some aspects of the risk management plan. The key is monitoring the plan to ensure that it is effective and being aware of any new risks that might appear and cause the project to be thrown off course.

## What Is Uncertainty?

The dictionary definition of *uncertain* contains at least five different concepts: indefinite, problematical, untrustworthy, doubtful, and variable. We claim to be uncertain about what other people or organizations are going to do (cut our project's funding), about what the environment is going to do (rain tomorrow), about what the future holds (our project's cost might go up or down). Uncertainty can arise about some future issue for many reasons—from lack of information to ambiguity in understanding of the issue to the basic unpredictability of the processes involved, even including deception by an untrustworthy person or an adversary.

Many discussions of uncertainty suggest that the causes or sources of uncertainty are information that is missing, ambiguous, complex, conflicting, or not trustworthy. Many people feel that they can eliminate uncertainty by collecting more and more information. However, a great deal of uncertainty cannot be eliminated; often the most important uncertainty cannot be eliminated. In fact, quite a large percentage of the really troubling uncertainty related to project management can barely be reduced.

Ayyub (2001) maps the ignorance underlying uncertainty with the concept map shown in Figure 9-4. The concepts in this map address both conscious and unconscious reasons for ignorance. (The word *partial* under Incompleteness replaces Ayyub's use of the word uncertainty; otherwise *uncertainty* would be a subset of *uncertainty,* which is a tautology.)

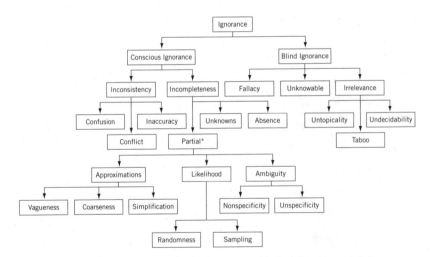

**FIGURE 9-4:** Concept Map for Ignorance Underlying Uncertainty

# How Do People Address Uncertainty?

In some situations, uncertainty is minimal, meaning that one possible resolution of the issue is much more likely than any other. Other situations raise much greater uncertainty and present many equally likely possibilities with very different consequences. Every once in a while there is quite an unlikely event that could cause a nearly catastrophic outcome.

Many people have great difficulty in dealing with uncertainty. Some procrastinate in making any decisions until they have enough information to resolve their uncertainty. Other people become very risk-averse and try to ensure the potential negative outcomes do not occur. A few ignore the uncertainty and act as if the future were known. What is the right way to decide in decisions fraught with high uncertainty? To answer this question, we will address how best to consider and gather information and how to weigh alternatives in terms of uncertainty. We introduced risk and how to reduce the risk for a selected alternative earlier in the chapter.

## Gathering Information

First, consider the issue of how much information is enough. People always want as much information as possible; recall the information bias at the end of the previous chapter. As discussed earlier, there are many people who believe that uncertainty can be eliminated by gathering information. In fact, most project management decisions contain important topics about which there will always be uncertainty, no matter how much information is collected.

For example, will the contractor (or subcontractor) deliver the product on schedule, within cost, and in a way that meets the performance requirements? Will the funding for next year and the year after be cut, and if so, by how much? Will a key supporter of the project move to a better job or retire? The answers to these and many more questions are critical to success but are seldom known for sure. There is also very little information that can be gathered to produce certainty. The project manager can talk to the key supporter and be told the key supporter has no plans to take another job. But that key supporter might get an unexpected and great job offer a week or month or year later and be unable to turn it down.

Second, how do people synthesize information? In the section titled "Approaches to Decision Making" in Chapter 4, we mentioned the bias of people for a selective search of evidence. We quickly adopt a belief about a resolution and then search for evidence that confirms this position. In addition, a confirmation bias can occur when people actually misinterpret evidence (information) to confirm their preconceived position on the issue. Several groups of people have been led to adopt different positions on the same issue at the beginning of an experiment and then all groups were given the same information, one piece at a time. Members of each group formed stronger views that their position was correct based on the same information.

Third, people exhibit "overconfidence" about issues for which there is uncertainty, whether they are experts or novices. Overconfidence means that we are likely to believe there is a greater chance than justified that an event will happen. Some of us overcompensate by believing that unlikely events are less likely to happen than they actually are. More details are provided later, but first let's talk about experts and novices.

Experts are often characterized as having at least 10 (some say 20) years of experience in an area, or over 10,000 hours of deliberate practice, although experience is not a guarantee of expertise. Expertise is also characterized as performance that exhibits high discrimination ability and consistency. Because of their extensive experience in an area, as well as the effort they have made to organize their knowledge, experts can quickly examine a situation, identify the most relevant variables, and develop a strategy for action. That is, the experts can easily recognize the situation and identify the appropriate response. Even experienced non-experts cannot attain this level of performance.

However, the characteristics of the domain of expertise place limits on the levels of discrimination and consistency that experts can attain. To illustrate this fact, Shanteau (1992 and 2001) summarized previous research that evaluated the predictive performance of experts in several different domains, noting substantial differences in expert performance between domains. Table 9-3 presents the results of this review, as refined by Weiss and Shanteau (2003).

The highest level was called "Aided Decisions" because the experts in these domains often relied on aids, models, or decision support systems to inform their judgments. The second level of performance was called "Competent"; in these domains, experts made skilled but unaided judgments. The third level was called "Restricted"; here, experts performed somewhat better than chance, but the accuracy of predictions was quite limited. In the domains in the final category, expert predictions were essentially as accurate as random guessing.

**TABLE 9-3:** Assessment of Domains by Four Levels of Performance

| Performance Level | | | |
|---|---|---|---|
| **Aided Decisions** | **Competent** | **Restricted** | **Random** |
| Short-term weather forecasters | Chess masters | Clinical psychologists | Polygraphers |
| Astronomers | Livestock judges | Pathologists | Managers |
| Test pilots | Grain inspectors | Psychiatrists | Stockbrokers |
| Auditors | Photo interpreters | Student admissions | Parole officers |
| Physicists | Soil judges | Intelligence analysts | Court judges |

David J. Weiss and James Shanteau, Table 8-1, "The Vice of Consensus and the Virtue of Consistency," *Psychological Explorations of Competent Decision Making* (New York: Cambridge University Press): 232. Copyright © 2008 by Cambridge University Press. Reprinted with permission.

In which of the four columns of Table 9-2 do you think project management falls? Are there different types of project management (commercial versus government, product development) for which a different column is most appropriate?

Project management requires a great deal of interaction with people, just as management does. Yet there are technical aspects to most pure management jobs. In some cases, such technical activity is related to physics, in other cases, the technical activity is related to geology or psychology, or any other area requiring technical knowledge. So project management might correctly fall into all four columns. Our conclusion is that there are different types of projects and some project managers have an inherently more difficult job than others.

Weiss and Shanteau (2003) summarized performance measures for two domains in each category in terms of the inter-expert consensus and the intra-expert consistency, producing the results shown in Table 9-4. Note that in this instance, "Consensus" measures the average agreement of two or more experts who make the same judgment. It does not refer to a group or organizational process for reaching agreement. Consensus of expert judgments was closely related to the performance level of a domain, indicating that experts in high-performing domains of expertise are more likely to agree with each other than those in domains associated with lower performance.

In general, internal consistency of expert judgments followed the same pattern, but there were several domains—most notably, livestock judges and polygraphers—that had high internal consistency, although they had relatively low inter-expert consensus. These domains appear to be ones in which there are several schools of thought that guide analysis and predictions. Adherents to different schools of thought will likely disagree with each other on predictions, even though each individual was highly consistent within his or her own predictions. Based on these results, Weiss and Shanteau argue against the idea that consensus is a necessary condition for expertise.

**TABLE 9-4:** Levels of Performance for Domains of Expertise

| Performance Level | | | |
|---|---|---|---|
| **Aided Decisions** | **Competent** | **Restricted** | **Random** |
| Short-term weather forecasters<br>Consensus: 0.95<br>Inter. consis.: 0.98 | Livestock judges<br>Consensus: 0.50<br>Inter. consis.: 0.96 | Clinical psychologists<br>Consensus: 0.40<br>Inter. consis.: 0.44 | Stockbrokers<br>Consensus: 0.32<br>Inter. consis.: 0.40 |
| Auditors<br>Consensus: 0.76<br>Inter. consis.: 0.90 | Grain inspectors<br>Consensus: 0.60<br>Inter. consis.: 0.62 | Parole officers<br>Consensus: 0.55<br>Inter. consis.: 0.50 | Polygraphers<br>Consensus: 0.33<br>Inter. consis.: 0.91 |

David J. Weiss and James Shanteau, Table 8-2, "The Vice of Consensus and the Virtue of Consistency," *Psychological Explorations of Competent Decision Making* (New York: Cambridge University Press): 233. Copyright © 2008 by Cambridge University Press. Reprinted with permission.

The research cited earlier indicates that different domains place varying restrictions on the ability of experts to make accurate predictions of the likelihood of future events and suggests that these restrictions might be fairly severe for intelligence analysis. The domains with high performance are relatively stable in terms of their facts—the objects judged, the rules of judging, and the objectivity and reliability of the tools and rules used to make judgments—compared to those characterized by lower predictive performance.

In general, these higher-performing domains possess a more elaborate and stable structure of knowledge to support analysis and judgment. These highly structured domains tend to deal more with science, logic, and inanimate objects, while the less-structured domains are more heavily skewed toward behavior of individuals and social or political organizations. Finally, in higher-performance domains such as weather forecasting and livestock judging, experts have more extensive experience making predictions and getting timely feedback on accuracy. In other domains, including intelligence analysis, feedback is often delayed or even absent.

In a completely separate but related body of research on expertise and judgment, Tetlock (2005) addressed the limited ability of political science analysts to make correct judgments about future events. Again, political science experts appear to be little better than chance and are subject to significant overconfidence. However, in a study of 284 experts in international affairs over 18 years, Tetlock was able to differentiate the abilities of experts with two different cognitive styles—termed foxes and hedgehogs—defined by Isaiah Berlin (1953).

According to this definition, a fox knows many little things, while a hedgehog knows one big thing. In Tetlock's words, the fox "pursues many ends, often unrelated and even contradictory ... entertains ideas that are centrifugal rather centripetal; ... without seeking to fit them into, or exclude them from, any one all-embracing inner vision." A fox avoids grand theories and is reluctant to forecast. A hedgehog "relates everything to a single central vision ... in terms of which all that they say has significance." A hedgehog readily extends his favorite theory into all domains and has great confidence in his ability to forecast. Tetlock showed that foxes making short-term predictions are far better calibrated than hedgehogs under any condition. Hedgehogs outperform foxes in one category—they assign higher probabilities to big changes that do materialize. But this comes with a substantial cost of many false positive predictions.

In domains such as intelligence analysis, experts should be very cautious in expressing confidence in predictions. Rather than asserting an event might occur, the analyst could take a more subtle, informed approach, after becoming familiar with the principles of probability and the conditional relationships between sources of uncertainty. Recognizing that certainty comes in degrees, the analyst would craft a more useful analysis by specifying the conditions that affect the likelihood of an occurrence, the separate and combined effects of those conditions, and the indicators that could serve as warning signs that such probabilities are rising or falling. This approach could inform policy makers of opportunities and warning signs, and thus put them on a better footing than they would otherwise be if they had only speculation that an event might or might not happen.

Regarding overconfidence, substantial research has confirmed the strong general tendency for overconfidence when making predictions or statements of uncertainty. In other words, the predicted probability of an event is often not calibrated with its actual likelihood of occurring. When a set of probabilistic predictions are calibrated, then the proportion of the events predicted to occur with a given probability should be the same as the assessed probability. For example, 90 percent of the events predicted to occur with a probability of 0.9 should actually happen if the prediction probabilities are calibrated. Similarly, 70 percent should occur for events assigned a probability of 0.7, and so on. One can plot the probabilities that an expert assigns and the percentages of events occurring, as shown in Figure 9-5 (Koehler, Brenner, and Griffin 2002). Here, the analyst's stated probabilities are on the horizontal axis and the frequencies of occurrence are on the vertical axis. Many people are well-calibrated at the 50-50 point; however, most do not make well-calibrated predictions for events that are either more or less likely.

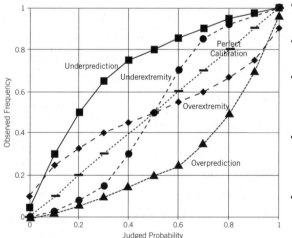

- Overprediction: Always assigning probabilities that are high
- Underprediction: Always assigning probabilities that are low
- Overextremity: Overestimating high probabilities and underestimating low probabilities
- Underextremity: Underestimating high probabilities and overestimating low probabilities
- Overconfidence: May take the form of overprediction or overextremity

**FIGURE 9-5:** Representation of Calibration of Probability Judgments

Figure 9-5 depicts four ways that judgments can fail to be calibrated. Two of these ways—overprediction and overextremity—indicate overconfidence in the judgments. Overprediction occurs when the assessed probabilities of events are higher than the actual event likelihoods throughout the range of probabilities. Overextremity occurs when individuals overestimate the probability of likely events and underestimate the probability of unlikely events. The corresponding conditions of underprediction and underextremity are also shown in the figure, although these do not occur nearly as frequently as the conditions representing overconfidence.

It is well known that people are overconfident in making most probability judgments; that is, they think they know more than they do. There is some evidence that people are likely to be overconfident on hard questions but underconfident on easy questions. The overconfidence bias manifests itself in at least two ways. First, people tend to express greater confidence that they are right than is justified by the data (including their own real-life experiences). Second, when asked for a probability distribution on a variable, the variance for that variable will tend to be too small; that is, the distribution will be too narrow.

Short-term weather forecasting is one domain in which predictions have demonstrated good calibration. The standard reason given for this usually good calibration is that short-term weather forecasters get nearly immediate feedback about whether they were right or wrong on a continuous basis. In addition, forecaster performance is scored in a way that encourages calibration. The adoption of these scoring rules and the incorporation of predictive ability into the determination of weather forecaster salaries, the calibration of predictions of temperature and precipitation has improved substantially. This example illustrates the importance of feedback and incentives in encouraging well-calibrated prediction probabilities.

## Weighing Options

Most people agree that uncertainty should be included in decision-making if we are to claim that we are good decision makers. For example, if we have several really good alternatives and there is relatively strong certainty associated with one of them but quite a bit of uncertainty about the others, we tend to pick the alternative with less uncertainty. Similarly, if we have several extremely poor alternatives, but one of them has some chance of a good outcome, we are likely to select the one that includes some hope (uncertainty). So uncertainty should be addressed when making a decision. But how?

The field of decision analysis suggests that we quantify our uncertainty using probability theory and then calculate an expected value or expected utility (if we are risk-averse). This area of decision analysis also asserts that values can be quantified so that these calculations can be performed. The authors of this book have decided not to present this quantitative material here but suggest the interested reader consult Buede (2000), Howard and Abbas (2007), and Schuyler (2001).

When the rigors and efforts associated with a full decision analysis are not justified by the stakes of the decision, we should still include the issue of uncertainty in our decision. We can do this by hedging the relative value we assign an alternative by the degree of the uncertainty associated with its outcomes. We strongly caution the reader that this is easier to say than to do, because people have those persistent and debilitating cognitive biases discussed earlier. This task of mentally downgrading an alternative because the uncertainties associated with it are greater than those of other alternatives is fraught with peril. In fact, the differential degrees of uncertainty associated with the alternatives for a particular decision are nearly enough to justify using a quantitative approach such as decision analysis.

This chapter addressed risk and uncertainty as being omnipresent in every project and project organization. We first defined risk and identified the different types of risk that have to be managed. We stressed that to manage risk, a risk management plan must be developed or risk has the potential to wreak havoc on project and product performance. How to develop a risk management plan was presented for the various types of risks that might pose a threat to the project. The plan we suggested contains four essential elements. A good risk management plan includes at least three: (1) risk identification, (2) risk analysis, and (3) risk response and the answers to six key questions. The risk management plan is an effective tool in managing risk, but handling risk is not quite as simple as developing a plan. We ended the section on risk with the idea that risk management is continual. The unexpected happens, especially when you least expect it.

Next, we addressed the subject of uncertainty. We began with defining uncertainty. How do people deal with uncertainty? Do they try to gather more information before making a decision? We stressed the fact that uncertainty cannot be eliminated by collecting more information. Due to the uncertainty of the information received, caution should be used when basing actions on it.

The following specific points were made in this chapter:

- A sufficient amount of accurate information is needed to make successful decisions.

- Risk can be mitigated, that is, minimized or reduced, but it can never be eliminated because it constitutes a lack of knowledge of future events.

- When making managerial decisions, project managers must (1) identify potential risks, (2) determine their probability of occurrence, (3) determine their consequences to the project, and (4) decide which risks they will respond to and which they will ignore.

- Project management risks traditionally falls into four categories: (1) schedule risks, (2) cost risks, (3) technical risks, and (4) programmatic risks. Each is equally dangerous to the welfare of a project.

- Risk management identifies many areas of project cost, schedule, and technical risk and gives the project manager the information with which to make educated decisions; risk management includes: (1) risk identification, (2) risk analysis, and (3) response to risk.

- Risk response involves a decision about which risks to prepare for and which to ignore and simply accept as potential threats.

- Because not all risks are equal and should not receive an equal amount of attention, project managers will need to prioritize risks according to their potential threat to the project. Even then, minor risks can easily develop into major risks.

- Most project management decisions contain important topics about which there will always be uncertainty, no matter how much information is collected.

- Most people agree that uncertainty should be included in decision-making if we are to claim that we are good decision makers.

In Chapter 10, we highlight the deficiency of much current project management training in the areas of decision-making and decision analysis. The chapter focuses on the need for including these areas as part of project management training courses.

# CHAPTER 10

# Training Project Managers as Decision Makers

Although the conventional project management body of knowledge (*PMBOK® Guide*) forms a good foundation for basic training and initial learning, it does not address the decisions and decision analysis techniques required to manage the complex problems of today's projects. If you apply the traditional tools, and follow the rules and processes as prescribed, will your project be successful? As we have found, the answer is "not always." Even if project managers do everything by the *PMBOK® Guide*, they might still fail. The fact that most projects still fail suggests that traditional project management training is not enough. The *PMBOK® Guide*, considered the bible of project management, emphasizes the following knowledge areas:

- Integration

- Scope

- Time

- Cost

- Quality

- Human resources

- Communications

- Risk

- Procurement.

These knowledge areas are critical to project management, yet even more critical—as this text has suggested—are decisions and decision-making. This chapter focuses on the need for including decision-making and decision analysis in project management training courses. Training courses currently reflect business principles but do not include elements of decision-making and decision-making techniques as they relate to managing projects. When project managers do receive training related to decision-making, it is generally not presented in the context of project management.

This chapter presents the following sections:

- The Elements of Traditional Project Management Training

- The Pitfalls of Project Management Training

- A Decision Analysis Curriculum.

## The Elements of Traditional Project Management Training

Project management training currently includes rules, tools, and procedures. During training, project managers are taught how to overcome the typical pitfalls of poor project management that result in not achieving objectives, overspending, and late delivery. The core elements in many programs that support these efforts include:

(1) Planning the project (the focus is on business results)

(2) Gathering requirements (the focus is on how to collect requirements)

(3) Developing the plan (the focus is on identifying resources)

(4) Developing and using the work breakdown structure (the focus is
on using Microsoft Project® or similar software)

(5) Managing resources (the focus is on task duration and task assignments)

(6) Optimizing the project (the focus is on shortening project duration)

(7) Managing conflict (the focus is on handling conflict)

(8) Tracking progress and reporting (the focus is on controlling the
project)

These and other elements are often referred to as the tools of project
management. Project managers are taught the implementation and application of each tool. We understand that project managers cannot be
taught how to improve their decision-making skills overnight; this is
learned through experience. However, there is quite a bit that people can
learn about decision-making to sharpen their skills and help them put a
process in place to support decision-making. We consider this the "how
to" in project management. Including the "how to" in project management training is critically important to managing projects; however, good
management cannot be performed without good decision-making.

## The Pitfalls of Project Management Training

Decision-making is not included in most project management texts. It should thus come as no surprise that it is also not included in project management training. In the early years of project management, there were very few training programs. The few programs that did exist emphasized only the technical aspects of project management and left out the behavioral aspects. However, over the past few years more companies have been offering project management training that covers the technical and the behavioral topics. Although project management training is more complete than ever, decision-making is *still* not included.

We hope this book has demonstrated the importance of decision-making to project management. How important is it? The fact is that the success of a project turns on the decisions made or not made. These decisions can be informed by all the technical and behavioral information generated by the rules, tools, and procedures taught in most project management training courses. But decisions that are made without considering all the alternatives over a complete set of objectives will likely turn out more poorly than needed.

Decisions affect whether a project meets its primary objectives—budget, schedule, and product performance. Decisions also affect the ability of the project to contribute to the organization's financial portfolio. When poor decisions are made, projects run the risk of not meeting budget, not meeting the schedule, and not attaining product performance; projects also run the risk of failing to meet financial objectives. The sober truth about decisions is that decisions can cost human lives.

This was evidenced by the space shuttle *Challenger* disaster. In 1986, the Rogers Commission found that NASA's organizational culture and decision-making processes were a key contributing factor in the tragic fate of the *Challenger*. The project had initially proved successful from a financial perspective, but in the end, at the launch of the *Challenger*, earlier faulty decision-making led to its failure and the deaths of its seven American crew members.

Perhaps the time is ripe for project management organizations to take a hard look at revising project management training and education programs so that they do include decision-making and decision analysis techniques. What elements should be included? A proposed curriculum is outlined in the next section.

## A Decision Analysis Curriculum

The following topics should be considered for most, if not all, project management training:

- Introduction to project management decision-making
  - The range of decisions that are made or should be made as part of project management.
  - The important aspects of a good decision-making process.
  - Decisions should not be judged on the basis of the outcomes but on the basis of the process used. Why is this true?
  - Different types of decision-making processes are needed for different decision situations.

- The key elements of any decision are the alternatives that could be selected, the objectives and values that enable determination of which alternative is most preferred, the information that is available at the time, and the remaining uncertainty associated with limited information. Determining which alternative will provide the best future objective results is the hard part.

- Defining objectives

  - Separating fundamental objectives from means objectives

  - Knowing when more objectives are needed

  - Using several techniques, including brainstorming and metaphors, to generate potential objectives

  - Turning means objectives into fundamental objectives

  - Developing measures for your objectives

- Defining alternatives

  - Using several techniques, including brainstorming, strategy tables (aka morphological boxes), and metaphors to generate new alternatives

  - Using Value-Focused Thinking to improve the alternatives after an analysis has been completed

- How and when to consider critical linkages between decision problems

  - Defining decision levels

  - Defining decision types

  - Defining decision order

  - Developing interdependency between decisions

- Using a decision frame to improve your assessment of the decision
  - Building the context for the decision
  - Defining decision objectives
  - Analyzing risks and uncertainties
  - Determining information sources
- Using decision aids to understand difficult choices and trade-offs
  - Building decision trees to evaluate uncertain situations
  - Using tornado diagrams to find the expected value of a decision
  - Developing risk profiles for decision alternatives
  - Defining the required information
  - Determining the sensitivity of the decision
- Addressing risk and uncertainty in important decision situations
  - Developing risk mitigation options for the selected alternative
  - Capturing the degree of uncertainty that exists in a decision problem and identifying when that uncertainty is an issue to be addressed
  - Finding information that might change the decision and focusing collection efforts on those variables
- Selecting and using a method for evaluating alternatives on the objectives
  - Developing and using a pros and cons matrix
  - Performing a qualitative assessment of the alternatives on the objectives

- Building a consequence table from a qualitative assessment

- Using Even Swaps after the decision has been narrowed down to two or three alternatives

- Understanding the basics of a quantitative analysis of the alternatives

■ Being aware of the biases and heuristics that affect decision-making quality

- Dealing with information bias

- Dealing with mental errors

- Handling the negative effect of biases

■ Determining when you should spend more time and money on a decision

- Buying additional information to remove uncertainty

- Understanding the value of additional information

- Understanding the value of perfect and imperfect information

This book is a resource for training efforts that wish to introduce topics about decision-making into existing training programs in project management. The integration of most elements of this training into existing training program requires the expertise of a trained decision analyst.

The following specific points were made in this chapter:

■ Discussions of decision-making are mostly absent from the project management literature and training courses.

■ There are many important pitfalls associated with decision making; in fact, many high-profile project failures can be traced back to poor decisions.

■ A training curriculum related to decision-making and decision analysis should address the importance of decisions and decision processes, defining objectives and alternatives, consideration of linkages between decisions, using a decision frame to improve the decision process, using other decision aids, assessing risk and uncertainty, making a wise choice in selecting an approach for evaluating alternatives in light of objectives and uncertainty and risk, the impact that biases and heuristics can have on degrading or improving decision-making, and considering the impact of delaying the decision so that more information can be collected with an emphasis on how to determine which information has value.

# Project Success Case Studies

This appendix provides two additional case studies that describe success stories for project managers. The first describes the development of the Z3 by BMW (Shenhar and Dvir 2007). The second describes Sony's effort to create the Walkman (Shenhar and Dvir 2007).

## The BMW Z3

(**What is the problem?**) In the late 1980s, BMW struggled with slowing sales imposed by new Japanese luxury car competitors. The company also suffered from the decline of worldwide motorcycle markets. (**What are the organizational goals?**) In an effort to reverse this trend, BMW decided to reposition itself as a producer of quality-oriented luxury vehicles having a unique and definitive identity in the marketplace. It defined its product as "the ultimate driving machine," built for people seeking excitement and a unique expression of individuality. (**What are user needs?**) Among other things, BMW needed a product that would satisfy the same needs that motorcycles do and would represent an exciting, aesthetically pleasing product. Several alternatives were considered, among them race cars, dune buggies, sport utility vehicles, and roadsters. (**What is the set of feasible concepts?**) The roadster concept was finally adopted in 1992 because it allowed BMW to maintain its goal of producing superior and exciting vehicles. The vehicle was dubbed Z3.

(**What are the design challenges?**) BMW understood the complexities of car production. It was accustomed to overcoming the difficulties associated with the design, development, and production of new cars as complex systems, a process involving the integration of many subsystems produced by numerous internal and external subcontractors. However, the Z3 presented additional levels of complexity. (**What are the project goals?**) The first was the decision to launch the Z3 as the first BMW car designed in Germany but produced in the United States, thereby aligning with a long-term company objective of becoming a truly global brand. (**What is the project organization required to achieve project goals?**) This decision required adapting to a different culture of concurrent cross-functional teams in a matrix organization. The goal was to use a new lean and flexible manufacturing environment, a lesson learned from Honda.

Second, BMW decided to leverage the buzz of the Z3 and invest 60 percent of its marketing efforts in nontraditional venues. (**What is the marketing goal and strategy?**) The goal was to generate interest in the Z3 two years before product launch. The nontraditional approach included, among other things, launching a tie-in with the new James Bond movie, *Golden Eye*, featuring the Z3 as a gift item in the Neiman Marcus catalog, and featuring the car in an interactive BMW home page on the web.

(**What are user needs?**) To cope with these complexities, managers attempted to make the design as simple as possible. (**What are the design goals?**) They used an existing 3-series car platform and very few new components. (**What is the prototype building and testing plan?**) However, to make sure everything went right, BMW produced 150 integration and testing prototypes. This number was much higher than with any previous project. (**What is the manufacturing and assembly plan?**) (**What is the optimal project location and layout?**) Parts for initial units were made in Germany, but integration took place in the United States, and when completed, these cars were put in U.S. showrooms before product release. This action gave joint German and U.S. teams the opportunity to identify and resolve design and manufacturing problems early in the product's life cycle. It also enabled redesign work without the need to shut down production, and it created market interest before the official launch.

(**What are the success criteria?**) When all bugs had been removed, and in spite of supply delays, the Z3 captured 32 percent of the estimated target market in its first year of sales, exceeding revenue forecasts by 50 percent. Featuring the Z3 in the James Bond movie and other nontraditional marketing techniques resulted in nine thousand preproduction orders and caused a marketing paradigm shift at BMW.

## A Market Revolution Created by Sony

The first Walkman was born out of frustration. (**What is the user need?**) Masaru Ibuka, the cofounder and honorary chairman of Sony in the 1970s, told some of his subordinates, "I wish it was easy to listen to recorded music on an airplane. Whenever I fly on business I take a heavy tape deck and headphones onto the airplane." (**Define feasible concepts**) To please their boss, a team of Sony employees removed the recording

Aaron Shenhar and Dov Dvir, *Reinventing Project Management: The Diamond Approach to Successful Growth and Innovation* (Boston: Harvard Business School Press, 2007): 41–42. Copyright © 2007 by Harvard Business School Press. Reprinted with permission.

components from an existing handheld Sony tape recorder, making it lighter and smaller, and added a set of earphones. What was left became a prototype for the first Walkman—small enough to carry onto an airplane or listen to music while taking a walk.

Even though he had no marketing research support, CEO Akio Morita decided in 1979 to develop and market the Walkman as a commercial product. As Morita put it, "The market research is all in my head; we *create* markets!" **(What are the product objectives?)** With no clear specifications, the development team worked for months, with two objectives: good sound quality and small headphones that felt like you weren't wearing them at all.

Although the technology was not new, the product represented a new-to-the-world concept. Initial customer reaction was lukewarm. **(What are the success criteria?)** Of 30,000 units produced, only 3,000 were sold, and Sony managers understood that they needed an innovative marketing strategy. But how could they convince people they needed a product that they'd never seen, owned, or even thought of before?

**(What is the marketing strategy?)** The first step was to get the word out to people who influence the public, such as celebrities and music industry people. Sony sent free Walkmans to Japanese recording artists and to TV and movie stars. Targeting younger people and active folks, Sony employees rode the trains, wearing their Walkmans and listening to music. On Sundays, they walked around in Tokyo shopping centers and cultural and sports events. Each employee wearing a Walkman became a walking sales demonstration.

Some people were skeptical at first, but when they tried out the new music system they were amazed. This was an entirely new experience. Japan was swept up in the Walkman wave, and soon visiting tourists were going home with these made-in-Japan souvenirs. Within a year, sales reached a million units and the Walkman revolution had begun. No wonder its brand name became generic and was admitted to the *Oxford English Dictionary* in 1986.

# Project Management Decisions

I n Chapter 5 our catalog of project management decisions was described at the top level. The entire catalog is reproduced here for your
reference.* The following tables appear in this appendix:

- Table B-1: Operational System Decisions—Needs Analysis

- Table B-2: Operational System Decisions—System Analysis and
  Concept Design

- Table B-3: Product System Decisions—Product System, Subsystem,
  and Component Requirements and Design

- Table B-4: Operational System Decisions—Test Planning

- Table B-5: Operational System Decisions—Product System, Subsystem, and Component Testing

- Table B-6: Operational System Decisions—Life Cycle Planning

- Table B-7: Development System Decisions—Management Structure

- Table B-8: Development System Decisions—Project Management
  Planning

- Table B-9: Development System Decisions—Development System
  Construction

*To download a poster-size document featuring all the tables in one layout, please go to
http://www.pmgooddecisions.com/downloads.

**TABLE B-1:** Operational System Decisions—Needs Analysis

| Category | Decisions |
|---|---|
| **Needs Analysis** | **Problem Definition**<br>• What are stakeholder needs?<br>• What is the set of relevant variables and factors?<br>• What is the market assessment strategy?<br>• Set of mission requirements?<br>• What is the consumer vision?<br>• What is the purpose (expectation) of the system?<br>• What is the operating environment definition?<br><br>**Problem Validation**<br>• What is the acceptable level of consistency between stakeholder needs and the mission requirement? |

**TABLE B-2:** Operational System Decisions—System Analysis and Concept
Design

| Category | Decisions |
|---|---|
| **Product System Analysis and Concept Design** | **Concept Definition**<br>*Set of operational scenarios*<br>• What is the user concept of operation?<br>• What is the system concept of operation?<br>• What is the system employment definition?<br>• What is the set of generic concepts?<br>• What is the set of feasible concepts that meet stakeholder need, cost, schedule and initial performance?<br>• What are the risks?<br>• What is the set of prototyping requirements?<br>• What is the set of technology requirements?<br>• What is the product system boundary?<br>• What are the product system constraints?<br>• What is the product definition?<br>• What is the initial product design?<br><br>**Concept Evaluation**<br>• What is the methodology for determining concept and technical feasibility?<br>• What are the evaluative tools, methods, and objectives for evaluating concept design alternatives?<br>• What is the set of trade-off objectives required to satisfy the problem definition and cost requirements?<br><br>**Concept Validation**<br>• What is the set of concept validation criteria?<br>• What is the concept validation methodology?<br>• What are the validation tools for concept designs, e.g., modeling and simulation? |

**TABLE B-3:** Product System Decisions—Product System, Subsystem, and Component Requirements and Design

| Category | Decisions |
|---|---|
| **Product System, Subsystem, and Component Requirements and Design** | **Requirements Definition**<br>• What are the source and method for defining requirements?<br>• What is the method for requirements validation?<br>• Define the method for validating requirements<br>• What are the intended functions and operations of the product system?<br>• Acceptance of sets of product-level requirements<br>• What are user interface and coupling/decoupling requirements?<br>• What are performance requirements?<br>• What are imposed external requirements e.g., security, OSHA?<br>• What are functional redundancy requirements?<br>• What are version two product requirements?<br><br>**Design Definition**<br>• What are the additional design cycles (redesign, rebuild, retest)?<br>• What is the concept/supplier selection?<br><br>**Design Requirements of the Subsystems and Components**<br>• What are the design thresholds and baselines?<br>• What are the values of the key design parameters (Krishnan and Ulrich 2001)?<br>• What are the design constraints and limitations?<br>• What are the physical attributes of the system?<br>• What are the configuration of the components and assembly precedence relations?<br>• What is the detailed design of the components, including material and process selection (Krishnan and Ulrich 2001)?<br>• What are the technologies to be employed (Krishnan and Ulrich 2001)?<br>• What are the available COTS elements?<br>• What is the level of the product system hierarchy requiring technology flexibility?<br><br>**Design Changes (Trade-offs) Required to Meet Key Performance Parameters**<br>• What are the "must cost" changes?<br>• What are the "customer desire" changes?<br>• What is the prototype building and testing plan? |

**TABLE B-3:** Product System Decisions—Product System, Subsystem, and Component Requirements and Design (Cont'd)

| Category | Decisions |
|---|---|
| | **Test Definition**<br>• What are the design test requirements?<br>• What are the test performance and evaluation criteria?<br>• What are the conditions for new technology testing?<br>• What are the data collection requirements to support design trade-offs?<br>• What are the data collection mechanisms?<br><br>**Validation Definition**<br>• What is the set of validation benchmarks?<br>• What is the set of design test criteria, e.g., stakeholder perspective?<br>• What is the set of design validation mechanisms?<br>• What is the set of acceptable stakeholder risks? |

**TABLE B-4:** Operational System Decisions—Test Planning

| Category | Decisions |
|---|---|
| Test Planning | **Product System, Subsystem, and Component**<br>• What is the strategy for proving the product will meet its key performance targets and perform its intended functions?<br>• What is the strategy for prototyping methods and technologies?<br>• What will the project test strategy include?<br>• Set of testing purposes?<br>• Testing strategy for new technologies?<br>• Operational test environment and test conditions?<br>• Required risk scenarios and their test requirements?<br>• Set of test constraints?<br>• Data collection requirements?<br>• Set of metrics to be used and how?<br>• Set of functional testing requirements?<br>• Set of test facility requirements?<br>• Selection of test participants?<br>• Selection of roles/responsibilities for test participants?<br>• Set of test mechanisms?<br>• Amount of testing to be conducted?<br>• Allowable extent of combining design and operational testing?<br>• Stakeholder role during testing?<br>• What to test and how to test as defined by performance indicators?<br>• Test cycle time for product system, subsystem, and components?<br>• What is the risk management plan? |

**TABLE B-5:** Operational System Decisions—Product System, Subsystem, and Component Testing

| Category | Decisions |
|---|---|
| **Product System, Subsystem, and Component Testing** | **Integration (Product System through Components)**<br>What are the assembly process and methodology?<br>What is the set of product system integration test criteria?<br><br>**Verification (Product System through Components)**<br>What is the set of product system verification criteria?<br>What are the sets of subsystem verification criteria?<br>What are the sets of component verification criteria?<br><br>**Product Validation**<br>What are the aspects of the product system to be validated?<br>What is the set of product system validation benchmarks?<br>What is the set of operational test conditions?<br>What are the stakeholder satisfaction criteria?<br>What validation tools and mechanisms are required?<br><br>**Market Validation**<br>What is the market validation strategy? |

**TABLE B-6:** Operational System Decisions—Life-Cycle Planning

| Category | Decisions |
|---|---|
| **Life Cycle Planning** | **Life-Cycle Requirements and Architecture**<br>• What are the stakeholder roles in determining life-cycle requirements?<br><br>**Manufacturing**<br>• What is the set of manufacturing requirements?<br>• What is the manufacturing architecture?<br><br>**Operation, Support, Maintenance, Upgrades**<br>• What is the set of product system support requirements as determined by:<br>  – Configuration management strategy?<br>  – Data requirements to define support requirements?<br>  – Support data purchasing?<br>  – Support provider and length of support?<br>• What are the maintenance concept and architecture?<br>• What is the operational support architecture?<br>• What is the set of upgrade and replacement requirements? |

**TABLE B-7:** Development System Decisions—Management Structure

| Category | Decisions |
|---|---|
| **Management Structure** | **Project Definition**<br>• What is the project process plan?<br>• What is the set of goals for the project, product, processes, organization, and environment?<br>• What are the schedule goals?<br>• What are the cost goals?<br><br>**Success Criteria**<br>• What is the set of success criteria for the project, product, processes, organization, and environment?<br>• What are the project risks?<br>• What is the project type?<br>• What is the project team structure?<br>• What are the project risks?<br><br>**Stakeholder System**<br>• What is the strategy for defining:<br>  – Operational users?<br>  – Elements influenced by product development?<br>  – Elements impacted by product development?<br>  – Stakeholders' activities and roles?<br>• Who are the stakeholders?<br><br>**Project Manager Construction**<br>*Role Definition*<br>• What are the set of roles and the authority of the project manager with respect to the requirements of planning the product and development systems?<br>• What is the set of project manager criteria with respect to project requirements?<br><br>*Evaluation*<br>• What is the strategy for evaluating organizational competency factors?<br><br>*Training*<br>• What is the training plan? |

**TABLE B-8:** Development System Decisions—Project Management Planning

| Category | Decisions |
|---|---|
| **Project Management Planning** | **Information Definition and Validation**<br>• What is the strategy for getting information from stakeholders?<br>• What is the set of information-gathering tools?<br>• What data have to be purchased?<br>• What is the set of baselines to be designed and managed?<br>• What is the strategy for interacting with stakeholders?<br>• What is the strategy for handling trade-offs with the stakeholders (cost versus performance, cost versus schedule)?<br>• What is the method for clarifying the consumer's vision and need?<br>• What is the requirements analysis strategy?<br>• What is the method for validating organizational processes?<br>• What are the reporting structure and meeting schedule?<br>• What are the means and technology of communication—local and global?<br><br>**Resource Definition and Validation**<br>• What are the management requirements?<br>• What is the method for defining task durations?<br><br>**Identification of Resources Required to Maintain Cost, Schedule, and Performance**<br>• What are the funding allocation requirements?<br>• What are the facilities required to support product development?<br>• What is the training budget and what is its impact on the project?<br>• What is the strategy for obtaining resources?<br>• What are the selection and allocation of available resources (amounts and timing)?<br>• What is the reserve allocation, e.g., money, parts, schedule?<br>• What are the actual and reserve cost requirements as matched to stakeholder requirements as determined by:<br>  – Project requirements?<br>  – Project risks for the development and product systems?<br>  – Schedule requirements and risks?<br>  – Cost and schedule estimate strategy?<br>• What is the strategy for determining consistency between requirements and available resources?<br>• What is the project feasibility with respect to imposed costs, schedule, and performance measures?<br>• What is the convergence goal among skills and resources on hand, schedule, and costs?<br>• What are the required decision aids?<br>• Who are the suppliers? |

**TABLE B-8:** Development System Decisions—Project Management Planning
(Cont'd)

| Category | Decisions |
|---|---|
| **Project Management Planning** | **Control Structure Definition and Validation**<br>• Define the method for validating the project plan.<br>• Define the project tasks.<br>• What are the negotiated contractual agreements?<br>• What is the set of major project milestones and planned prototypes?<br>• What is the project monitoring plan, e.g., reviews, plans, and decisions, needed at gates?<br>• How will user requirements be managed?<br>• What is the risk to project completion?<br>• What is the risk to project costs?<br>• What are the planned timing and sequence of development activities:<br>  – Timeline for concept development?<br>  – Commencement of product design?<br>• What are the means for controlling project costs, schedule, and performance?<br>• What is the critical path?<br>• What is the management and reporting system?<br>• What are the data and information requirements?<br>• What is the strategy for controlling requirements?<br>• What is the strategy for measuring project performance?<br>• What are the change effects of requirements on schedule and costs?<br>• What is the strategy for project review requirements?<br>• Definition of project checkpoints?<br>• Purpose of project checkpoints?<br>• Checkpoint participants?<br>• What are the organizational meeting requirements and strategy?<br>• What is the project validation strategy for costs, schedule, and performance?<br>• What is the strategy for continually validating development activities?<br>• What is the strategy for maintaining flexibility relative to system cost, schedule, and performance to handle system design changes and risks?<br>• What are the project termination criteria?<br>• What is the relative priority of development objectives?<br>• When are the planned project reviews?<br><br>**Termination**<br>• What are the project termination requirements? |

**TABLE B-9:** Development System Decisions—Development System Construction

| Category | Decisions |
|---|---|
| **Development System Construction** | **Organizational Structure**<br>• What is the project team structure?<br>• What organizational components are required?<br>• What is the reporting structure as defined by:<br>  – Communication strategy among team members?<br>  – Communication mechanisms among team members and among organizational components?<br>• What are the interrelated requirements between organizational components?<br>• What are the organizational risks and risk mitigation measures?<br><br>**Role Definition**<br>• What is the organizational responsibility matrix (who does what)?<br><br>**Makeup**<br>• What are the organizational team composition requirements as defined by:<br>  – Required degree of efficiency?<br>  – Allocated personnel cost budget?<br>• What is the set of core skill competencies?<br>• What is the set of experience, skill requirements, and interpersonal style requirements for organizational team individuals?<br>• What is the time phasing of project personnel into the project?<br>• What is the process for team staffing?<br>• What is the set of external components, e.g., contractors, subcontractors?<br><br>**Resources**<br>• What are the resource requirements necessary to perform tasks?<br>• What are the infrastructure and tool requirements, e.g., software, computer support, building, office space?<br>• What are the resource constraints? |

**TABLE B-9:** Development System Decisions—Development System
Construction (Cont'd)

| Category | Decisions |
|---|---|
| | **Evaluation**<br>• What is the objective basis for evaluating organizational competency factors, e.g., required skills, experience, and personal attributes?<br>• What are the risk factors?<br><br>**Validation**<br>• What is the team composition validation methodology?<br>• What is the strategy for validating organizational processes?<br><br>**Location**<br>• What are the physical arrangement and location of the team as influenced by:<br>– Communication objectives?<br>– Technological capabilities?<br>• What is the optimal project location and layout?<br><br>**Training**<br>• What is the required training?<br>• What is the timing of required training for organizational team members? |

# An Introduction to Decision Trees

I n this appendix, Robert Dees and Ken Gilliam briefly describe some of the fundamental concepts of decision analysis and move to a discussion about one of the favorite *structural models* of decision analysts: the decision tree.

## Decisions and Outcomes

To think about decision analysis, we must begin with the decision. A *decision*, as already stated, is an irrevocable allocation of resources. In the project manager's world, this means that the decision is not made until contracts are signed or money changes hands. We know that we have made a decision when we cannot go back, or at least that we cannot go back without incurring a penalty. Going back would be another decision, and in this case we have at least decided to commit resources up to the amount of the penalty. This penalty could be time, money, public opinion, or any other resource.

On the flip side, when we do nothing or wait to decide, we are choosing to allocate resources in a particular way right now, and we might incur an opportunity cost. We must decide about not only what to do but also when to do it. This definition of a decision also implies that a decision is more than just thought; a decision is an action.

We would like our decision to be characterized by logical thought, but it isn't a decision until action takes place. Consider a person who says that he or she is on a diet but routinely visits the pantry for junk food; the dieter hasn't truly decided on the diet until the actions performed reflect his or her spoken words. Along the same lines, a project manager hasn't decided on a project management plan, or anything else, until it is implemented.

The most important, and still most commonly misunderstood, distinction in decision analysis is that between a decision and an outcome (Howard 2007). We have already defined a decision; we say that an *outcome* is a future state of the world, and that a *good outcome* is one that we prize relative to other possibilities (Howard 1988), as shown in Figure C-1.

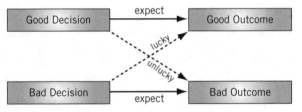

**FIGURE C-1:** Decision and Outcome Relationships

When we make a good decision, we expect to have a good outcome but might experience an unlucky bad outcome. If we play the roulette game with an 80 percent chance of winning, we can still get unlucky and lose. When we make a bad decision, we expect to have a bad outcome, but we might get lucky and have a good outcome. As decision makers, we are unable to eliminate all uncertainty in the world, and we face the possibility of bad outcomes after making good decisions.

## Decision Trees—"Hammer V-12 Roadster" Case

Confusing the tools of decision analysis with decision analysis itself has contributed to the loss of precision. Because uncertainty is at the heart of most perplexing decision problems, decision analysts frequently use specialized tools, such as decision tree techniques, to evaluate uncertain situations. Unfortunately, many people, some of them educators, have confused decision analysis with decision trees. This is like confusing surgery with the scalpel. Although decision tree techniques are extremely useful in solving problems where uncertainty is critical, in a real decision analysis, most of the effort and creativity is focused on finding and formulating the correct problem and on interpreting the results rather than on performing computations. (Howard and Matheson 2004)

Decision trees are only one tool; in Chapter 4, we mentioned other tools, including decision matrices, decision hierarchies, influence diagrams, spreadsheets, tornado diagrams, risk profiles, and sensitivity analyses. In this section, we proceed through a systematic development of necessary distinctions that must be understood in order to effectively use decision trees. We will use a hypothetical case about a product development decision to demonstrate these distinctions.

You are currently a lead project manager working for Startup Motors. Startup Motors makes performance vehicles and unveiled a new model called the "Hammer" on last year's auto show circuit. The Hammer is a V-12 roadster designed to compete with the likes of the Dodge Viper and Chevrolet Corvette ZR-1. The estimated selling price is $85K to $95K. Based on the buzz at the auto shows, Startup Motors has decided to continue the development of the Hammer into a production model.

You have been hired as the lead project manager for Hammer development. Up to this point, Startup Motors has spent $30M in development of the Hammer, and you estimate that it will take an additional $80M to get the Hammer to market. In the past, 80 percent of vehicles introduced in this segment of the market have been a "Success." If the Hammer is successful, then you believe that Startup Motors will realize a $120M profit over the current product planning horizon. If the Hammer experiences "Failure," then Startup Motors will realize only a $10M profit over the same time period.

You, along with the top-level management of Startup Motors, hire an outside market research company to assess whether the Hammer will be a "Success." In the past, this market research company's predictions have been 90 percent accurate in this segment of the market.

## Possibilities

To begin, we have said that the Hammer can turn out to be either a "Success" or a "Failure." This distinction has two *degrees*, or levels, that we could realize. We easily could have defined more degrees; we could have rated the level of success on a scale from 1 to 10. We have kept it to two degrees for simplicity in our first example. "Success" and "Failure" are *mutually exclusive*, meaning that they cannot both happen at the same time. It makes sense that only one of our degrees of any distinction could happen. "Success" and "Failure" are also *collectively exhaustive*, meaning that there are no additional possibilities. Because "Success" and "Failure" are mutually exclusive and collectively exhaustive, exactly one of the two degrees on this distinction will happen. We represent this distinction in a *possibility tree* (see Figure C-2).

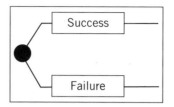

**FIGURE C-2:** Initial Possibility Tree

As we identify other relevant distinctions, we can add more branches to our tree. Using our Hammer example, we now decide that the marketing firm will conduct a market test and predict whether the Hammer will be a "Test Success" or a "Test Failure." We see that there are now four possibilities that could happen. It is important to note that we could experience "Success" even if the Hammer is a "Test Failure." Additionally, the Hammer could be a "Failure" even if we are told that it is a "Test Success."

The order of the possibility tree (Figure C-3) shows that we are first going to think about whether the Hammer is a "Success," and then whether the marketing firm reports a "Test Success."

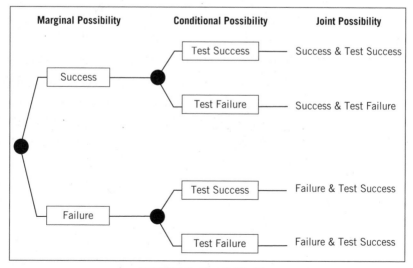

**FIGURE C-3:** Possibility Tree

This is the *order of the information that we have* at this point. As we progress, we would like to think about the results of the market test before we think about success of the Hammer because this is the *order that the events will happen.*

## Outcomes and Value

We have said that outcomes are future states of the world. As of now, we have four possible outcomes in our Hammer example. We need to assess the value of each one of these future states. In this case, we are told that if the Hammer is a "Success," then we will experience a profit of $120M. If the Hammer is a "Failure," then we will experience a profit of only $10M.

Value is not always expressed in dollars; project managers continually care about cost, performance, and schedule. None of these are valued in the same units, and currently we are considering only one measure of value—dollars. Multiple objective decision analysis (MODA) can be used to assign value to our joint possibilities when we face a decision for which we have multiple and competing objectives (Parnell and Driscoll 2008). One of the attractive features of MODA is that it helps us to get everything into the same units so that we can compare apples to apples. For our current discussion of the Hammer, we make the assumption that our only value is money. We now move to include value in our possibility tree (Figure C-4).

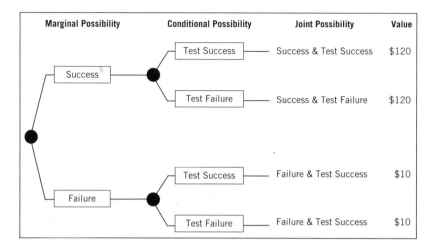

**FIGURE C-4:** Possibility Tree with Value (the order we have information)

We have recorded the value of "Success" and "Failure" along the branches of the tree. We then add Value to the right through our tree to arrive at the Value associated with our joint possibilities. We note that our profit, in this case, doesn't change based on what the marketing company says about the Hammer. We can record Value in the tree like this for problems with a single objective; we can add the Value to the right to come up with the Value of each possibility. Alternately, we can assign Value to each of our joint possibilities (prospects).

## Probabilities

We now add our probabilities, or beliefs, to the possibility tree (Figure C-5). Notice that the probabilities sum to 1.0 on any individual branch of the tree; this is because our distinctions are mutually exclusive and collectively exhaustive. As mentioned in the Hammer case, the chance of success in this market segment is 80 percent; this is recorded as a probability of 0.80 in the tree. Additionally, we said that the marketing company has been 75 percent accurate at predicting "Success" and 25 percent accurate at predicting "Failure" in this segment. We *sum* value to the right; we *multiply* probability to the right. We see that the probability of "Success" and "Test Success" happening is (0.80 × 0.75) = 0.60. The probabilities of our four joint possibilities also sum to 1.0.

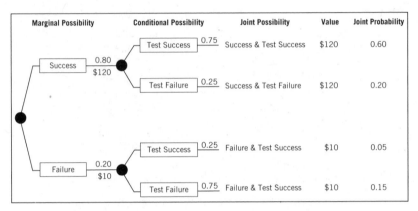

**FIGURE C-5:** Probability Tree with Value

In the information we have, the probability of "Test Success" is conditioned on "Success." This works, but thus far we have talked about the information in the order that *we have it,* and we want to get the information in the order that *the events will happen.* Figure C-6 explains how to get the information in the order that the events will happen.

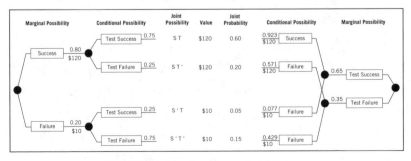

**FIGURE C-6:** Flipping the Probability Tree

This figure shows a process that we call "tree flipping." We changed the notation for our joint possibilities. S indicates "Success," and S' indicates "Failure." T indicates "Test Success," and T' indicates "Test Failure." The tree on the left is identical to the previous figure, and we used the following steps to flip the tree:

■ We first drew the tree to the right in order to depict the information in the order that the events will happen. Hammer "Test Success" is now the marginal possibility, and Hammer "Success" is the conditional possibility. The joint possibilities (prospects) are the same as they were previously. Note that ST = TS; they are the same prospect.

■ We then use probability theory to compute the probabilities of "Test Success" and "Test Failure," as well as the conditional probabilities of "Success given Test Success" and "Failure given Test Success." (See Buede 2000, Howard and Abbas 2007, or Schuyler 2001 for more information on how this is done.)

Figure C-7 shows the final version of our probability tree. This tree shows the information in the order that the events will actually occur.

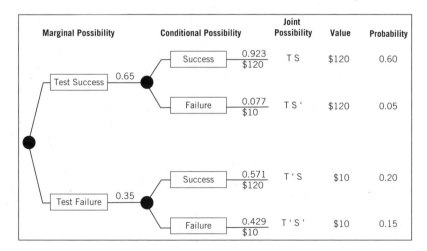

**FIGURE C-7:** Probability Tree with Value

The most counter-intuitive result that we have found thus far is that when the 75 percent accurate marketing company indicates that the Hammer is a "Test Failure," we still have a 57.1 percent chance of "Success." This is a well-known example based on the law of conditional probability, and it is used extensively in the field of medical testing. Right now, we have an 80 percent chance of "Success"; this is known as the *prior probability* of "Success." If we get back "Test Success," then we have a 92.3 percent chance for "Success"; this is called the *posterior probability* of "Success." We have gained some information from the marketing test, and we will later talk about how much the test is worth to us.

## Decisions and Decision Trees

We are now at a point where we can represent our decisions in the Hammer tree. We will insert our decisions in the order that they happen. Decision trees inherently grow in the order that things will happen, and we advocate modeling the decision this way when attempting to build a new tree. We use circles to represent chance nodes in the tree; we use squares to represent decisions. Additionally, we use triangles to denote terminal nodes (Figure C-8).

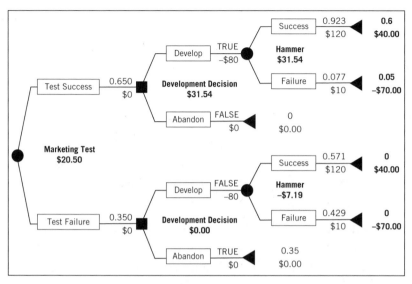

**FIGURE C-8:** Decision Tree

After we get the results of the marketing test, we will make a decision about whether to continue development of the Hammer. Notice that we have inserted the future development cost of $80M on the decision branches. We solve the decision tree by using the following steps:

***Sum value from left to right.*** In our example, if we decide to continue development and the Hammer is successful, we will realize an outcome of –$80M + $120M = $40M. If we continue development and the Hammer is a failure, we will realize an outcome of –$80M + $10M = –$70M. If we decide to abandon the Hammer, we will realize an outcome of $0M from where we are now. We said that we have already spent $30M on the Hammer, but this is a sunk cost and should not be considered in future decisions.

***Fold the tree.*** When we fold the tree, we (1) calculate the *expected value* of chance nodes and (2) *choose* the better alternative when we encounter a decision node (Clemen and Reilly 2001). Expected value is given by:

$$\sum_i p_i V_i$$

where $p_i$ is the probability of event i and $V_i$ is the value of event i. An *expected value* is what we would expect to get as a long-run average if we were to make the same decision over and over again. When the chance node is at the end of the tree, we use the terminal value in our calculations. We illustrate these steps for our Hammer case:

We first calculate the expected value of our chance nodes relating to Hammer success. If the Hammer is a "Test Success" and we decide to "Develop" it, the expected value of our chance node is $(0.923 \times \$40M)$ + $(0.077 \times -\$70M) = \$31.54M$. We complete the same operation for our other chance node with different probabilities and have the resulting tree (Figure C-9).

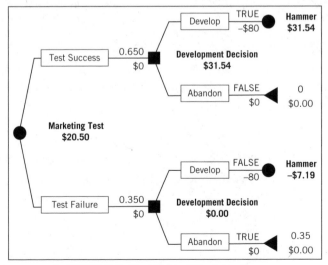

**FIGURE C-9:** First Fold of Decision Tree

We choose the better alternative when faced with the development decision. In the "Test Success" case, we see that the expected value of the decision to continue development is greater than the certain terminal value of $0M if we choose to abandon the Hammer. We also notice that we should abandon the Hammer if the marketing company says "Test Failure," because the expected value of deciding to develop is $7.19M less than that of abandoning the Hammer. This is indicated by "TRUE" or "FALSE" on our tree, and we can prune the tree back as shown in Figure C-10.

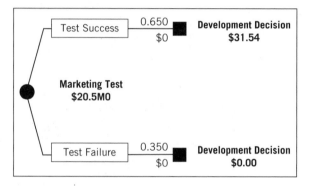

**FIGURE C-10:** Second Fold of Decision Tree

Finally, we might take heart in our current situation at Startup Motors; we have an expected value of $20.5M for our current situation. An expected value does not guarantee what we will get as the situation unfolds. From our initial tree, we can see that our only possible outcomes are -$70M, $0M, and $40M. As stated earlier, an *expected value* is what we would expect to get as a long-run average if we were to make the same decision over and over again. Once again, we choose based on expected value only when we agree to be risk-neutral over our prospects.

# References

Archibald, R.D. 2004. "Project environment impact on the life cycle model," *Project management state of the art – 2004, Part 2: Project management applications, practices and tools.* Online at "Max's project management wisdom," http://www.maxwideman.com/guests/stateofart/specific.htm#table4 (accessed August 21, 2008).

Axelrod, R., ed. 1976. *Structure of decision: the cognitive maps of political elites.* Princeton, NJ: Princeton University Press.

Ayyub, B. 2001. *Elicitation of expert opinions for uncertainty and risks.* Boca Raton, FL: CRC Press.

Barnard, C. 1938. *Functions of an executive.* Boston: Harvard University Press.

Barnhart, D. 1993. "Decision analysis software helps Boeing select supercomputer," *OR/MS today,* 62–63.

Bell, Jr., W.J., and L.W. Labaree, eds. 1956. *Mr. Franklin: a selection from his personal letters.* New Haven: Yale University Press.

Belton, V., and T.J. Stewart. 2002. *Multiple criteria decision analysis.* Norwell, MA: Kluwer Academic Publishers.

Berlin, I. 1953. *The Hedgehog and the Fox.* New York: Simon and Schuster.

Bernoulli, D. 1738. "Exposition of a new theory on the measurement of risk," trans. in *Econometrica* 22 (1954): 23–36.

Black, F., and M. Scholes. 1973. "The pricing of options and corporate liabilities," *Journal of political economy* 81.3: 637–654.

Blanchard, B.S., and W.J. Fabrycky. 1998. *Systems engineering and analysis.* Upper Saddle River, NJ: Prentice-Hall.

Bocquet, J., J.S. Cardinal, and M. Mekhilef. 1999. "A systematic decision approach for capitalizing dysfunctions in design processes," *Proceedings of DETC '99* in Las Vegas, Nevada, September 12–15, 1999, by the American Society of Mechanical Engineers (ASME), 1175–1183. New York: American Society of Mechanical Engineers.

Boehm, B. 2000. *Spiral development: experience, principles, and refinements,* CMU/SEI-2000-SR-008. Pittsburgh: Carnegie Mellon Software Engineering Institute.

Braverman, J.D. 1980. *Management decision-making: a formal/intuitive approach.* New York: AMACOM.

Bronzite, M. 2000. *System development: a strategic framework.* London: Springer.

Buchanan, L., and A. O'Connell. 2006. *A brief history of decision-making.* Boston: Harvard Business Review.

Buede, D.M. 2000. *The engineering design of systems: models and methods.* Hoboken, NJ: John Wiley & Sons, Inc.

Buede, D.M., and D.O. Ferrell. 1993. "Convergence in problem solving: a prelude to quantitative analysis," *IEEE transactions on systems, man and cybernetics* 23.3: 746–765.

Carroll, L. 1865. *Alice's adventures in wonderland.* Oxford: Clarendon Press.

Clarke, D. 2000. "*Strategically evolving the future,*" *Technological forecasting and social change* 64 (June/July): 133–153.

Clemen, R.T., and T. Reilly. 2001. *Making hard decisions with decision tools.* Florence, KY: Duxbury Press.

DeMarco, T., and Lister, T. 2003. "*Risk management during requirements,*" *IEEE software* 20.5.

Descartes, R. 1641. *Meditations on first philosophy.* J. Cottingham, trans., 1996. Cambridge, UK: Cambridge University Press.

Dewey, J. 1933. *How we think.* Boston: D.C. Heath.

Driscoll, P.J. 2008. "*System life cycle,*" *Decision-making in systems engineering and management.* G.S. Parnell, P.J. Driscoll, and D.L. Henderson, eds., 55–77. Hoboken, NJ: John Wiley & Sons, Inc.

Edgeworth, F. 1881. *Mathematical psychics: an essay on the application of mathematics to the moral sciences.* London: C. Kegan Paul.

Eppinger, S.D., D.E. Whitney, R.P. Smith, and D. Gebala. 1990. "Organizing the tasks in complex design projects," *Design theory and methodology* 27: 39–46.

Fairhurst, G.T., and R.A. Sarr. 1996. *The art of framing: managing the language of leadership.* San Francisco: Jossey-Bass.

Fienberg, R.T. 1990. "The space telescope: picking up the pieces," *Sky & Telescope* 80.4: 352–358.

Fisher, Irving. 1907. *The rate of interest: its nature, determination, and relation to economic phenomena.* New York: Macmillan.

Forsberg, K., H. Mooz, and H. Cotterman. 2000. *Visualizing project management,* 2nd ed. Hoboken, NJ: John Wiley & Sons, Inc.

Frost, R. 1916. "The road not taken," *Mountain interval.* New York: Henry Holt & Company.

Hammond, J. S., R.L. Keeney, and H. Raiffa. 1999. *Smart choices*. New York: Broadway Books.

Harrison, E.F. 1987. *The managerial decision-making process*, 3rd ed. Boston: Houghton Mifflin Co.

Hartmann, D. "Interview: Jim Johnson of the Standish Group," August 25, 2006. Online at http://www.infoq.com/articles/Interview-Johnson-Standish-CHAOS (accessed June 17, 2008).

Haugan, G.T. 2006. *Project management fundamentals: key concepts and methodology*. Vienna, VA: Management Concepts, Inc.

Heuer, Jr., R.J. 1999. *Psychology of intelligence analysis*. Washington, D.C.: Center for the Study of Intelligence, Central Intelligence Agency.

Howard, R.A. 2007. "The foundations of decision analysis revisited," *Advances in decision analysis*. W. Edwards, R.F. Miles, Jr., and D. von Winterfeldt, eds. Cambridge, UK: Cambridge University Press.

Howard, R.A. 2000. *"Decisions in the face of uncertainty," Visions of risk.* C. Alexander, ed. London: Pearson Education Limited.

Howard, R.A. 1988. "Decision analysis: practice and promise," *Management science* 34.6.

Howard, R.A. 1968. "The foundations of decision analysis," *IEEE transactions on systems, science*, and *cybernetics* 4: 211–219.

Howard, R.A. 1966. "Decision analysis: applied decision theory," *Proceedings of the fourth international conference on operational research*, 55–71. Hoboken, NJ: Wiley-Interscience, Inc.

Howard, R.A., and A. E. Abbas. 2007. *Foundations of decision analysis*. Upper Saddle River, NJ: Prentice-Hall.

Howard, R.A., and J.E. Matheson, eds. 2004. *Readings on the principles and applications of decision analysis, volume I: general collection*, viii. Palo Alto, CA: Strategic Decisions Group.

Hulett, D., and D. Hillson. 2006. "Branching out," *PM network* 20: 36–40.

Hume, D. 1739. *A treatise of human nature*, 1967 ed. Oxford: Oxford University Press.

Jackson, S. 1997. *Systems engineering for commercial aircraft*. Brookfield, VT: Ashgate.

Janis, I.J., and L. Mann. 1977. *Decision-making: a psychological analysis of conflict, choice, and commitment*. New York: Free Press.

Jet Propulsion Laboratory. 1999. *Mars climate orbiter mishap investigation board Phase I report*. Online at ftp://ftp.hq.nasa.gov/pub/pao/reports/1999/MCO_report.pdf (accessed October 15, 2008).

Keeney, R.L. 2004. "Making better decision makers," *Decision analysis* 1:4 (December): 193–204.

Keeney, R.L. 1992. *Value-focused thinking*. Boston: Harvard University Press.

Keeney, R.L. and H. Raiffa. 1976. *Decisions with multiple objectives: preferences and value trade-off*. Hoboken, NJ: John Wiley & Sons, Inc.

Kerzner, H. 2006. *Project management: a systems approach to planning, scheduling, and controlling*, 9th ed. Hoboken, NJ: John Wiley & Sons, Inc.

Kirkwood, C.W. 1997. *Strategic decision-making*. Belmont, CA: Duxbury Press.

Kleefeld, Eric. 2005. "UW working to salvage multimillion HR software project." Wisconsin Technology Network. Online at http://wistechnology.com/articles/2137 (accessed June 18, 2008).

Klein, G. 1998. *Sources of power: how people make decisions*. Cambridge, MA: The MIT Press.

Knight, F.H. 1921. "Risk, uncertainly, and profit," *Hart, Schaffner, and Marx prize essays*, no. 31. Boston and New York: Houghton Mifflin.

Koehler, D.J., L. Brenner, and D. Griffin. 2002. "The calibration of expert judgment: heuristics and biases beyond the laboratory," *Heuristics and biases: the psychology of intuitive judgment*. T. Gilovich, D.W. Griffin, and D. Kahneman, eds. Cambridge, UK: Cambridge University Press.

Krishnan, V., and K.T. Ulrich. 2001. "Product development decisions: a review of literature," *Management science* 47.1: 1–21.

Leigh, A. 1983. *Decisions, decisions: a practical management guide to problem solving and decision-making*. Brookfield, VT: Gower Publishing Co.

Mantel Jr., S.J., J.R. Meredith, S.M. Shafer, and M.M. Sutton. 2001. *Project management in practice*. Hoboken, NJ: John Wiley & Sons, Inc.

Markowitz, H.M. 1952. "Portfolio selection," *Journal of Finance* 7.1: 77–91.

Matheson, D., and J. Matheson. 1998. *The smart organization: creating value through strategic R&D*. Cambridge, MA: Harvard Business School Press.

Mazda, F. 1998. *Engineering management*. New York: Addison-Wesley.

McLean, W.B. 1960. "Management and the creative scientist," *California management review* 3.1: 9–11.

McLean, W.B. 1962. "The Sidewinder missile program, in science, technology, and management," *The proceedings of the national advanced-technology management conference* 4–7 September 1962. F. Kast and J. Rosenzweig, eds., 166–176. New York: McGraw-Hill.

Mintzberg, H., D. Raisinghani, and A. Theorot. 1976. "The structure of 'unstructured' decision processes," *Administrative sciences quarterly* 21: 246–275.

Mintzberg, H., and F. Westley. 2001. "Decision-making: it's not what you think," *MIT sloan management review* 42.3: 89–93.

Pariseau, R., and I. Oswalt. 1994. "Using data types and scales for analysis and decision-making," *Acquisition review quarterly* (Spring): 145–159.

Parks, R. 1994. *Quiet strength*. Grand Rapids, MI: Zondervan.

Parnell, G.S., and P.J. Driscoll. 2008. "Introduction," *Decision-making in systems engineering and management*. G.S. Parnell, P.J. Driscoll, and D.L. Henderson, eds., 1–15. Hoboken, NJ: John Wiley & Sons, Inc.

Paté-Cornell, M.E. 1996. "Uncertainties in risk analysis: six levels of treatment," *Reliability engineering and system safety* 54: 95–111.

Payne, J.W., J.R. Bettman, and E.J. Johnson. 1993. *The adaptive decision maker*. Cambridge, UK: Cambridge University Press.

Petersen, C.C., and J.C. Brandt. 1995. *Hubble vision: astronomy with the Hubble space telescope*. Cambridge, UK: Cambridge University Press.

Plas, J.V. 2006. "UW system says goodbye to Lawson after 5 years, $26 million." Wisconsin Technology Network. Online at http://wistechnology. com/articles/3120 (accessed August 21, 2008).

Pugh, S. 1991. *Total design – integrating methods for successful product engineering*. Reading, MA: Addison-Wesley.

Powell, R.A. 2008. "Solution implementation," *Decision-making in systems engineering and management*. G.S. Parnell, P.J. Driscoll, and D.L. Henderson, eds., 399–427. Hoboken, NJ: John Wiley & Sons, Inc.

Powell, R.A. 2002. *A definition of high-level decisions in the engineering of systems*. Hoboken, NJ: Stevens Institute of Technology.

Powell, R.A., and D.M. Buede. 2006. "Decision-making for successful product development," *Project management journal* 37.1: 22–40.

Raiffa, H. 1968. *Decision analysis: introductory lectures on choice under uncertainty*. Reading, MA: Addison-Wesley.

Ramsey, F.P. 1931. "Truth and probability," *The foundations of mathematics and other logical essays.* R.B. Braithwaite, ed. New York: Harcourt Brace.

Richards, C. 2004. *Certain to win: the strategy of John Boyd, applied to business.* Philadelphia: Xlibris Corporation.

Richards, C. 2002. "PR blitzkrieg: maneuver warfare for marketing communications." Online at http://www.jaddams.com/culture_fourth_ edition.pdf (accessed October 15, 2008).

Russo, J.E., and P.J.H. Schoemaker. 2002. *Winning decisions: getting it right the first time.* New York: Doubleday.

Savage, L.J. 1954. *The foundations of statistics.* Hoboken, NJ: John Wiley & Sons, Inc.

Schuyler, J. 2001. *Risk and decision analysis in projects.* Newtown Square, PA: Project Management Institute.

Sculley, J., and J. Byrne. 1987. *Odyssey: Pepsi to Apple... a journey of adventure, ideas, and the future.* New York: Harper Collins.

Shanteau, J. 2001. "What does it mean when experts disagree?" *Linking expertise and naturalistic decision-making.* E. Salas and G. Klein, eds. Mahwah, NJ: Lawrence Erlbaum Associates.

Shanteau, J. 1992. "Competence in experts: the role of task characteristics," *Organizational behavior and human decision processes* 53: 252–266.

Shenhar, A.J., and D. Dvir. 2007. *Reinventing project management: the diamond approach to successful growth and innovation.* Boston: Harvard Business School Press.

Shewhart, W.A. 1939. *Statistical method from the viewpoint of quality control.* New York: Dover.

Simon, H.A. 1965. *The shape of automation.* New York: Harper and Row.

Simon, H.A. 1955. "A behavioral model of rational choice," *Quarterly journal of economics* 69: 99–118.

Sinnott, R.W. 1990. "HST's magnificent optics... what went wrong?" *Sky and telescope* 80.4: 356–357.

Smith, J.E., and D. von Winterfeldt. 2004. "Decision analysis in management science," *Management science* 50.5: 561–574.

Smith, P.G., and D.G. Reinertsen. 1998. *Developing products in half the time.* Hoboken, NJ: John Wiley & Sons, Inc.

Standish Group International. 2001. *Chaos.* Online at http://www. standishgroup.com/chaos (accessed October 16, 2008).

Suh, N.P. 2001. *Axiomatic design: advances and applications.* New York: Oxford University Press.

Tetlock, P. 2005. *Expert political judgment: how good is it? how can we know?* Princeton, NJ: Princeton University Press.

Trainor, T., and G.S. Parnell. 2008. "Problem definition," *Decision-making in systems engineering and management.* G.S. Parnell, P.J. Driscoll, and D.L. Henderson, eds., 263–313. Hoboken, NJ: John Wiley & Sons, Inc.

Tversky, A., and D. Kahneman. 1981. "The framing of decisions and the psychology of choice," *Science* 211: 453–463.

Tversky, A., and D. Kahnaeman. 1974. "Judgment under uncertainty: heuristics and biases," *Science* 185: 1124–1131.

von Neumann, J., and O. Morgenstern. 1947. *Theory of games and economic behavior.* Princeton, NJ: Princeton University Press.

Weiss, D.J., and J. Shanteau. 2003. "The vice of consensus and the virtue of consistency," *Psychological explorations of competent decision-making.* J. Shanteau, P. Johnson, and C. Smith, eds. New York: Cambridge University Press.

West, P. 2008. "Solution Design," *Decision-making in systems engineering and management*. G.S. Parnell, P.J. Driscoll, and D.L. Henderson, eds., 317–354. Hoboken, NJ: John Wiley & Sons, Inc.

Westrum, R. 1999. *Sidewinder: creative missile development at China Lake*. Annapolis, MD: Naval Institute Press.

Yates, J.F. 2003. *Decision management: how to assure better decisions in your company*. San Francisco: Jossey-Bass.

# Additional Reading

Covey, S.R. 1989. *The seven habits of highly effective people: restoring the character ethic.* New York: Simon & Schuster.

Edwards, W. 1954. "The theory of decision-making," *Psychological bulletin* 51: 380–417.

Edwards, W., R.F. Miles, Jr., and D. von Winterfeldt. 2007. "Introduction," *Advances in decision analysis.* W. Edwards, R.F. Miles, Jr., and D. von Winterfeldt, eds. New York: Cambridge University Press.

Eisner, H. 2002. *Essentials of project and systems engineering management,* 2nd ed. Hoboken, NJ: John Wiley & Sons, Inc.

Hulett, D., and D. Hillson. 2006. "Branching out," *PM network* 20: 36–40.

Keeney, R.L. 1982. "Decision analysis: an overview," *Operations research* 30.5 (September/October): 803–838.

Parnell, G.S., and P.D. West. 2008. "Systems decision process overview," *Decision-making in systems engineering and management.* G.S. Parnell, P.J. Driscoll, and D.L. Henderson, eds., 243–262. Hoboken, NJ: John Wiley & Sons, Inc.

Project Management Institute. *A guide to the project management body of knowledge,* 3rd ed. Newtown Square, PA: Project Management Institute.

Saaty, T.L. 1980. *The analytical hierarchy process.* New York: McGraw-Hill.

U.S. Department of the Army. 2005. *Field manual 5-0: army planning and orders production.* Online at http://armyrotc.msu.edu/resources/ FM5-0ArmyPlanningOrdersProd.pdf (accessed October 16, 2008).

van Gigch, J.P. 1991. *System design modeling and metamodeling.* New York: Plenum Press.

# Index